Programming via Pascal

Also in the series

1   An Introduction to Logical Design of Digital Circuits
    C.M. Reeves 1972
2   Information Representation and Manipulation in a Computer
    E.S. Page and L.B. Wilson, Second Edition 1987
3   Computer Simulation of Continuous Systems
    R.J. Ord-Smith and J. Stephenson 1975
4   Macro Processors
    A.J. Cole, Second Edition 1981
5   An Introduction to the Users of Computers
    Murray Laver 1976
6   Computing Systems Hardware
    M. Wells 1976
7   An Introduction to the Study of Programming Languages
    D.W. Barron 1977
8   ALGOL 68 – A first and second course
    A.D. McGettrick 1978
9   An Introduction to Computational Combinatorics
    E.S. Page and L.B. Wilson 1979
10 Computers and Social Change
    Murray Laver 1980
11 The Definition of Programming Languages
    A.D. McGettrick 1980
12 Programming via Pascal
    J.S. Rohl and H.J. Barrett Second Edition 1990
13 Program Verification using Ada
    A.D. McGettrick 1982
14 Simulation Techniques for Discrete Event Systems
    I. Mitrani 1982
15 Information Representation and Manipulation using Pascal
    E.S. Page and L.B. Wilson 1983
16 Writing Pascal Programs
    J.S. Rohl 1983
17 An Introduction to APL
    S. Pommier 1983
18 Computer Mathematics
    D.J. Cooke and H.E. Bez 1984
19 Recursion via Pascal
    J.S. Rohl 1984
20 Text Processing
    A. Colin Day 1984
21 Introduction to Computer Systems
    Brian Molinari 1985
22 Program Construction
    R.G. Stone and D.J. Cooke 1986
23 A Practical Introduction to Denotational Semantics
    Lloyd Allison 1986
24 Modelling of Computer and Communication Systems
    I. Mitrani 1987
25 The Principles of Computer Networking
    D. Russell 1989
26 Concurrent Programming
    C.R. Snow 1990

12 Cambridge Computer Science Texts

Programming via Pascal
Second edition

J.S. Rohl and H.J. Barrett

Department of Computer Science, The University of Western Australia

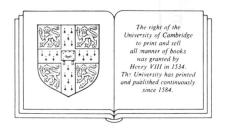

*The right of the
University of Cambridge
to print and sell
all manner of books
was granted by
Henry VIII in 1534.
The University has printed
and published continuously
since 1584.*

Cambridge University Press

Cambridge
New York   Port Chester
Melbourne   Sydney

Published by the Press Syndicate of the University of Cambridge
The Pitt Building, Trumpington Street, Cambridge CB2 1RP
40 West 20th Street, New York, NY 10011, USA
10 Stamford Road, Oakleigh, Melbourne 3166, Australia

First published 1980
Reprinted 1982, 1984
Second edition 1990

Printed in Great Britain at the University Press, Cambridge

British Library Cataloguing in Publication Data
Rohl, J.S.
    Programming via Pascal. – 2nd ed. –
    (Cambridge computer science texts; 12).
    1. PASCAL (Computer program language)
    I. Title   II. Barrett, H.J.
    005.13'3   QA76.73.P2

Library of Congress Cataloguing in Publication Data
Rohl, J.S. (Jeffrey Soden), 1938–
    Programming via Pascal
    (Cambridge computer science texts; 12).
    Includes index.
    1. PASCAL (Computer program language)
I. Barrett, H.J.   II. Title.   III. Series.
QA76.73.P2R63   1988   005.13'3   87-32589

ISBN 0 521 35558 3 hard covers
ISBN 0 521 35661 X paperback

Contents

Preface   x

1 Introduction   1
1.1 A simple payroll example   2
1.2 The compiler   6
1.3 Preparing a program   6
1.4 Running programs   7
1.5 What happens when you get it wrong?   8
    Exercises   8

2 Variables and arithmetic   10
2.1 Variables and variable declarations   11
2.2 Program layout   13
2.3 Comments   13
2.4 Types   14
2.5 Constants   15
2.6 Expressions   15
2.7 Operators   16
2.8 Precedence and brackets   18
2.9 Functions   20
2.10 Assignments   21
2.11 The importance of assignment-statements and expressions   23
    Exercises   24
    Problems   24

3 Specifying Pascal's syntax   26
3.1 Syntax diagrams   26
3.2 Extended Backus Naur Form   29
3.3 A note on the syntax diagrams used here   32
    Exercises   32
    Problems   32

4 Alternatives   34
4.1 The if-statement   34
4.2 Indentation   36
4.3 Boolean-expressions   36

4.4	Extended if-statements	37
4.5	Nested if-statements	39
4.6	Logical operations	40
4.7	Set notation	42
4.8	The compound-statement	42
4.9	The case-statement	44
4.10	Tree diagrams	46
	Exercises	46
	Problems	47
5	**Repetition**	50
5.1	The for-statement	51
5.2	The loop as a fundamental building block	53
5.3	Using the control-variable within the loop	55
5.4	Nested loops or loops within loops	57
5.5	The specification of the for-statement	57
5.6	Unnecessary loops	59
	Exercises	59
	Problems	60
6	**Program design**	62
6.1	Producing a table of dates for Summer-time	62
6.2	Drawing a board for Noughts-and-Crosses or Tic-Tac-Toe	65
	Exercises	68
	Problems	68
7	**Constants and types**	71
7.1	Constant-definitions	71
7.2	Types	74
7.3	Enumerated-types	76
7.4	Subrange-types	82
7.5	The ordinal-types	83
	Exercises	83
	Problems	83
8	**Procedures and functions**	85
8.1	Structuring the payroll program with procedures	85
8.2	Stylistic conventions	87
8.3	The relative independence of procedures	90
8.4	Storage allocation	93
8.5	Formal-parameters and actual-parameters	94
8.6	The design of procedures	97
8.7	Functions	99
8.8	The design of procedures and functions	101
	Exercises	103
	Problems	104

9   Iteration and Booleans   105
9.1   Euclid's algorithm   105
9.2   The while-statement   106
9.3   The *Boolean-type*   107
9.4   Operations on Booleans   108
9.5   Operator priorities   112
9.6   The relationship between for- and while-statements   112
9.7   A strategy for writing loops   114
9.8   The repeat-statement   117
9.9   State variables   118
      Exercises   119
      Problems   120

10   Program design with procedures   122
10.1   Writing out PIN numbers   122
10.2   Easter day   127
      Problems   132

11   Program development   134
11.1   Testing the programs we designed earlier   134
11.2   The philosophy of testing   135
11.3   Testing assignment-statements   135
11.4   Testing compound-statements   137
11.5   Testing conditional-statements   137
11.6   Testing repetitive-statements   138
11.7   Other considerations   140
11.8   Checking that the algorithm is implemented   141
11.9   A testing strategy   141
11.10 Correcting the program that is found to be faulty   143
11.11 If all else fails: debug printing   145
11.12 A caveat   146
      Problems   146

12   Characters   149
12.1   The required type *char*   149
12.2   Operations on characters   150
12.3   Slightly more realistic employee code numbers   153
12.4   Two examples   154
      Exercises   156
      Problems   157

13   Records and arrays   159
13.1   Records   159
13.2   Records of records   162
13.3   Storage of records   163
13.4   Arrays   164
13.5   Strings   166

13.6   Arrays of records, records of arrays   166
13.7   Storage of arrays   169
13.8   Entire- and component-variables   170
13.9   The with-statement   171
13.10   The payroll program with sorted output   172
13.11   Multi-dimensional arrays   178
13.12   Variant-records   179
13.13   Structures as parameters   181
13.14   Packed arrays and records   182
        Exercises   183
        Problems   184

14 Sets   186
14.1   The set-types   186
14.2   Operations on sets   187
14.3   Examples   191
        Exercises   195
        Problems   196

15 Files   197
15.1   File definitions   197
15.2   Creating a file   199
15.3   Accessing a file   200
15.4   External files   202
15.5   Textfiles   204
15.6   Input and output   205
15.7   A more typical example – the *Payroll* program   206
15.8   Arrays or files?   208
        Exercises   208
        Problems   209

16 Program design with data structures   213
16.1   *Bibit Magus* winery   213
16.2   The type definitions for records on the file   213
16.3   Producing a summary   215
16.4   The type definitions for the summary record   215
16.5   The summary program   216
        Problems   223

17 Program structure and scope   226
17.1   Static structure diagrams   227
17.2   The accessibility of variables   227
17.3   The accessibility of type-denoters and constants   229
17.4   Scope   229
17.5   Accessing procedures and forward references   229
17.6   Dynamic structure diagrams   231
17.7   Procedure structure and top-down design   232
17.8   Parametric procedures   232

	Exercises	237
	Problems	237

18 Recursion 239
18.1 A simple recursive function: *Factorial* 239
18.2 How it works 240
18.3 Another simple recursive function: *Greatest Common Divisor* 243
18.4 A third simple recursive function: *Integer Powering* 244
18.5 More powerful recursive functions 246
18.6 A classical counter-example 248
18.7 Recursive procedures 250
18.8 Simulating nested loops 254
18.9 The power of recursion 259
Exercises 259
Problems 260

19 Dynamic storage 261
19.1 Conway's *Game of Life* 261
19.2 Pointer-variables and identified-variables 263
19.3 Interchanging rows of a matrix 268
19.4 Linked lists 270
19.5 Recursive list-processing procedures 276
19.6 Binary trees 278
19.7 Managing the heap 280
19.8 The power of the pointer 281
Exercises 282
Problems 282

Appendices
1 The syntax of Pascal 284
2 Reserved words, required-identifiers and operators 299

Solutions to exercises 303

Index 326

Preface

It is now ten years since the first edition of this book was completed – over half of Pascal's lifetime ago. Consequently, this edition is not so much a revision as a complete rewrite. The most noticeable change is the increased emphasis on structure. The idea of structuring at the statement level, using compound-statements, conditional-statements and repetitive-statements, is well accepted – even by Basic programmers – though there are periodic outbursts against it in the literature. The idea of structured data is less well accepted, and certainly the idea that a program may have only one or two global structures, which its procedures transform, is almost radical, Wirth's excellent *Algorithms + Data Structures = Programs* notwithstanding. The main changes can be summarized as follows.

- Procedures are covered very much earlier, before any of the structured-types. This means that all the examples are new, since their parameters are all of a simple-type. Parameters are introduced in the same chapter, and all procedures are fully parameterized, unless they are internal procedures in recursive situations. It was our experience that, if parameterless procedures are introduced first, then it is difficult to motivate the use of parameters, unless we fall back onto the use of procedures as subroutines, a view much less fruitful than that of procedures as structuring devices.

- Types and constants are introduced much earlier, with subranges being included from the first chapter. All variables are declared with as strong a type as possible. Almost no variables are of integer-type.

- Arrays and records are introduced later, after procedures in fact. They are discussed together to enable a full discussion of typical structures, in which fields of records may be arrays, whose elements may in turn be records, whose fields may be ... . This positioning enables us to write many procedures operating over these data structures, to reinforce the idea that in many situations the structure of the data determines the structure of the program.

- Top-down design is emphasized, with three chapters being devoted to the design of programs. These chapters are strategically placed after the introduction of the key structuring concepts of repetition, procedures, and records and arrays.

Of course, much of the philosophy of the original edition remains. The experience that has suggested the changes above has confirmed the worth of the remainder, and suggested extensions and improvements. The important retentions are described below.

- The development of a payroll program from a rudimentary, one-person version has been extended so that it now is developed into a full-blown system using files. As well the reader is encouraged to follow a similar development on a program to handle examination marks. This is the first problem in each chapter in which the payroll is enhanced.

- The book is still in a form that is directly useful for a lecture course. Almost all the chapters fit comfortably into a 40- to 45-minute period, and those that do not can be covered in two such periods.

- The emphasis on the use of diagrams is retained. Syntax diagrams, structure diagrams and store layout diagrams are used extensively. It is still our belief that Pascal is best understood in terms of the Pascal machine on which it runs. Flow diagrams, not very prominent in the first edition, have withered away.

With one exception, the programs are all in Standard Pascal. That exception relates to program-parameters. Because we are using micro-computers in the programming laboratories rather than mainframes, the assignment of permanent files to a program must be done differently, by means of statements within the program, rather than by operating system commands. Accordingly, we have dispensed with the *(input, output)* on program-headings. We have, too, omitted to describe the label and goto facilities – they have, in our view, no place in a first course on programming.

For those interested in running and perhaps modifying the programs, they are available on disc from *Sophisters and Calculators, 29 Viewway, Nedlands, WESTERN AUSTRALIA 6009* at a price of $US10. The current disc formats are 3.5" suitable for MacPascal or LightSpeed Pascal and 5.25" suitable for Turbo Pascal running on IBM PCs or their clones.

I should like to thank Joyce Fisher, who entered the text of the first edition into my computer, Christine Gatti, Lisa McAllister, Frank O'Connor and Lisa Beckley, who did a great deal of the manuscript checking, and Casper Boon, who ensured that the programs had not become corrupted in the transfer and editing process.

Oxford, October 1989   J. S. Rohl

1

Introduction

The computer is a very powerful device, since it can be turned into a machine for performing any particular specific computing task at will. This transformation is effected by providing the computer with a *program*, which is a set of instructions defining precisely the operations to be performed. (As technical terms are introduced they will appear in *italics*.) We cannot yet talk to a computer in English, and so a program is expressed in what is called a *programming language*. There are a number of these in existence: the one this book uses is called *Pascal*.

Let us look at the broad structure of a computer, shown in Fig 1.1.

Fig 1.1 A broad schematic of a computer

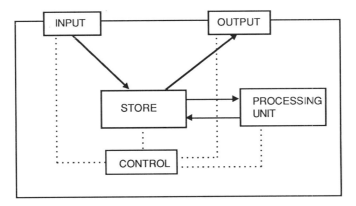

It consists of five components. The program is held in part of the *store* and we assume that it is there initially. (How it gets there we will consider later in this chapter.) At the heart of the computer is the *control* unit which has a very simple operation: it takes an instruction from the program in the store and causes it to be obeyed; then it takes the next instruction from the store and causes it to be obeyed; and so on. The dotted lines in Fig 1.1 illustrate this. The instruction may:

- Cause data to be read into the store from the *input* device.

- Cause *processing* to take place on data held in the store.

- Cause answers to be written out from the store via the *output* device.

The solid lines in Fig 1.1 illustrate the flow of information.

1.1   A simple payroll example

All programs are built from such instructions. Let us illustrate this by a very simple example of a program (Prog 1.1) for use by an employee who wishes to calculate his gross pay. In detail, the program will:

- Ask the employee for his personal code number (of 4 digits), his rate of pay in dollars per hour and the number of hours worked. These last two may have a decimal point in them to allow for a rate of pay which consists of dollars and cents, and a time which includes a fraction of an hour.

- Calculate from these the gross pay.

- Write out the gross pay together with the personal code number.

The overtime pay provisions are quite simple: overtime is paid at time and a half after 37$\frac{1}{2}$ hours have been worked. Further, the program assumes that the employee works at least the regulation 37$\frac{1}{2}$ hours. The program, as written, follows very precise rules (and much of this book is concerned with specifying these) but for the moment we are concerned only with explaining how it works. Let us assume therefore that this program is in the machine and consider what happens when the program runs. The output which is produced when employee

Prog 1.1   A very simple payroll program

```
program Payroll;
  var
    code : 1000..9999;
    rate, hours, gross, overtime : real;
begin
  writeln('This program calculates your weekly wage.');
  write('What is your employee code number? ');
  readln(code);
  write('What is your basic rate of pay? ');
  readln(rate);
  write('For how many hours did you work? ');
  readln(hours);
  overtime := hours − 37.5;
  gross := hours * rate + overtime * 0.5 * rate;
  writeln('Employee ', code : 4, ' your wage is $', gross : 6 : 2, '.')
end.
```

2134, whose pay rate is $8.26 per hour and who has worked 42³/₄ hours, runs
the program is given below:

```
This program calculates your weekly wage.
What is your employee code number? 2134
What is your basic rate of pay? 8.26
For how many hours did you work? 42.75
Employee 2134 your wage is $374.80.
```

We now describe step by step how the program produces this result. With the
description of the action we will give some pictorial representation of the part of
the store that contains the data. Initially the store contains the program and
whatever data was left there by the previous program.

The segment:

program Payroll;

is called the *program-heading*. (When describing parts of the Pascal language
we use hyphenated phrases.) This introduces the program giving it the name
Payroll. No action is taken by the computer. Note that **program** is in bold type
and does not start with a capital letter. Note, too, that precise punctuation is
important: the semi-colon is necessary. The spacing is rather more flexible, but
for the moment we will simply put blanks in as we would when writing English.
You may find this need for precision daunting: a good idea is to model your early
programs on those given here. As this book progresses we will explain all the
details, and in an interlude shortly we will introduce a way of defining the form of
Pascal quite precisely.

The rest of the program has the form of a *block* and is terminated by a *full
stop*. The block consists of a variable-declaration-part followed by a statement-
part. The *variable-declaration-part*:

var
    code : 1000..9999;
    rate, hours, gross, overtime : real;

defines the characteristics of the quantities that the program operates on, the so-
called *variables*. Here there are five. One, called *code*, can have integral
values only in the range 1000..9999. That is, it must be a 4-digit integer. The
other four called *rate*, *hours*, *gross* and *overtime*, may take on *real* values,
which allows them to have a fractional part. Clearly the variables of this program
correspond to the real world quantities described above. For example, the
variable *gross* corresponds to gross pay. There is a certain freedom of choice in
the naming of variables, as we shall see in Chapter 2, and we could have
chosen, say, *grosspay*, instead of *gross*. Note the punctuation marks used in
the variable-declaration-part. There are commas between variables in groups of
the same type, and semi-colons between the groups.

The effect of the variable-declaration-part is that five pieces (or *locations* as
they are generally called) of storage are allocated, one to each of the variables.

Pictorially we can imagine that the name of the variable is attached to the locations as shown below.

code	rate	hours	gross	overtime
?	?	?	?	?

No value is associated with any of the variables as yet: each location still contains whatever value happened to be in the store when the program was started. We will indicate this by a question mark though later on we will merely leave the location blank.

The *statement-part* extends from the **begin** to the **end**, which enclose ten *statements* separated by *semi-colons*. (Again the punctuation is important.)

The first statement is a *writeln-statement*.

writeln('This program calculates your weekly wage.')

When this statement is obeyed, the sentence within the quotation marks (') is written on the screen. The significance of the "ln" in "writeln" is that any following output goes onto a new line. This line of the output tells the user what the program does. Although it seems a little pedantic here, we will always do this in our programs as a help to the user.

The second statement:

write('What is your employee code number? ')

is a *write-statement*. Note that there is no "ln" after the "write". When obeyed, this statement causes the question within the quotation marks to be written onto the screen, but does not move to the next line. The intention, of course, is to prompt the user to answer that question by typing his code number, here 2134, so that it can be read into the computer.

The third statement:

readln(code)

achieves this. It is a *readln-statement* and its effect is as follows. A *cursor*, a winking rectangle or vertical line, appears on the screen immediately beyond the last character written to the screen. The user types his response, followed by pressing the return key. The number is read in and its value is assigned to the variable *code*. The significance of the "ln" is that that the whole of the rest of the line is read: if more than one number is typed on the line, then the second and subsequent numbers are simply ignored. Subsequent output appears on the next line. At the end of the first three statements, the store is as shown below.

code	rate	hours	gross	overtime
2134	?	?	?	?

The next four statements consist of two pairs, each of which resembles the last pair.

```
write('What is your basic rate of pay? ');
readln(rate);
write('For how many hours did you work? ');
readln(hours)
```

The first of each pair writes out a question on the screen: the second reads the user's response. If the answers are the same as those used earlier, then at the end the store looks like this:

code	rate	hours	gross	overtime
2134	8.26	42.75	?	?

The next two statements:

```
overtime := hours − 37.5;
gross := hours * rate + overtime * 0.5 * rate
```

are *assignment-statements*. Each causes appropriate operations (here arithmetic) to take place and the result assigned to a variable. Thus, in the first, 37.5 is subtracted from the value of *hours* (which is 42.75) giving 5.25, this value being assigned to *overtime*. Similarly, the value 42.75 * 8.26 + 5.25 * 0.5 * 8.26 = 374.7975 is assigned to *gross.* Below is a picture of the store after these two.

code	rate	hours	gross	overtime
2134	8.26	42.75	374.7975	5.25

The final statement, another writeln-statement:

writeln('Employee ', code : 4, ' your wage is $', gross : 6 : 2, '.')

is somewhat more complicated than earlier ones. It is clear from the output that the statement produces a line of output which has five parts. In the statement the five parts are separated by commas. The first, third and fifth parts contain strings of words and other characters within quotation marks, and as we saw earlier, these are written out exactly as typed. The second and fourth parts of the writeln-statement consist of variables, *code* and *gross* respectively, and it is their values that are written. The style in which they are written is determined by the *field-width.* Consider the second part. The 4 specifies that *code* shall be written out using a *TotalWidth* of 4 spaces on the screen. Since *code* is a 4-digit number, this is quite sensible. But note that the string to its left ends with a space, and that to its right starts with one. Thus the number, here 2134, fits properly into the line. In the fourth part of the statement, *gross* has two field-widths specified, a TotalWidth of 6 of which the *FractionalPart* is 2. In this case 2 is clearly sensible because it gives the gross to the nearest cent, and the 6 is adequate if the gross is in the range $100.00 to $999.99. If TotalWidth is too big then spaces will be added in front of the number: if it is too small, then enough extra space will be used to write out the number in full. As we shall see later, if you are producing tables rather than sentences then the layout will be spoiled in the latter case.

1.2   The compiler

We have assumed here that the program is initially in the store. The question is: how does the program get into the machine? The answer is that it is read by another program which resides in the machine, called a *compiler* or an *interpreter.* The compiler or interpreter not only reads in the program but also converts it from Pascal (the so-called *source language*) into the language of the machine (the so-called *object language*). We can usually forget this conversion process and pretend, as we have here, that the machine obeys Pascal. It will be convenient, though, to refer to the compilation process throughout this book to explain some of the features of Pascal.

1.3   Preparing a program

A Pascal program contains certain words which, when written in manuscript or typescript, are generally underlined, and when printed appear in bold face. This convention serves two purposes:

• Experience with similar languages shows that the emboldening makes it easier to read programs.

• It reminds us that the emboldened words are *word-symbols,* which have a fixed meaning and can be used only in a fixed context.

Except for the Macintosh, however, no popular computer allows emboldening or underlining, and so this convention is not available to users of those machines. To gain similar advantages many programmers use the fact that, except within strings, upper and lower case letters are not differentiated by the compiler and write all their word-symbols in upper case. Prog 1.2 shows this with the payroll program. You may find that some of the older Pascal texts present their programs in this style.

While the word-symbols are immutable, there is a certain amount of flexibility allowed to the programmer in the choice of *identifiers*, as we mentioned earlier. Note that there are some identifiers such as *real*, *read* and *write* that the compiler is required to provide. (As you might imagine they are called *required-identifiers*.) They are meant for a specific purpose, and although they could be used for another purpose it would be difficult to find a good reason for doing this. Thus we have three related concepts: word-symbols, required-identifiers and ordinary, user-chosen identifiers. As is the case with most other programming languages, you simply have to learn which words are required-identifiers and which are word-symbols. Appendix 2 contains a list of both classes.

1.4 Running programs

Programs can be run either interactively or in batch mode. In the *interactive mode*, which we assumed for the payroll program, and will generally use throughout this book, the program is entered into the machine and then set running. During the running it will ask the user for the data as required. This is the normal mode for micro-computers. In *batch mode*, the program and data are entered together, and the program runs without user intervention. Batch mode programs are generally shorter than the equivalent interactive ones, because they do not need to conduct a dialogue with the user. On mainframe computers, batch processing is still quite often the norm. On micros, too, there are many

Prog 1.2 The payroll program with upper case word-symbols

```
PROGRAM payroll;
  VAR
    code : 1000..9999;
    rate, hours, gross, overtime : real;
BEGIN
  writeln('This program calculates your weekly wage.');
  write('What is your employee code number? ');
  readln(code);
  write('What is your basic rate of pay? ');
  readln(rate);
  write('For how many hours did you work? ');
  readln(hours);
  overtime := hours - 37.5;
  gross := hours * rate + overtime * 0.5 * rate;
  writeln('Employee ', code : 4, ' your wage is $', gross : 6 : 2, '.')
END.
```

situations where running in batch mode is desirable, especially where the data for a program already exists within the computer. In later chapters we shall write such programs. In either case, the *operating system* of the computer demands that certain other information be supplied by the user, either from the keyboard or in *control lines* which are attached to the program. The details vary from computer to computer and you must consult your system's manual for this information.

1.5   What happens when you get it wrong?

It may be, of course, that your program is not correct. What happens when you present it to the computer for running? One of three things may happen, and we will consider these in turn.

(i) Suppose that you had misspelled the word *rate* as *rat* in the read-statement of the payroll program. The compiler will discover this error by noting that you have referred to the variable *rat* though no such variable has been declared. There could be many other such errors. The compiler will always give some indication of the symptoms: you then have to diagnose the problem. While this is difficult at first it becomes fairly easy after a little experience. The means by which these *syntax errors* are reported to the user are so numerous that little purpose is served by describing any of them here. Consult your Pascal manual.

(ii) Suppose that you had typed the program correctly but had accidently typed an employee number that was out of range, 12345 say. Then when obeying the (translated version of the) statement:

readln(code)

the machine would stop running the program, give a message indicating where in the program the error was detected and perhaps write out the values of the variables to help in diagnosing the error. We call these *run-time errors*.

(iii) Suppose, finally, you had mistyped a + as a − in an assignment-statement. The program would run to a conclusion: it just would give the wrong answer! This is always a difficult mistake to correct. We will discuss it in some detail in Chapter 11 but at this stage the only thing to do is to work through the program step by step (like the computer) using diagrams of the store like those used earlier (or at least stylized forms of them) until you find the cause.

Note that you must have known that there was an error before you could have corrected it. That is, you must have known the correct answer in order to determine that the program-produced answer was wrong. We will return to the subject of testing programs in Chapter 11. For now, whenever you test a program, use simple data which you check either by hand or with a calculator.

Exercises

1.1   Write a program which simply writes out a menu for your favourite meal. It will use only writeln-statements.

1.2 Tradesmen who come to work at private residences usually charge a fixed fee, for being called out, and an hourly fee for the time spent on the job. Write a program which will ask the user for the call-out fee, the hourly rate and the number of hours worked, and write out the total bill payable. Use the *Payroll* program as a model.

2

Variables and arithmetic

In Chapter 1 we looked at a Pascal program, the payroll program, which is reproduced as Prog 2.1, and sketched out both its broad structure and the way it works. We now start on the problem of writing a program. There are many places where we might start: we will choose to consider the facilities provided for performing arithmetic, postponing consideration of input and output until later.

Arithmetic is performed in the *assignment-statement*, two examples of which we have seen already:

```
overtime := hours − 37.5;
gross := hours * rate + overtime * 0.5 * rate
```

The form of the assignment-statement is quite simple. On the left-hand side of the *becomes symbol*, :=, is what is called a *variable-access*. It is just the name of one of the variables of the program. On the right-hand side is an *expression*. The effect is simple, too. The expression is evaluated and the result is *assigned* to the variable accessed. The structure of a typical assignment-statement, the

Prog 2.1 The simple payroll program

```
program Payroll;
  var
    code : 1000..9999;
    rate, hours, gross, overtime : real;
begin
  writeln('This program calculates your weekly wage.');
  write('What is your employee code number? ');
  readln(code);
  write('What is your basic rate of pay? ');
  readln(rate);
  write('For how many hours did you work? ');
  readln(hours);
  overtime := hours − 37.5;
  gross := hours * rate + overtime * 0.5 * rate;
  writeln('Employee ', code : 4, ' your wage is $', gross : 6 : 2, '.')
end.
```

---

assignment to *gross* above, is illustrated in Fig 2.1.

Fig 2.1   The structure of the assignment-statement

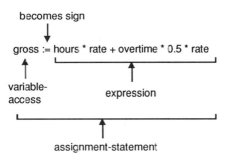

The arithmetic is performed in expressions, which we now consider.   The important question is: how can we express a computation in terms of Pascal expressions?   We answer this by posing two simpler questions:

- What are the available forms of operand for the expression?

- How may these operands be combined to form an expression?

Firstly, we consider variables, which occur both as operands in expressions and as the variable-access of assignment-statements.

2.1   Variables and variable declarations

A *variable* is a quantity on which the program operates.   Its value is the value *last assigned to it*, either by an earlier assignment-statement (as is the case with *overtime* in the second of the pair of statements above) or by a read-statement (as is the case with *hours* and *rate*).   In a program we refer to a variable by a name, called its *identifier*, such as *overtime* or *hours*.   (We clearly cannot refer to it by its value since that changes throughout the course of the program.)   There is a great deal of freedom in the choice of identifier.   It must start with a (Roman) letter and may be followed by a sequence of letters and/or digits. No other characters may be used.   Thus:

overtime	hours	
t0	t1	t2
XMS711	ETU952K	

are all valid identifiers.   It is important to note that a blank may not appear in an identifier.   Thus none of the following:

XMS 711   ETU 952 K   Gross pay

is valid.   It can be seen that this restriction is a little inhibiting since it discourages identifiers made of a number of words. If you want multi-word identifiers then you must write them without spaces; the use of upper case for the first letter of each word improves their readability. Our general strategy for choosing identifiers shall be as follows. For programs and procedures, which will be introduced later, we will use multi-word identifiers, capitalizing the first letter of each word. For variables we shall be more subtle. We will not create long identifiers just for the sake of it: we will be concerned with creating identifiers which are meaningful. Sometimes, where the program is an abstract one, we will use suitably general identifiers; and where the program is mathematical, we shall use single letters if that is what the mathematical formulation uses.

The programmer specifies the existence of the quantities of his program in the *variable-declaration-part*. In this he specifies not only the identifier of each variable but also its *type*. In the payroll program we have:

        var
            code : 1000..9999;
            rate, hours, gross, overtime : real;

which is verbalized as "the variables are *code* of *integer-type* in the range 1000..9999; and *rate, hours, gross* and *overtime* of *real-type*". Let us take a close look at the structure of this statement, which is illustrated in Fig 2.2.

Fig 2.2   The structure of the variable-declaration-part

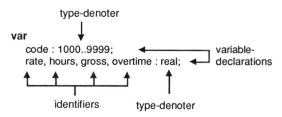

It consists of the delimiter-word **var** (short for "variables") followed by a series of what are called *variable-declarations* which are separated by semi-colons. In this example the variable-declarations are *code : 1000..9999* and *rate, hours, gross, overtime : real*. Each variable-declaration consists of a series of identifiers separated by commas (not semicolons). These are followed, after a colon, by a *type-denoter*. In simple programs, an identifier may not be used for more than one purpose. It cannot, for example, be used both as an integer variable and as a real variable. Within the variable-declaration-part, the order of the identifiers is irrelevant as is the order in which the types are introduced. Further, a type can be associated with more than one list of identifiers. Thus:

        var
            hours, overtime : real;
            code : 1000..9999;
            rate, gross : real;

is precisely equivalent to:

```
var
  code : 1000..9999;
  rate, hours, gross, overtime : real;
```

Clearly the latter is more straightforward and rather easier to understand, especially when coming back to a program after a period, since variables of a given type are declared together.

2.2 Program layout

In Pascal, a change to a new line has no effect on the meaning of a program. We have already noted that spaces may be added to a program if that improves readability. Perhaps now is the time to describe the situation more formally. A space and a change to a new line are considered as *token-separators*. They have the following properties:

- None may appear inside a word-symbol, identifier or constant.

- At least one must appear between consecutive word-symbols, identifiers and constants.

- Any number of them may appear anywhere else.

Thus it has become traditional to indent programs to help readability. Since all the programs of this book have been developed using Macintosh Pascal, and since that compiler enforces its own conventions, those are the ones that we shall use. We shall explain them as they arise. Authors of other text-books (including the current authors in the first edition of this book) develop their own conventions, as undoubtedly will many of our readers. An example of a layout of the variable-declaration-part which is often used is:

```
var
  code :
            1000..9999;
  rate,
  hours,
  gross,
  overtime :
            real;
```

which has some advantages, especially when used with comments.

2.3 Comments

A comment is a sequence of characters enclosed within braces, { and }, which is ignored by the compiler, and which therefore can be used by the programmer to document his program. The above declaration-part might in a large program be commented as below.

```
var
   code:                      {The employee's code number}
            1000..9999;
   rate,                      {The employee's rate of pay}
   hours,                     {The number of hours worked}
   gross,                     {The gross pay earned}
   overtime :                 {The amount of overtime worked}
         real;
```

As long as the layout convention is sensible, and is adhered to, it doesn't much matter what it is. The Macintosh convention for the variable-declaration-part is:

- **var** is on a separate line, indented one unit of space from **program**.

- Each variable-declaration is on a new line indented one further unit.

2.4   Types

The payroll program contains variables of only two types, the integer-type and the real-type, and we will confine ourselves to these for the next few chapters. Most often, as in the payroll program, integer variables are within some well-defined range such as 1000 to 9999, and will be declared as such. Sometimes, however, we cannot easily predict in advance what values an integer will range over. In this case we give it the integer-type. For example:

```
var
   random : integer;
```

There is a special constant, *maxint*, whose value is the largest integer in the computer. Thus variables of integer-type range over −*maxint..maxint*. Two subranges occur quite often. If a variable is known not to be negative, then it should be declared:

```
var
   natural : 0..maxint;
```

Similarly, a variable known to take only positive integral values could be defined:

```
var
   posint : 1..maxint;
```

With real numbers there is no subrange facility: all real variables are of real-type. Reals can take on values over a much larger range than integers, though only to a certain accuracy. It is usually quite obvious whether a quantity should be of integer-type or real-type. In the example we have been using, an employee's personnel code number is clearly of integer-type, and, since it is a 4-digit number, is equally clearly in the range 1000 to 9999. On the other hand, his salary expressed in dollars is of real-type. Had we chosen to express it in cents, it would, of course, have been of integer-type. On most (probably all) computers, integers and reals are stored differently, and different operations are required to perform the arithmetic. When processing a variable-declaration, a compiler:

- Ensures that the appropriate storage is allocated to each variable.

- Remembers the type so that it can ensure that the correct machine instructions are used for subsequent operations on the quantity. It also checks that only operations appropriate to the type are used.

2.5   Constants

We have considered in the last few sections the first form of operand, the variable. The second sort of operand is the *unsigned-constant*. Associated with the types integer and real are the unsigned-constants called, naturally enough, the *unsigned-integer* and the *unsigned-real*. An unsigned-integer consists simply of digits. For example:

       3   17   6092

The only thing to note is that it must not contain a decimal point. An unsigned-real, on the other hand, contains a decimal point. For example:

       37.5   7.0   0.2818

Not only must there be a decimal point, there must also be at least one digit either side of the point. For very large or very small numbers this can be tedious and a further form of the unsigned-real allows scientific notation. For example:

       1.0e7   27.3e−6   3.14e+2   4e11

Here the *e* is part of the constant, as is the *scale-factor* which follows. This is a signed-integer stating the power of 10 by which the initial part of the constant must be multiplied to give the correct value. Thus 1.0e7 can be read as "1.0 times 10 to the power of 7". The scale-factor can be attached to an integer (as in the last example) but the resulting constant is an unsigned-real.

2.6   Expressions

Now that we have considered the operands we can return to the main theme of the chapter, *expressions*, to consider the other problem: how can the operands be combined to form an expression? To motivate the discussion, consider the following formulae (the first of which concerns loan repayments, the second the area of a triangle):

$$p = \frac{A * \dfrac{r}{100} * (1 + \dfrac{r}{100})^3}{(1 + \dfrac{r}{100})^3 - 1}$$

$$\text{Area} = \sqrt{s(s-a)(s-b)(s-c)}$$

The question is: how can we write an expression to evaluate the right-hand side? There are three problems to be considered:

- How do we represent the operations of addition, subtraction, multiplication, division and raising to a power?

- How do we write displayed formulae in a one-dimensional format (as we have to do in Pascal) without introducing ambiguity?

- How do we represent functions such as taking the square root?

Before we discuss these problems, we give assignments for the examples above.

p := A*r/100*(1+r/100)*sqr(1+r/100)/((1+r/100)*sqr(1+r/100)−1)

Area := sqrt(s*(s−a)*(s−b)*(s−c))

See if you can interpret these two expressions. Note that *sqrt* means "take the square root of what appears within the following brackets" and *sqr* means "square what appears within the following brackets".

One important point to note is that, just as there are two types of variable (so far), so there are two types of expression, integer and real. In an integer expression all operands must naturally be of integer-type; in a real expression, on the other hand, the operands may be of either integer-type or real-type, since the integers are a subset of the reals. As a general rule we can say that wherever a real value is required an integer value is acceptable. We consider the three problems mentioned above in turn.

2.7   Operators

We represent addition by +, subtraction by −, and multiplication by *. In an integer expression both operands will be of integer-type; in a real expression they will generally be of real-type but one or both may be of integer-type. The latter is relatively rare except where one of the operands is an unsigned-integer. This much has been obvious from the payroll example. To make absolutely sure let us now extend the example so that it calculates tax at a rate of 20%, and writes out the tax deducted and the nett pay as well as the gross pay. An appropriate program, which produces the following output, is given in Prog 2.2.

```
This program calculates your weekly wage.
What is your employee code number? 2134
What is your basic rate of pay? 8.26
For how many hours did you work? 42.75
Employee 2134 your wage is $374.80.
After tax of $ 74.96 this leaves $299.84.
```

Division is represented in two ways since there are essentially two different forms of division. The operator / produces a real value regardless of whether either operand has an integer or a real value. Thus *17/5* has the value 3.4. This is what we generally want in programs where we are dealing predominantly with real values. In other programs we may be concerned mainly with integers. In this context, when we divide two integers we require an integer result, the accurate (real) result rounded down. In Pascal the operator **div** performs this function so that *17 div 5* is 3. There is another operator relevant only to integers called **mod**, which gives the remainder after the division. Thus *17 mod 5* is 2. More generally, for any two integers *i* and *j*, $i = i\ div\ j * j + i\ mod\ j$. If one or both of the operands of **div** or **mod** is real, then the compiler will detect the error and write out an appropriate message.

Exponentiation (or raising to a power) cannot be explicitly performed in Pascal, and must be created by multiplication (for integer powers) or by the log and exp functions described in the next section (for real powers). However, a squaring function, *sqr*, is provided to help. Thus:

Prog 2.2 The payroll program with 20% tax rate

---

program Payroll;
  var
    code : 1000..9999;
    rate, hours, gross, overtime, tax, nett : real;
  begin
    writeln('This program calculates your weekly wage.');
    write('What is your employee code number? ');
    readln(code);
    write('What is your basic rate of pay? ');
    readln(rate);
    write('For how many hours did you work? ');
    readln(hours);
    overtime := hours − 37.5;
    gross := hours * rate + overtime * 0.5 * rate;
    tax := 0.20 * gross;
    nett := gross − tax;
    writeln('Employee ', code : 4, ' your wage is $', gross : 6 : 2, '.');
    writeln('After tax of $', tax : 6 : 2, ' this leaves $', nett : 6 : 2, '.')
  end.

$$x^2 + y^2$$

is written:

sqr(x) + sqr(y).

2.8   Precedence and brackets

In algebra, formulae are displayed in two dimensions because of exponentiation and division (both of which we have discussed) and special functions such as square root (to be discussed next). All expressions in Pascal, on the other hand, must be written in one-dimensional format. This linearization leads to the following problem. In the *formula*:

$$\frac{pv}{rt}$$

it is clear that the product of *p* and *v* is to be divided by the product of *r* and *t*. The Pascal *expression*:

p*v/r*t

on the other hand, is potentially ambiguous, in that it could mean either:

$$\frac{pv}{rt} \quad \text{or} \quad \frac{pv}{r}t$$

(In fact it means the latter.) This potential ambiguity is resolved by two rules. Firstly, operators are assigned a *priority* or *precedence*. The *multiplying-operators* (*, /, **div**, **mod**) have higher precedence than the *adding-operators* (+, −), just as in algebraic formulae. Secondly, where operators have equal precedence, they operate from left to right (as in algebra). These rules can be overcome by the use of brackets (again as in algebra). We give below some formulae and their Pascal expression equivalents.

Formula	Pascal expression
u + ft	u + f * t
$ut + \frac{1}{2} ft^2$	u * t + f * sqr(t) / 2
$\frac{-b}{2a}$	−b/(2*a)
h(f0 + 4f1 + f2)	h*(f0 + 4*f1 + f2)

Note that the brackets must be round, not square or curly.

Let us consider a program which uses the facilities of the last two sections. Prog 2.3 reads a time expressed as minutes since midnight on Sunday and calculates the number of days, hours and minutes in that time. A sample of its output is given below.

```
Midnight Sunday was how many minutes ago? 5000
That's 3 days, 11 hours and 20 minutes.
```

Let us see how the calculating part of the program works. Forgetting the days part for the moment, the total number of hours in the time is given by:

hours := time **div** 60

and the number of minutes left over by:

minutes := time **mod** 60

Similarly, from the total number of hours we calculate the number of days, and the number of hours left over:

days := hours **div** 24;
hours := hours **mod** 24

With a little bit of manipulation we can reduce this to three statements:

minutes := time **mod** 60;
hours := time **div** 60 **mod** 24;
days := time **div** 60 **div** 24

Note in Prog 2.3 the use throughout of a field-width of 1. This means that regardless of their values, the expressions are written out using the minimum

Prog 2.3 A program to convert minutes to days, hours and minutes

---

program ConvertTime;
  var
    time : 0..10079;
    minutes : 0..59;
    hours : 0..23;
    days : 0..6;
  begin
    write('Midnight Sunday was how many minutes ago? ');
    readln(time);
    minutes := time **mod** 60;
    hours := time **div** 60 **mod** 24;
    days := time **div** 60 **div** 24;
    writeln('That''s ', days : 1, ' days, ', hours : 1, ' hours and ',
                                         minutes : 1, ' minutes.')
  end.

---

amount of space. This technique is often used when the output is in a narrative form. Note, too, the use of what is called the *apostrophe-image*, ", to get a single apostrophe in the output. It consists of consecutive apostrophes, or quote signs, ', not a double quote. A single apostrophe or quote sign would be seen by the system as the terminator of the string to be written.

2.9   Functions

Many formulae are expressed in terms of functions, such as square root, sine and so on. Pascal implementations are required to provide a number of functions. The required real functions are given in Table 2.1, in which * means "or integer-type", and the required integer functions in Table 2.2.

Table 2.1   The required real functions

Name	Argument type	Comment
abs	real-type	The absolute value of the argument
sqr	real-type	The square of the argument
sin	real-type*	The argument is in radians
cos	real-type*	The argument is in radians
exp	real-type*	Antilog (exponentiation)
ln	real-type*	Natural logarithm (base e)
sqrt	real-type*	The positive square root
arctan	real-type*	The result is in radians

Table 2.2   The required integer functions

Name	Argument type	Comment
abs	integer-type	The absolute value of the argument
sqr	integer-type	The square of the argument
succ	integer-type	The successor (i.e. argument +1)
pred	integer-type	The predecessor (i.e. argument −1)
ord	integer-type	Its value
trunc	real-type	The truncated integer value
round	real-type	The rounded integer value

Note that there are two *abs* functions and two *sqr* functions, the type of the function being that of its argument. The functions *succ, pred* and *ord* are redundant but we will see in later chapters situations where they are useful. We give a description of *trunc* and *round* in the next section. In an expression, a *function-designator* (as it is called) takes its argument in brackets. The argument may itself be an expression. For example:

sqrt(x)   sin(n*pi/180)   ,   log(sin(x))

2.10   Assignments

Consider a general triangle whose sides are *a*, *b* and *c*. The classical formulae for the area of the triangle is:

$$Area = \sqrt{s(s-a)(s-b)(s-c)} \quad \text{where} \quad 2s = a+b+c.$$

A program which will calculate the area using this formula is given in Prog 2.4. Note that although in the description we defined *s* by:

$$2s = a + b + c$$

we did not express this in the program as:

$$2*s := a + b + c$$

because that is not the sense of the assignment-statement. In assignments an expression is evaluated and assigned to a variable. It is important to appreciate the difference between an equation and an assignment-statement. The equation:

$$r = \frac{-b + \sqrt{b^2 - 4ac}}{2a}$$

expresses the relationship between four quantities *a*, *b*, *c* and *r*, and if the values of any three are explicitly known, then the value of the fourth is implicitly known. The assignment-statement:

$$r := (-b + sqrt(sqr(b) - 4*a*c))/(2*a)$$

on the other hand, specifically causes *r* to be calculated, and requires, therefore,

Prog 2.4   A program which finds the area of a triangle

```
program Triangle;
  var
    a, b, c, s, area : real;
  begin
    writeln('This program finds the area of a triangle given the sides.');
    write('What are the sides? ');
    readln(a, b, c);
    s := (a + b + c) / 2;
    area := sqrt(s * (s - a) * (s - b) * (s - c));
    writeln('Its area is ', area : 8 : 2, '.')
  end.
```

that the values of *a*, *b* and *c* be known. If we had values for, say, *a*, *c* and *r* and required to calculate *b*, we would first have to manipulate the expression to give:

$$b = -ar - \frac{c}{r}$$

from which we immediately arrive at the assignment-statement:

$$b := -a^*r - c/r$$

In an assignment-statement, if the left-hand side variable is of integer-type, then the expression on the right-hand side must also be of integer-type. By contrast, if the left-hand side is of real-type, then the right-hand side may be of integer-type or real-type. Thus, even if *a*, *b*, *c* and *s* were of integer-type, and the product *s(s–a)(s–b)(s–c)* had an integral value, the assignment:

$$area := sqrt(s^*(s–a)^*(s–b)^*(s–c))$$

would be invalid if *area* were of integer-type, since the value of the sqrt function is of real-type. How can we get the integer equivalent of a real? The answer is by means of a *transfer function* which effects the transfer of a value from one type to another. There is a problem though, in that we need to be precise about which integer is the "integer equivalent" of a real. There are at least three candidates, two of which are available in Pascal. These, *trunc* and *round*, were given earlier as two of the required integer functions. Their meanings are the traditional ones, so that, for example:

trunc(3.7)	= 3	round(3.7)	= 4
trunc(–3.7)	= –3	round(–3.7)	= –4

As an example of the use of *round*, consider Prog 2.5 which reads in 2 natural numbers, representing the number of feet and inches in a distance, and writes out

Prog 2.5   A program to convert from feet and inches to millimetres

---

```
program ImperialToMetric;
  var
    feet, millimetres : 0..maxint;
    inches : 0..11;
begin
  writeln('This program converts feet and inches to millimetres.');
  write('Type the number of feet and inches. ');
  readln(feet, inches);
  millimetres := round(25.4 * (12 * feet + inches));
  writeln(feet : 1, 'ft ', inches : 1, 'ins = ', millimetres : 1, 'mm.')
end.
```

---

the distance and its metric equivalent to the nearest millimetre.

Sometimes we wish to round an integer to, say, the nearest hundred. If *n* is that integer then:

> 100*round(n/100)

achieves that effect by dividing *n* by 100, rounding it (to the nearest integer) and then multiplying by 100.

2.11   The importance of assignment-statements and expressions

The assignment statement is the only mechanism we have for performing any operation (except for input and output). Thus we shall find special cases of assignments such as:

> i := 0

which merely assigns 0 to *i*. We talk of "setting *i* to 0" or "initializing *i* ". We also find:

> x := y

which assigns *y* to *x*. We talk of "setting *x* to *y*" or "remembering *y* in *x*", or just "remembering *y*". When these arise in later chapters we will comment on them.

Expressions for overtly mathematical problems are usually very easy to write. For non-mathematical problems though they can sometimes be less than obvious until you have some experience with them. Below are a few examples which often prove useful.

English description	Pascal expression
The units digit of *n* of type 0..999	n **mod** 10
The tens digit of *n* of type 0..999	n **div** 10 **mod** 10
The hundreds digit of *n* of type 0..999	n **div** 100
The number of minutes in a time, *t*, expressed in the 24-hour clock system	t **div** 100 * 60 + t **mod** 100

Exercises

2.1 Write assignment-statements which perform the calculation of the following formulae. Assume s and n are of integer-type and all others are of real-type.

(i) $s = \frac{1}{2}n(n+1)$

(ii) $d = \sqrt{(E1-E2)^2 + (N1-N2)^2}$

(iii) $c = \sqrt{a^2 + b^2 - 2ab \cos C}$

2.2 Write arithmetic assignment-statements for the following formulae, which give the volume of a cylinder, a cone and a sphere respectively:

(i) $V = \pi r^2$

(ii) $V = \frac{\pi r^2 h}{3}$

(iii) $V = \frac{4}{3}\pi r^3$

2.3 Write an expression to round a real variable x of real-type to 2 decimal places.

2.4 Write arithmetic expressions whose values are:

(i) The largest even number not greater than some integer M. For example, if $M = 300$ or $M = 301$, the value is 300.

(ii) The largest odd number not greater than some integer M. For example, if $M = 300$ the value is 299; if $M = 301$ the value is 301.

Problems

2.1 Expand the very simple payroll program so that it also deducts a social services levy of 1.5%.

2.2 Consider a computing course in which the final mark awarded, an integer in the range 0 to 100, is obtained from two projects each weighted at 20%, and an exam mark with a weight of 60%. For the examiners' convenience, each component is marked as an integer out of 100. Write a program which will ask the user for 4 numbers: a four-digit student number and the 3 component marks, and write out the final mark, which should be rounded to the nearest percent. The conversation should go like this:

```
This program works out your final mark.
What is your student number? 8479
What are the marks for the 2 projects and exam?
86   75   59
Your final mark is 68.
```

Note that this problem will be continually extended in scope from chapter to chapter.

2.3 Consider again a general triangle with sides of length *a*, *b* and *c*. The circle which goes through its three vertices is called its *circumscribed circle*, and its radius *R* is given by:

$$R = \frac{abc}{4\sqrt{s(s-a)(s-b)(s-c)}}$$

The circle which touches all three sides is called its *inscribed circle*, and its radius *r* is given by:

$$r = \sqrt{\frac{(s-a)(s-b)(s-c)}{s}}$$

where *s* is, as before, half the sum of the sides. Write a program which will read in the values of *a*, *b* and *c* and print out the values of *R* and *r*.

2.4 A 12-metre yacht must conform to the formula:

$$\frac{L + 2(d_1-d_2) + \sqrt{s} - F}{2.37} \leq 12 \text{ metres}$$

where:

L is the length of the hull,
d_1 is the skin girth,
d_2 is the chain girth,
s is the sail area,
F is the average freeboard.

Write a program for use by a yacht measurer, which asks for the appropriate data and writes out the value of the formula to 2 decimal places.

3

Specifying Pascal's syntax

We have emphasized the importance of precision in writing programs and have gone to considerable lengths to spell out the precise form of the constructs as we introduced them. We refer to the rules describing the structure of a language as *syntax*. So far, this has all been done in English. For example, in Chapter 1 we described the broad structure of a program. We could have condensed the description to:

> "A program consists of a program-heading followed by a program-block terminated by a full stop; the program-block consists of a variable-declaration-part followed by a statement-part; and the statement-part consists of a sequence of statements separated by semi-colons and enclosed between the symbols **begin** and **end**."

This method has two disadvantages:

- It is not very concise so that it is relatively difficult when reading it to distill out its essence. This is compounded by the tendency of English writers to vary both vocabulary and syntax from sentence to sentence in order to achieve an acceptable style.

- There is an inherent difficulty in using English (words and punctuation marks) to describe the structure of another language (Pascal) containing those same words and marks. The difficulty is not insuperable, and the quoted paragraph is not ambiguous, but it is a demanding task to get it right.

Thus we seek another method which is both concise and precise and which avoids the second problem above.

3.1   Syntax diagrams

The technique we shall use throughout this book is a pictorial one using *syntax diagrams*. We start with the simplest one, and give in Fig 3.1 the diagram for *digit*. Note that each diagram has a name (here, of course, *digit*) attached to it. Even at a first glance, this has something to do with decimal digits, but how do we interpret it? Suppose we have a string of characters and wish to know whether it starts with a digit (presumably as part of the larger question of whether the original string is a Pascal program). If a path through a diagram can be found then the string indeed starts with a digit. To find a path through a circle (or later, a box with rounded ends) we simply have to find the circled (or boxed) symbol at the start of the string. There are clearly 10 paths through the *digit* diagram, corresponding to the 10 decimal digits – as you would expect.

Fig 3.1 The syntax diagram for *digit*

digit

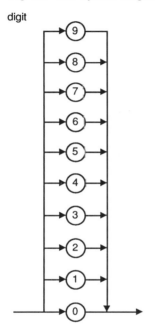

There is a similar diagram for *letter*. It has 52 alternatives corresponding to the upper and lower case letters of the Roman alphabet, and inclusion would simply waste space. These two diagrams are very simple, since they consist entirely of circles, and so the construct, here *digit* or *letter*, is defined directly. More complicated constructs refer to other diagrams. Consider, for example, Fig 3.2,

Fig 3.2 The syntax diagram for *identifier*

identifier

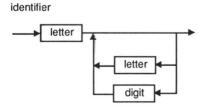

which is a diagram for *identifier*. Note the rectangular boxes. Each of these represents a diagram whose name is the same as that within the box, here *digit* or *letter*. Any path through that diagram closes the path through the box. So *a* is an *identifier*, because it is a *letter*, and closing a path through the letter box closes a path through the *identifier* diagram. Similarly, *t0* is an identifier, because *t* closes a path through the *letter* diagram and *0* closes a path through the *digit* diagram, thus closing a path through *identifier*.

As a more detailed example, Fig 3.3 gives the syntax diagram for *unsigned-real*. Compare this with the description given in the last chapter.

Fig 3.3   The syntax diagram for *unsigned-real*

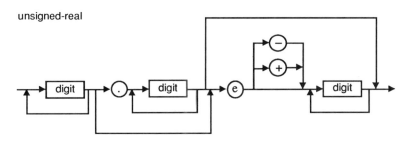

unsigned-real

To help in interpreting syntax diagrams, the following conventions are adopted:

(i) There is a main line of flow from left to right. Alternatives, especially empty alternatives, are drawn above this line; repetitions are drawn below it. The only exception to this is in Fig 3.3 above: an alternative line is drawn below the main line to avoid lines crossing.

(ii) An asterisk against the name indicates a diagram which is abridged because of the restricted facilities we have met and which will be explained later. A complete set of diagrams is given in Appendix 1.

(iii) The syntax of identifier is simply that given in Fig 3.2. However, identifiers are used for different purposes (so far we have used them for variables and for programs); and in the diagrams it is convenient to indicate which class of identifier is being referred to by preceding it with an adjective such as *variable* or *procedure*. The same is true of the syntax of *variable*, there being a number of different classes of variable, each having the same syntax but being used in a different context, of *block* and of *function-designator*.

(iv) Conversely, there are different classes of expression, each having a different syntax but sometimes used in the same context. We will use diagrams to describe the syntax of arithmetic expression (and later Boolean-expression and so on), but when describing the common contexts (here procedure-statement) we will omit the adjective. This applies to *assignment-statement* and *relation* (see later) as well.

(v) The precedence of operators is indicated by including the loop containing the higher priority operators within that containing the lower priority operators. As an example consider the syntax of arithmetic expression given in Fig 3.4.

Fig 3.4 The syntax of *arithmetic expression*

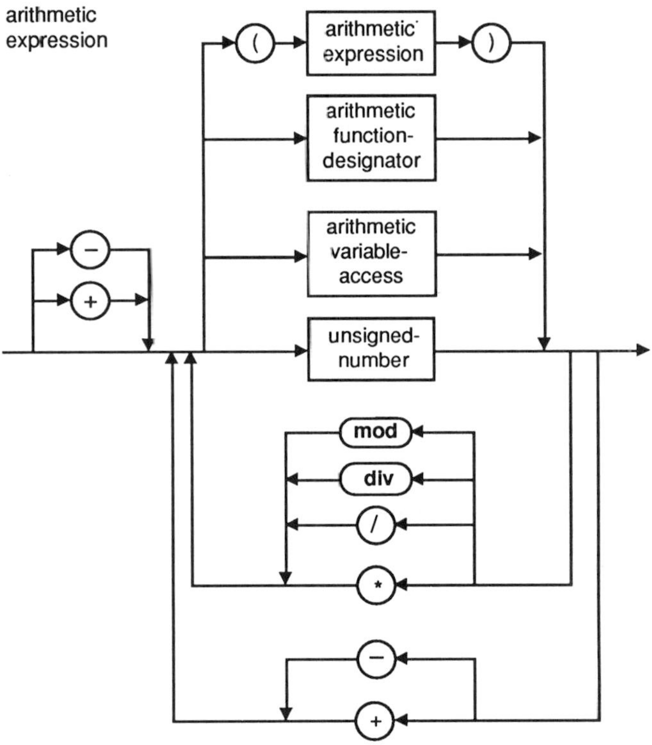

A set of syntax diagrams for the top level of a Pascal program is given in Fig 3.5.

3.2   Extended Backus Naur Form

The Pascal Standard uses an alternative method of describing syntax, a formalism called Extended Backus Naur Form (EBNF). In this notation, syntax is defined by equations. For example, *digit* is defined:

digit = "0"|"1"|"2"|"3"|"4"|"5"|"6"|"7"|"8"|"9".

Fig 3.5 The top-level syntax of Pascal

program

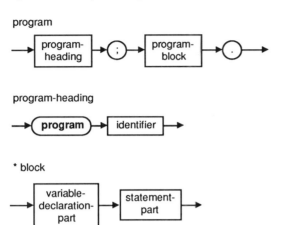

program-heading

program-heading diagram

* block

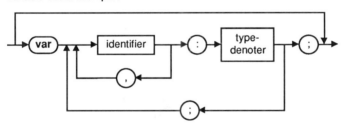

variable-declaration-part

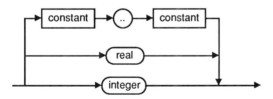

* type-denoter

type-denoter diagram

statement-part

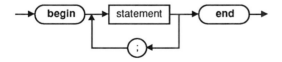

Here the vertical bar means "or", Pascal symbols appear inside quotation marks and the equation is terminated by a full stop. Thus we can read the above as:

> "A *digit* is defined to be either the symbol 0, or the symbol 1, or the symbol 2, or the symbol 3, or the symbol 4, or the symbol 5, or the symbol 6, or the symbol 7, or the symbol 8, or the symbol 9."

It is easy to see that this corresponds directly to the syntax diagram for *digit* given in Fig 3.1. Consider, now the definition of *block*:

> block = variable-declaration-part statement-part.

Remember that we use hyphenated phrases to describe the syntactical components of Pascal. The side-by-side appearance of two such components, or of one of them and a string of characters within quotes, can be read as "followed by". Thus the definition of block can be read as:

> "A *block* is a *variable-declaration-part* followed by a *statement-part.*"

The repetition of some syntactical component is indicated by means of curly brackets as in:

> identifier = letter {letter | digit}.

which is read as:

> "An *identifier* is defined to be a letter followed by any number of occurrences (including 0) of *letter* or *digit.*"

The optional occurrence of some syntactical component is indicated by means of square brackets. Thus:

> variable-declaration-part = [**"var"** variable-declaration ";"
> { variable-declaration ";" }].

indicates that the *variable-declaration-part* may be empty.
    We give below the EBNF definitions of the top level of Pascal.

> program = program-heading program-block ".".
> program-heading = **"program"** identifier ";".
> block = variable-declaration-part statement-part.
> variable-declaration-part = [**"var"** variable-declaration ";"
> { variable-declaration ";" }].
> variable-declaration = identifier-list ":" type-denoter.
> identifier-list = identifier { "," identifier }.
> statement-part = **"begin"** statement {";" statement} **"end"**.

3.3   A note on the syntax diagrams used here

The syntax diagrams used here are somewhat more expansive than those generally given (see, for example, Wilson & Addyman, 1983) and those implied by the EBNF definitions of the Standard (BS6192:1982). The main difference occurs in expressions (and later on in relations). The Standard has a single definition which covers all classes of expression. Unfortunately, it also covers a whole host of invalid expressions. The definition is adequate for a competent Pascal programmer, but during the learning stages, more precise definitions, one for each class of expression, seems preferable. As a consequence, we introduce notions such as *arithmetic expression*, which are not present in the Standard. In this case we will not use a hyphen between the adjective and the Standard name.

Exercises

3.1   Determine from the diagrams given earlier whether the following is a legitimate Pascal expression:

t **div** 100 * 60 + t **mod** 100

3.2   Given the syntax diagrams of Fig 3.6, determine whether each of the following is a *string*:

ab +   ab + −   ab   ab + cd + *

3.3   Write syntax equations corresponding to the syntax diagrams of Fig 3.6.

Problems

3.1   Go a step further towards precision by giving syntax diagrams for *integer expression* and *real expression* instead of *arithmetic expression*.

Fig 3.6   The syntax of string

string

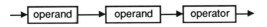

operand

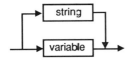

variable

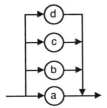

operator

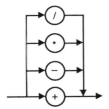

4

Alternatives

Let us consider the payroll program again and see what happens if an employee, whose hourly rate is $7.54, works for 12$1/2$ hours. Here is the output:

```
This program calculates your weekly wage.
What is your employee code number? 7105
What is your basic rate of pay? 7.54
For how many hours did you work? 12.5
Employee 7105 your wage is $  0.00.
After tax of $  0.00 this leaves $  0.00.
```

He gets no pay! Why not? First let us skip over the dialogue, and work through the assignment-statements to see what happens. Thus:

$$\text{overtime} = \text{hours} - 37.5$$
$$= 12.5 - 37.5$$
$$= -25,$$
$$\text{gross} = \text{hours} * \text{rate} + \text{overtime} * 0.5 * \text{rate}$$
$$= 12.5 * 7.54 + (-25) * 0.5 * 7.54$$
$$= 0$$

He gets penalized for working negative overtime, that is for working fewer than the standard hours. Clearly the problem is that two different calculations are involved in the determining of overtime, one for the case where the employee works fewer hours than the standard (in which case his overtime is 0), and another where he works more (in which case the previous formula is still correct).

4.1   The if-statement

Clearly we need a facility to be able to distinguish between these two cases. The solution is given in Prog 4.1. Instead of calculating *overtime* by a single assignment-statement we use a form of *conditional-statement*.

```
if hours > 37.5 then
   overtime := hours - 37.5
else
   overtime := 0
```

Its effect is as follows. If the condition being tested (here *hours* > 37.5) is true, the first statement is obeyed and the second is skipped, so that *overtime* is set to *hours* – 37.5. Conversely, if the condition is false (that is *hours* ≤ 37.5), the first statement is skipped and the second obeyed, and *overtime* is set to 0. Thus one or other of the statements is obeyed but not both. This gives the correct result shown below.

```
This program calculates your weekly wage.
What is your employee code number? 7105
What is your basic rate of pay? 7.54
For how many hours did you work? 12.5
Employee 7105 your wage is $ 94.25.
After tax of $ 18.85 this leaves $ 75.40.
```

The formal term for a condition is a *Boolean-expression*. There are two forms. The **if** ... **then** ... **else** ... form was used above. With this form, there are two statements, of which only one is obeyed. In the alternative **if** ... **then** ... form, there is only one statement, which is obeyed if the Boolean-expression is true, and skipped if it is false. Fig 4.1 gives the syntax diagram of the if-statement. We illustrate the alternative form in a different sequence for calculating the gross

Prog 4.1   The payroll program to deal with short working

```
program Payroll;
  var
    code : 1000 .. 9999;
    rate, hours, gross, overtime, tax, nett : real;
  begin
    writeln('This program calculates your weekly wage.');
    write('What is your employee code number? ');
    readln(code);
    write('What is your basic rate of pay? ');
    readln(rate);
    write('For how many hours did you work? ');
    readln(hours);
    if hours > 37.5 then
      overtime := hours – 37.5
    else
      overtime := 0;
    gross := hours * rate + overtime * 0.5 * rate;
    tax := 0.20 * gross;
    nett := gross – tax;
    writeln('Employee ', code : 4, ' your wage is $', gross : 6 : 2, '.');
    writeln('After tax of $', tax : 6 : 2, ' this leaves $', nett : 6 : 2, '.')
  end.
```

---

income in the payroll program:

```
gross := hours * rate;
if hours > 37.5 then
    gross := gross + (hours – 37.5) * 0.5 * rate;
```

This sequence calculates the "normal" pay (assuming a fixed rate per hour regardless of whether or not overtime is worked); and then, if overtime is worked, adds on the extra pay. In what follows we return to the form of the payroll program used in Prog 4.1, that is the one which uses the **if** ... **then** ... **else** ... form of the if-statement. The conditional-statement is one form of *structured-statement*, so called because it is constructed out of other statements (here assignment-statements).

4.2   Indentation

In both versions of the payroll program we have used another indenting convention: each of the alternative statements (or the one alternative in the **if** ... **then** ... case) is indented with respect to the **if** and the **else**. Thus the extent of any if-statement can be seen at a glance. Note the implication that each of the alternative statements occupies a line on its own. This will always be the case in this book, but when the statement is short some writers put it on the same line as the **if** or the **else**.

4.3   Boolean-expressions

The key concept in this new construct is the *Boolean-expression*, which is named after George Boole who first investigated what is now called Boolean algebra. We will generally use the term "Boolean-expression" instead of "condition" when we are describing parts of a Pascal program. A Boolean-expression can have one of only two values, *true* and *false*. In its simplest form it is the relation between two arithmetic expressions. The traditional six relational operators are available (though they may look unusual due to the inadequacies of the available character set). They and their meaning are given overleaf. Some examples are:

hours > 37.5   gross <= 100   sqr(b) = 4*a*c   x **mod** y <> 0

Fig 4.1   The syntax of *if-statement*

if-statement

Relational   Meaning
operator

=	equal to
<>	not equal to
<	less than
>	greater than
<=	less than or equal to
>=	greater than or equal to

It makes sense to talk of an *arithmetic relation* and Fig 4.2 gives its syntax. As a further example we expand the payroll program yet again, Prog 4.2, to deal with a taxation system which allows the first $100 of income each week to be tax-free.

4.4   Extended if-statements

Returning to the syntax diagram for if-statement we see that each of the alternative statements may be an if-statement. Thus the second alternative may be an if-statement whose second alternative may be an if-statement, and so on:

if ... then
  ...
else if ... then
  ...
else
  ...

Although, from the description given above, this is a highly structured statement, it is convenient to regard it as a single if-statement whose operation is as follows:

• If the first Boolean-expression is true the first statement is obeyed, and all the others skipped;

Fig 4.2 The syntax of *arithmetic relation*

arithmetic relation

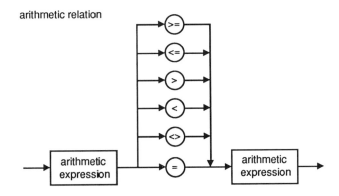

- If the first Boolean-expression is false and the second is true then the first statement is skipped, the second obeyed, and the others skipped;

- And so on.

In other words the Boolean-expressions are tested in turn until one is found to be true. If that Boolean-expression is the nth, then the nth statement is obeyed and all others skipped. If none of the Boolean-expressions is true, then none of the statements is obeyed unless the last of the alternatives is unconditional. As an example consider a more realistic tax system:

Weekly wage	Base tax	% on excess over column 1
0	0	0
78	0.32	32
331	81.28	46
662	233.54	60

Prog 4.2   The payroll with some tax exemption

```
program Payroll;
  var
    code : 1000..9999;
    rate, hours, gross, overtime, tax, nett : real;
begin
  writeln('This program calculates your weekly wage.');
  write('What is your employee code number? ');
  readln(code);
  write('What is your basic rate of pay? ');
  readln(rate);
  write('For how many hours did you work? ');
  readln(hours);
  if hours > 37.5 then
    overtime := hours - 37.5
  else
    overtime := 0;
  gross := hours * rate + overtime * 0.5 * rate;
  if gross <= 100 then
    tax := 0
  else
    tax := 0.20 * (gross - 100);
  nett := gross - tax;
  writeln('Employee ', code : 4, ' your wage is $', gross : 6 : 2, '.');
  writeln('After tax of $', tax : 6 : 2, ' this leaves $', nett : 6 : 2, '.')
end.
```

The interpretation of this table is: if the weekly wage is between, say $78 and $331, then the tax payable is the base tax, $0.32, plus 32% of the difference between the wage and $331. A sequence to calculate the tax is as follows:

> **if** gross < 78 **then**
>   tax := 0
> **else if** gross < 331 **then**
>   tax := 0.32 + 0.32 * (gross − 78)
> **else if** gross < 662 **then**
>   tax := 81.28 + 0.46 * (gross − 331)
> **else**
>   tax := 233.54 + 0.60 * (gross − 662)

Note that because the Boolean-expressions are tested in order, there is no need to test explicitly whether a value of *gross* is in within a range. For example, when the Boolean-expression *gross* < 331 is tested, *gross* is known to be at least 78, otherwise the first statement, *tax* := 0, would have been obeyed. We return to the simple tax scheme for now to keep the program small in size.

4.5   Nested if-statements

The first alternative of an if-statement can also be an if-statement. That is we can have statements whose structure is:

> **if** ... **then**
>   **if** ... **then**
>   ...
>   **else**
>   ...
> **else**
>   ...

The meaning of the statement is fairly clear. If the first Boolean-expression is true then either the first or the second statement is obeyed depending on the value of the second Boolean-expression. Conversely, if the first Boolean-expression is false, then the third statement is obeyed. In practice, however, this form of statement is not often used since experience shows that it is less easy to understand than the previous paragraph suggests. The alternative is to use an extended if-statement with three alternatives. Furthermore, there is a problem which may arise. What does the following mean?

> **if** ... **then**
>   **if** ... **then**
>   ...
>   **else**
>   ...

We cannot tell from the syntax diagram whether the statement after the **else** is to be obeyed as a result of the falsity of the first Boolean-expression or of the second. However the Pascal Standard defines its interpretation: each **else** is paired with the *last* unpaired **then**. Thus it is obeyed if and only if the second Boolean-expression is false.

4.6   Logical operations

Booleans are a pervasive concept and we shall study them in some detail in Chapter 9. For the moment we content ourselves with introducing two logical operators **and** and **or**. Each operand is a Boolean-expression and the result is of Boolean-type. Given the simple nature of the variables involved, the functions can be completely defined by extension as shown below:

x	y	x and y	x or y
false	false	false	false
false	true	false	true
true	false	false	true
true	true	true	true

Fig 4.3 gives the syntax of Boolean-expression. Note that the operands of the logical operators must be in (round) brackets. To test if a real variable, x, is between 0 and 1 we write:

$$(0 <= x) \textbf{ and } (x <= 1)$$

The interpretation of a Boolean-expression is also based on the precedence of the operators, **and** being of higher precedence than **or**. Thus:

$$(x = 1) \textbf{ and } (y = 1) \textbf{ or } (z < 0)$$

means the same as:

Fig 4.3   The syntax of *Boolean-expression*

* Boolean-expression

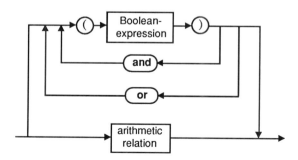

((x = 1) **and** (y = 1)) **or** (z < 0)

This example shows the use of brackets in enforcing the explicit ordering of operators. Here, of course, they are redundant, but they can be used to over-ride the normal operator priorities, for example:

(x = 1) **and** ((y = 1) **or** (z < 0))

It is clear that it is important to be able to express a condition as a Boolean-expression. Below we give some examples.

English	**Pascal**
x is a multiple of y	x **mod** y = 0
n is a 3-digit integer	(n >= 100) **and** (n <= 999)
y is a leap year	(y **mod** 4 = 0) **and** (y **mod** 100 <> 0)
	or (y **mod** 400 = 0)
p is a perfect square	sqr(round(sqrt(p))) = p

The last example is probably worth a sentence of explanation, though it is best explained by example. Suppose *p* were 50. We first take the square root of it, which is 7.0710... We then round it (to the nearest integer), giving 7. Next we square it to get 49. Finally we compare with *p* for equality, which is *false*.

To illustrate the use of Boolean-expressions, we consider a program for calculating a composite mark in some subject with three components. If a student passes all three components, he passes the subject as of right. He is given a conceded pass if he fails only the first component, provided that he scores at least 40% in that component and has an overall average of at least 55%. In all other situations he fails. In Prog 4.3 we give a program which reads in his three marks,

Prog 4.3 A concessional exam program

```
program ConcessionalExam;
  var
    x, y, z : 0..100;
begin
  write('This program will determine the result of a ');
  writeln('concessional exam.');
  write('What are the student"s marks? ');
  readln(x, y, z);
  if (x >= 50) and (y >= 50) and (z >= 50) or
    (x >= 40) and (y >= 50) and (z >= 50) and (x + y + z >= 165) then
    writeln('The student passes with a mark of ', (x + y + z)/3:1:1, '.')
  else
    writeln('The student fails.')
end.
```

---

and writes out the result, including the average (to one decimal place) if the student passes.

4.7   Set notation

We will find as we progress through this book that the conditions that arise can be quite complex. A particular example is that we may wish to test whether the value of a variable is one of a set of values. For example, suppose that *m*, of type 1..12, represents a month of the year. To test whether month *m* has 30 days in it, we have to test whether it is in the set {4,6,9,11} representing the months of April, June, September and November. One Boolean-expression which is true if *m* is a 30-day month is:

(m = 4) **or** (m = 6) **or** (m = 9) **or** (m = 11)

There is, however, an alternative which directly reflects the set involved:

m **in** [4, 6, 9, 11]

Note the use of square brackets to surround the set elements: the usual curly brackets are used in Pascal for comments, as we have already seen. Where some of the elements of a set are consecutive integers they can be represented by the subrange notion. For example:

m **in** [1..4, 9..12]

is true if month *m* has an "r" in its name − the traditional formula for determining whether it is safe to eat oysters. The elements of the set may be defined by expressions. For example, provided *t* is in the range 1..11, the expression:

m **in** [t..t+1]   or   m **in** [t, t+1]

is true if *m* represents the same month as *t* or the month after. Sets are an important concept in Pascal, which we discuss fully in Chapter 14.

4.8   The compound-statement

In many situations we require to do a sequence of things if a condition is satisfied (and a different sequence if it is not) rather than just one thing. We do this by making each sequence into a *compound-statement* by separating the statements by semi-colons and enclosing them between **begin** and **end**. Its syntax is given in Fig 4.4.

As an illustration consider a program which will read in three natural numbers *day*, *month* and *year*, representing any date after 1583 (the introduction of the Gregorian Calendar), and write out the day of the week on which the date falls. We are given that 1 March 1600 was a Wednesday. It is clear that, as a normal year has 365 days, the day on which 1 March falls advances by 1 each year, except for a leap year, when it advances by 2. Within any year, as we move forward by months, the day of the first of the month moves on by 3 for 31-day months, 2 for 30-day months, and 0 or 1 for February. Finally, within each month each day advances the day of the week by 1.

How do we represent the days of the week? At first thought it seems sensible to use an integer in the range 1..7 – after all, Sunday is the first day of the week. However, it is generally more convenient to start the counting at 0, since d **mod** 7 is always in the range 0..6.

When we come to implement this, it is the irregularity of the length of the months that causes the problem. If we consider January and February, not as the first and second months of a year, but as the eleventh and twelfth months of the previous year, with the year starting instead on the 1 March, then the problem simplifies for two reasons. Firstly, the leap year day appears at the end of the year. Secondly, the length of the months has a pattern, 31 30 31 30 31, which repeats twice (March to July, August to December) and starts again with January. The trick is to find an expression which advances by 2 or 3 appropriately, while still keeping it in the range 0..6. If we call the new month and year m and y, then one such expression is (13*(m–1) + 2) **div** 5 so that the day of the week is:

$$(3$$
$$+ y{-}1600 + (y{-}1600) \textbf{ div } 4 - (y{-}1600) \textbf{ div } 100 + (y{-}1600) \textbf{ div } 400$$
$$+ (13{*}(m{-}1) + 2) \textbf{ div } 5$$
$$+ (day{-}1)) \textbf{ mod } 7$$

With some trivial algebra this reduces to what is known as Zeller's Congruence:

$$(y + y \textbf{ div } 4 - y \textbf{ div } 100 + y \textbf{ div } 400 + (13{*}m{-}1) \textbf{ div } 5 + day) \textbf{ mod } 7$$

To write out the appropriate day name, we use an extended if-statement:

```
if dayofweek = 0 then
   writeln('It was a Sunday.')
else if dayofweek = 1 then
   writeln('It was a Monday.')
   .
   .
   .
else
   writeln('It was a Saturday.')
```

Fig 4.4   The syntax of compound-statement

compound-statement

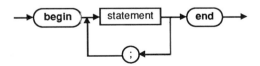

4.9   The case-statement

However, there is a more appropriate conditional-statement, the *case-statement*. To write out the days of the week, we use:

```
case dayofweek of
  0 :
    writeln('It was a Sunday.');
  1 :
    writeln('It was a Monday.');
  2 :
    writeln('It was a Tuesday.');
  3 :
    writeln('It was a Wednesday.');
  4 :
    writeln('It was a Thursday.');
  5 :
    writeln('It was a Friday.');
  6 :
    writeln('It was a Saturday.')
end {of cases on "dayofweek"}
```

The case-statement is appropriate where a single expression, here *dayofweek*, is being tested for one of a small set of values, here the range 0..6. Then depending on the value of that expression one statement, which may be a structured-statement, is chosen and obeyed. The syntax is given in Fig 4.5. Prog 4.4 gives the complete day-of-the-week program. Notice that in Prog 4.4, we have added a comment to the **end** of the case-statement. While not really necessary here, we will find as we progress through the book that the number of **end**s increases, and the information provided by the comments is a help in understanding the structure of the program. We will also add, from now on, a comment at the start of each program to explain its purpose.

In a case-statement, the integer constants are called *case-labels*, and Fig 4.5 shows that a series of case-labels may be associated with each statement. Note that, if the expression has a value which is not given as one of the case-labels, then the program is invalid. Consequently, the case-statement is sometimes

Fig 4.5   The syntax of case-statement

* case-statement

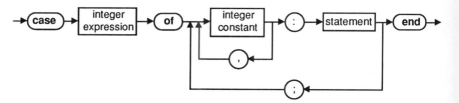

Prog 4.4 A program to determine the day of the week of a given date

---

program FindDayOfWeek;
{This program reads a date and writes out the day on which it fell.}
  var
    day : 1..31;
    month, m : 1..12;
    y : 1582..maxint;
    year : 1583..maxint;
    dayofweek : 0..6;
begin
  writeln('This program tells you on which day a date fell.');
  writeln('What year are you interested in?');
  readln(year);
  writeln('In what month of ', year : 1, ' (type a number 1..12)?');
  readln(month);
  writeln('What day of that month?');
  readln(day);
  if month **in** [1, 2] **then**
    begin
      m := month + 10;
      y := year − 1
    end {of sequence for Jan & Feb}
  else
    begin
      m := month − 2;
      y := year
    end; {of sequence for Mar..Dec}
  dayofweek := (y + y **div** 4 − y **div** 100 + y **div** 400 + (13*m − 1)
                                      div 5 + day) **mod** 7;

  case dayofweek **of**
    0 :
      writeln('It was a Sunday.');
    1 :
      writeln('It was a Monday.');
    2 :
      writeln('It was a Tuesday.');
    3 :
      writeln('It was a Wednesday.');
    4 :
      writeln('It was a Thursday.');
    5 :
      writeln('It was a Friday.');
    6 :
      writeln('It was a Saturday.')
  end {of cases on "dayofweek"}
end.

---

made conditional, for example:

if e **in** [1..5] **then**
  case e **of**
    1:
      ...
    2:
      ...

    5:
      ...
  end {of cases on "e"}
  else
    ...

4.10   Tree diagrams

Fig 4.6 is a tree diagram showing the relationship between the classes of statement introduced in this chapter such as structured-statement, if-statement and so on. It replaces a whole series of (uninteresting) syntax diagrams. It shows that a statement may be either a simple-statement or a structured-statement; that a structured-statement may be either a compound-statement or a conditional-statement; and so on. Note that we have used the more general term procedure-statement to include the read-statement, the readln-statement, the write-statement and the writeln-statement.

Fig 4.6   A tree-diagram for the statements so far met

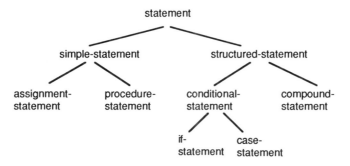

Exercises

4.1 Write Boolean-expressions (assuming the appropriate declarations) which have the value *true* if:

    (i) *p* is non-positive,
    (ii) *number* is divisible neither by 5 nor 7,
    (iii) *a*, *b* and *c* are the sides of a right-angled triangle.

4.2 Write a case-statement which, given the appropriate values of *month* and *year*, sets *days* to the number of days in that month of the given year.

4.3 Write a sequence based on a case-statement which, given the appropriate values of *day*, *month* and *year*, sets *daynumber* to the number of days between New Year's Day and that date. For example, the daynumber for 7 June 1988 is 159 and for 31 December 1988 is 366.

4.4 Given that *n* lies within the range 1..10, write Boolean-expressions which are true if:

    (i) *n* is an odd number,
   (ii) *n* is a prime number,
  (iii) *n* is a perfect square.

4.5 Extend the concessional exams program of Prog 4.3 so that a concessional pass is awarded if the overall average is at least 55%, any two subjects are passed, and at least 40% is obtained in the third.

Problems

4.1 Extend your exam marks program to deal with the following two situations. Firstly, the markers of the components are generally generous people and sometimes award a bonus, so that a student's mark may be up to 110. The Registrar is made of sterner stuff, however, and insists that the final mark must be in the range 0 − 100. Extend your program to allow for bonus marks, but ensure that a student with component marks of, say, 103, 104 and 99 gets 100 as his final mark. Secondly, suppose the mark must be converted into a grade using the table below.

Range of marks	Grade
80 − 100	A+
75 − 79	A
70 − 74	B+
65 − 69	B
60 − 64	C+
50 − 59	C
45 − 49	N+
40 − 44	N
0 − 39	NM

Thus if the marks entered are 86 75 59, the program should respond with:

```
Your final mark is 68.
Your grade is  B.
```

4.2 Consider the following problem which is more by nature of a puzzle than a serious problem. Fig 4.7 shows a number spiral, which is drawn on the co-ordinate axis, by placing 0 at the origin,1 immediately to its right at (1,0), 2 above 1 at (1,1), 3 immediately to the left of 2 at (0,1) and so on. (Ignore the shading of the spiral for the moment.) Produce a program which will read in a number and calculate and write out its co-ordinates. For example, for the number 46, it would write out the co-ordinates 1 and −3. One way to proceed is as follows. The spiral can be thought of as a series of (square) rings which we will number from 0 outwards from the centre. In Fig 4.7 ring 2 is shown shaded. The numbers in ring r range from $(2r-1)^2$ to $(2r+1)^2 - 1$. Thus given a number n, we can determine its ring by:

$r := \text{trunc}((\text{sqrt}(n) +1) / 2)$

From this the actual co-ordinates can be found quite easily.

Fig 4.7 A number spiral

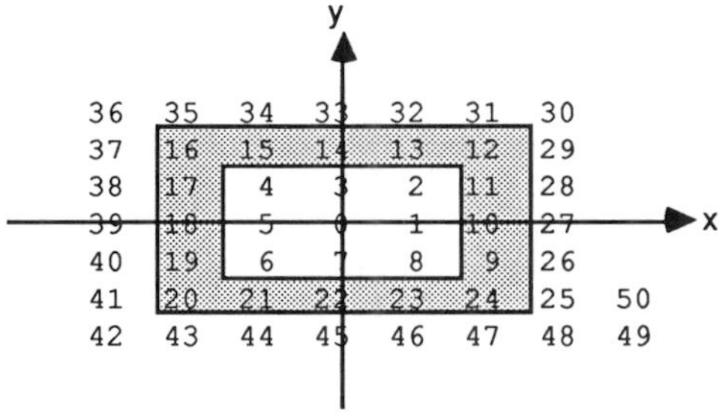

4.3 Consider the following description of Buley's law, which is said to determine the amount of rest (in days) necessary to overcome jet-lag.

$$\frac{\frac{T}{2} + (Z - 4) + DC + AC}{10}$$

where T is the number of hours in transit; Z is the number of time zones crossed; DC and AC are the Departure and Arrival Coefficients tabulated opposite.

	Departure Coefficient	Arrival Coefficient
0800 − 1159	0	4
1200 − 1759	1	2
1800 − 2159	3	0
2200 − 0059	4	1
0100 − 0759	3	3

with 0 being good and 4 being bad. Thus for the Perth–London flight, which crosses 8 time zones, takes 19 hours, leaves 2230 and arrives at 0930, the rest period is 2.15 days or 52 hours (to the nearest hour). Write a program which will ask the user the appropriate questions about the number of time zones crossed, the flight duration, the departure and arrival times, and, from the answers, determine and write out the rest period in hours. Note that the table is really two tables combined. One specifies DC in terms of the departure time, the other AC in terms of arrival time. You will find it easier to rearrange the table to start at midnight. Thus the period 2200–0059 will become two: 0000–0059 and 2200–2359.

5

Repetition

All the versions of the payroll program that we have written so far have been for use by an employee. Let us modify it so that it can be used by an employer. It is, of course, a trivial matter to change the write- and writeln-statements so that they refer to the employee rather than the user. In view of what we are about to do in the next section, we will make a further change. As the program stands, it asks for the three details for the employee in three distinct questions, and these and the answers occupy three lines. Let us change the program so that it asks the employer instead to give this information on one line like this:

```
This program calculates your employee's wages.
Give me code number, basic rate and hours worked,
on one line, separated by spaces.
2134 8.26 42.75
Employee 2134's wage is $374.80.
After tax of $ 54.96 this leaves $319.84.
```

The changes to the program are confined to the read- and write-statements. Rather than give the whole program, we give just the changed parts of it. First, the initial dialogue in which the program gives the user his instructions and then reads in the answers:

```
writeln('This program calculates your employee"s wages.');
writeln('Give me code number, basic rate and hours worked,');
writeln('on one line, separated by spaces.');
readln(code, rate, hours);
```

Second, the writing out of the results of the computer's calculations:

```
writeln('Employee ', code : 4, '"s wage is $', gross : 6 : 2, '.');
writeln('After tax of $', tax : 6 : 2, ' this leaves $', nett : 6 : 2, '.')
```

Unfortunately the program performs the calculation for just one employee. For an organization employing hundreds or thousands of people it would be desirable to have a program which did the calculation for all of the employees. Let us now extend the program so that it can deal with this. The first question that the program will ask the user is how many employees are involved. Then, for each employee in turn, it simply asks for the code number, rate of pay and hours worked as before, calculating the gross pay, tax payable and nett pay, which it writes out. A typical dialogue, for only two employees, is given below.

```
This program calculates your employees' wages.
How many staff do you have? 2
For each in turn give me code number, basic rate
and hours worked, on one line, separated by spaces.
2134 8.26 42.75
Employee 2134's wage is $374.80.
After tax of $ 54.96 this leaves $319.84.
7105 7.54 12.5
Employee 7105's wage is $ 94.25.
After tax of $  0.00 this leaves $ 94.25.
```

Referring back to the program we see that the sequence to read in the relevant data for an employee and calculate his gross salary, tax, and nett pay is:

```
readln(code, rate, hours);
if hours > 37.5 then
  overtime := hours − 37.5
else
  overtime := 0;
gross := hours * rate + overtime * 0.5 * rate;
if gross <= 100 then
  tax := 0
else
  tax := 0.20 * (gross − 100);
nett := gross − tax;
writeln('Employee ', code : 4, '''s wage is $', gross : 6 : 2, '.');
writeln('After tax of $', tax : 6 : 2, ' this leaves $', nett : 6 : 2, '.')
```

(Note that this does not include the initial dialogue. It should appear once initially, not once for each employee.) What we have to do now is to ensure that these seven statements are obeyed repeatedly, once for each employee.

5.1   The for-statement

We introduce now the third type of *structured-statement*, the *repetitive-statement*, often called simply a *loop*. The required effect can be achieved by the use of one of the repetitive-statements, called the *for-statement*. The complete program is given in Prog 5.1. To explain: if the part of the program which we wish to be repeated is not a single statement, it is made into one, a compound-statement, by enclosing it between **begin** and **end**. We refer to this as the *body* of the loop. It is then made into a for-statement by preceding it with, in the current example:

for employee := 1 **to** staffsize **do**

and, in line with our layout convention, indenting the body. This ensures the repetition of the compound statement *staffsize* times. More precisely, *employee* (the *control-variable*) is first set to 1 (the *initial-value*) and the body obeyed; then *employee* is set to 2, and the body obeyed; ... ; until finally *employee* is set to *staffsize* (the *final-value*) and the body obeyed. This completes the action of the for-statement. Thus, as the body is obeyed, *employee* effectively counts the number of times the body of the loop has been obeyed. That is, it counts the number of employees considered. Of course, the number of times the loop is to be obeyed must equal the size of the staff, and this value is obtained from the user by reading his answer to the appropriate question before the loop appears. Note that the control-variable is a variable like any other, and must be declared.

As this description suggests, the for-statement has much more power than is needed here: in Section 5.3 we shall see how to put the power to good effect. The for-statement, like the if-statement of the last chapter, is a single statement. It

Prog 5.1   The payroll program dealing with all employees

```
program Payroll;
{This program calculates the payroll for all employees.}
  var
    code : 1000..9999;
    rate, hours, gross, overtime, tax, nett : real;
    employee, staffsize : 1..maxint;
begin
  writeln('This program calculates your employees" wages.');
  write('How many staff do you have? ');
  readln(staffsize);
  writeln('For each in turn give me code number, basic rate');
  writeln('and hours worked, on one line, separated by spaces.');
  for employee := 1 to staffsize do
    begin
      readln(code, rate, hours);
      if hours > 37.5 then
        overtime := hours - 37.5
      else
        overtime := 0;
      gross := hours * rate + overtime * 0.5 * rate;
      if gross <= 100 then
        tax := 0
      else
        tax := 0.20 * (gross - 100);
      nett := gross - tax;
      writeln('Employee ', code : 4, "'s wage is $', gross : 6 : 2, '.');
      writeln('After tax of $', tax : 6 : 2, ' this leaves $', nett : 6 : 2, '.')
    end {of loop on "employee"}
end.
```

---

is composed of a number of statements, here seven, but is nevertheless a single statement. This theme, of statements being composed of, or structured from, simpler statements, is a recurring one in Pascal.

5.2 The loop as a fundamental building block

In the payroll example above, it was quite clear that the total calculation involved a number of calculations of precisely the same type, one for each employee. In many important situations the use of a loop is a little more subtle. For example, Prog 5.2 gives a program which will ask the user for a series of real numbers and write out the sum of those numbers. The numbers might represent sales to individual customers by a salesman, or scores by an Olympic skater, or component marks in an examination, or whatever. Because we are writing a general program, we use general words like *sum*, *i* and *n* for the variables. In specific applications, such as that of the next section, we use more specific identifiers such as *totalmark*, *judge* and *panelsize*.

In the initial dialogue, the user is asked how many numbers there are, and the loop is traversed that many times. The body of the loop is almost trivial. It consists of only two statements, the first causes a number to be read into *next*, and the second causes it to be added to *sum*. This latter statement:

sum := sum + next

deserves comment since it very succinctly underlines the statement of Chapter 2 that, in an assignment-statement, the expression is evaluated and the resulting

Prog 5.2 A program to sum some numbers

```
program FindSum;
{This program reads in some numbers and writes out their sum.}
  var
    i, n : 1..maxint;
    sum, next : real;
begin
  writeln('This program will sum a string of numbers.');
  write('How many numbers are there ? ');
  readln(n);
  sum := 0;
  writeln('Give them to me one to a line.');
  for i := 1 to n do
    begin
      readln(next);
      sum := sum + next
    end; {of loop on "i"}
  writeln('Their sum is ', sum : 1 : 2, '.')
end.
```

---

value assigned to the variable on the left hand side of the := symbol. Thus the above statement causes *next* to be added to *sum*, so that as the loop is being continually traversed, *sum* is at any point the sum of the numbers so far read. On the completion of the for-statement it is of course the sum of all the numbers. Note, too, that *sum* is initialized to 0 *outside the loop*. Let us see how the variables of the program change as execution progresses. Rather than use the diagrammatic model of Chapter 2, we give instead a tabular representation. Suppose that a user wishes to add the 4 numbers 2.6, 3.2, 1.7 and 6.1. Convince yourself that the values before the loop and at the end of the loop are as follows.

	i	n	next	sum
Before the loop	?	4	?	0.0
At the end of the first traverse	1	4	2.6	2.6
At the end of the second traverse	2	4	3.2	5.8
At the end of the third traverse	3	4	1.7	7.5
At the end of the fourth traverse	4	4	6.1	13.6

It is a good idea in the early stages of learning programming to draw out such tabulations to ensure that you understand the operation of Pascal's structured statements. Ultimately, though, you must be able to use them directly.

Consider now another general example, given in Prog 5.3. This program, closely related to the summation program above, reads in a series of numbers, finds and writes out the largest one. The basic idea is given opposite.

Prog 5.3   A program to find the largest of some positive numbers

```
program FindLargest;
{This program reads in some numbers and writes out the largest.}
  var
    i, n : 1..maxint;
    next, largest : real;
begin
  writeln('This program finds the largest of a string of numbers.');
  write('How many numbers are there? ');
  readln(n);
  writeln('Give them to me one to a line.');
  readln(largest);
  for i := 2 to n do
    begin
      readln(next);
      if next > largest then
        largest := next
    end; {of loop on "i"}
  writeln('The largest is ', largest : 1 : 2, '.')
end.
```

Largest is initialized to the first number since, at that point, it is the largest number so far read. Each subsequent number is read into *next*, and if it is greater than *largest*, then *largest* is set to it. Thus at any point, *largest* is always equal to the largest number read so far; and after all the numbers have been read, it is the largest of them all.

When the numbers are all greater than some given value, we often use a variant of this procedure in which *largest* is initialized to a constant less than that given value, and *all* the numbers are read and compared inside the loop. For example, if the numbers are known to be positive, as will be the case with examples later on, we can initialize *largest* to 0.

Finding the smallest of a sequence of numbers follows very similar lines. The identifier *largest* is replaced by *smallest* and the condition reversed so that the if-statement within the body of the loop becomes:

> **if** next < smallest **then**
> smallest := next

If we use the variant, in which all numbers are read within the loop, *smallest* is set to some number known to be equal to or greater than the largest possible number in the problem at hand.

5.3   Using the control-variable within the loop

There is more power in the for-statement than these examples have demonstrated. This is due to the fact that the control-variable can be used within the loop itself. The full significance of this will become clear when we introduce arrays in Chapter 13, but we can give a couple of simple examples now. Prog 5.4 gives a program which reads in a positive integer, *n*, and writes out its factorial. The factorial of *n* is defined as $1 \cdot 2 \cdot 3 \cdot \ldots \cdot n$, and the program has a loop which is traversed *n* times. If *count* is the control-variable and *p* is a variable in which

Prog 5.4 A factorial program

```
program Factorial;
{This program reads in a positive integer and writes its factorial.}
  var
    count, n, p : 1..maxint;
  begin
    writeln('This program calculates factorials.');
    write('What number would you like to try? ');
    readln(n);
    p := 1;
    for count := 1 to n do
      p := p * count;
    writeln(n : 1, '! = ', p : 1, '.')
  end.
```

the factorial is being accumulated, then *p* is multiplied by *count* within the loop.

To complete this section we consider a problem which includes the ideas of both the general programs given in the last section. In many artistic Olympic events, a competitor's performance is assessed by a panel of judges, typically 9, though our program will allow any number up to 9. Each judge awards a mark, typically in the range 1..10, the mark being expressed to the nearest tenth of a mark. For 9 judges a set of marks might be:

8.9 8.7 9.2 8.6 8.9 9.0 8.9 8.7 9.0

The candidate's score is obtained by discarding both the best and the worst mark, and summing the rest. For the data above this means discarding 8.6 and 9.2, resulting in a score of 62.1. In Prog 5.5 we give a program for this problem. It first reads in the size of the judging panel (no more than 9) and the competitor's number, assumed to be of three digits. It then asks for and reads the mark

Prog 5.5   Calculating a score in an Olympic artistic event

```
program OlympicScore;
{This program will calculate an Olympic artistic event score.}
  var
    number : 1..999;
    judge, panelsize : 1..9;
    nextmark, totalmark, bestmark, worstmark, score : real;
begin
  writeln('This program calculates an Olympic event score.');
  write('How many judges are there in the panel? ');
  readln(panelsize);
  write('What is the competitor''s number? ');
  readln(number);
  totalmark := 0;
  bestmark := 0;
  worstmark := 10;
  for judge := 1 to panelsize do
    begin
      write('Judge ', judge : 1, '''s mark is? ');
      readln(nextmark);
      totalmark := totalmark + nextmark;
      if nextmark > bestmark then
        bestmark := nextmark;
      if nextmark < worstmark then
        worstmark := nextmark
    end; {of loop on "judge"}
  score := totalmark – bestmark – worstmark;
  writeln('The score for competitor ', number : 1, ' is ', score:1: 1, '.')
end.
```

---

awarded by each of the judges, and calculates and writes out the score. Note that the program calculates the total and finds the best and worst marks all in one loop. It then calculates the score by subtracting these latter two marks from the total mark.

5.4 Nested loops or loops within loops

The body of a for-statement may be any statement; in particular it may be a for-statement. That is, for-statements may be nested too. We shall see many examples in this book. For now, we give one example, a program which will find all those three-digit numbers which are equal to the sum of the cubes of their digits. One such number is 153 since $1^3 + 5^3 + 3^3 = 1 + 125 + 27 = 153$.

There are two approaches: either generate each three-digit number, decompose it into its three digits, and then test for the desired property; or generate all combinations of the digits, determine the integer made up from those digits, and test for the desired property. We choose the latter, leaving the former as an exercise. If the digits are h, t, u then the integer is $100h + 10t + u$, and the test of the desired property is $100h + 10t + u = h^3 + t^3 + u^3$. In the absence of a generalized powering facility, we write this as:

$$100^*h + 10^*t + u = h^*h^*h + t^*t^*t + u^*u^*u$$

To generate all combinations of h, t and u we use three nested loops. Prog 5.6 gives the complete program. Note that h is constrained to be in the range 0..9, like t and u. Thus the program produces as answers 0 or 1, which are degenerate three-digit numbers with the required property.

Prog 5.6 The "sum of the cubes of the digits" program

```
program SumOfCubes;
{This program solves the "sum-cube-digits" problem.}
  var
    h, t, u : 0..9;
begin
  writeln('The following 3-digit numbers are all equal to');
  writeln('the sum of the cubes of their digits: ');
  for h := 0 to 9 do
    for t := 0 to 9 do
      for u := 0 to 9 do
        if h*h*h + t*t*t + u*u*u = 100*h + 10*t + u then
          writeln(100 * h + 10 * t + u : 3)
end.
```

5.5 The specification of the for-statement

In Fig 5.1 we give the syntax diagram of the for-statement.

Fig 5.1   The syntax of *for-statement*

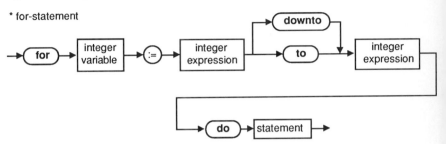

From the diagram we notice one facility not so far described. The control-variable can count down (using **downto**) as well as up (using **to**). The use of this facility is rather special, and it is difficult to give a simple example which is not contrived. Note that:

- The control-variable must be of integer-type (including a subrange of the integer-type) but not of real-type.

- Both initial-value and final-value may be expressions, of integer-type.

Although the syntax does not say so (indeed cannot say so):

- The initial-value and the final-value are evaluated once only.

- If the initial-value is greater than the final-value in the **to** case (or less than in the **downto** case), the body of the loop is not obeyed at all.

- After the loop, the value of the control-variable is undefined.

- The control-variable, the initial-value and the final-value must not be altered within the for-statement.

Fig 5.2 is the branch of the tree of statements containing structured-statements.

Fig 5.2   The tree of structured-statements

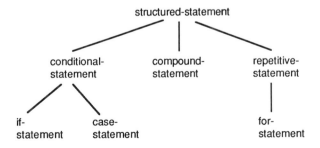

5.6   Unnecessary loops

Loops are enormously powerful, since they cause the body, which may be just a single assignment-statement, to be obeyed many times. We must be careful, however, not to use them when they are unnecessary, since they may take an excessive amount of time. For example, suppose we require a sequence to set s to the sum of the first n natural numbers. Our first thought might be to use a loop, in which a control-variable, i say, is added on each traverse to s, which is initialized to 0:

```
s := 0;
for i := 1 to n do
    s := s + i
```

However, the sum of the first n natural numbers is known to be:

$$\frac{n\,(n+1)}{2}$$

so that a single assignment suffices:

```
s := n*(n+1) div 2
```

Generally speaking this will be faster, because there are only 3 operations to be done, rather than n.

Exercises

5.1   The Fibonacci numbers are

0 1 1 2 3 5 8 13 ...

where, given the first two numbers 0 and 1, each subsequent number is the sum of its two predecessors. Thus 5+8 = 13. Assuming that we count from 0, so that the third Fibonacci number is 2, write a sequence to set *Fib* to the nth Fibonacci number.

5.2   Write sequences to set *sigma* to the sum of:

(i)   The first n cubes (i.e. $1^3 + 2^3 + 3^3 + ... + n^3$).
(ii) The first n factorials (i.e. $1! + 2! + 3! + ... + n!$)

5.3   Write a program to solve the "sum of the cubes of the digits" problem, using the alternative approach given in Section 5.4.

5.4   Write a program which will write out all perfect squares of the form *xxyy* where x and y are digits which may be the same. 7744 is a solution, since it is 88^2.

5.5 Rewrite the following loops as assignment-statements, assuming n to be positive.

   (i) sigma := 0;
        for count := 1 **to** n **do**
          sigma:= sigma + 2*count − 1;

   (ii) sigma := 0;
        for count := 1 **to** n **do**
          sigma:= sigma + sqr(count);

Problems

5.1 Expand your exam marks program so that it can be used by an examiner to process the marks of any number of students.

5.2 Now extend it (yet again), so that it writes out at the end the averages of the projects, the exam and the final mark to 1 decimal place.

5.3 A perfect number is one which is equal to the sum of its factors including 1 but excluding itself. Thus 6 is a perfect number because its factors are 6, 3, 2 and 1; and the sum of 3, 2 and 1 is 6. Conversely 12 is not a perfect number because its factors are 12, 6, 4, 3, 2, and $6 + 4 + 3 + 2 + 1 \neq 12$. Write a program to read in n and write out all perfect numbers less than n. (There are not many known, so that to avoid wasting computer time run with, say, $n = 1000$.)

5.4 Write a program which will find all those three-digit numbers which are equal to the sum of the factorials of their digits.

5.5 The mortgage calculation formula of Chapter 2 is more useful when generalized to allow for more than 3 years. Further, we can express it in terms of periods (of, say, months or years) rather than simply of years. The formula is:

$$p = \frac{A * \dfrac{r}{100} * (1 + \dfrac{r}{100})^n}{(1 + \dfrac{r}{100})^n - 1}$$

where:

   A is the amount borrowed
   n is the number of periods
   r is the interest rate per period in %

p is the repayment for the period.

Write a program which reads in sets of *A*, *n* and *r* and calculates and writes out the value of *p*.

5.6 In 12 metre fleet racing, as in most yachting competitions, the final placings are decided, not over just one race, but over seven. Furthermore, for each yacht, the worst result in a race is discarded. The points awarded for each race are determined as follows:

  • The winner receives no points,
  • The runner-up receives 3 points,
  • The third place-getter receives 5.7 points,
  • The fourth place-getter receives 8 points,
  • The fifth place-getter receives 10 points,
  • The sixth place-getter receives 11.7 points,
  • All other finishers receive 6 points more than their placing,
  • Yachts which do not enter, do not finish or are disqualified receive 1 point more than if they had finished last.

It is clear from this description that the yacht with the fewest points wins, and that a yacht's worst score is its largest one. Write a program to determine a yacht's score in a 12 metre championship. The program should ask for the number of yachts in the competition, and for the yacht's position in each race. Failure to enter or to finish, and disqualification will be represented by 0 as the position.

6

Program design

So far the programs we have written, and the programs you may have produced in attempting the problems, have been of two sorts. Like the payroll program, or the exam marks program, they have been expanded step by step; or like the calculation of a score in an Olympic artistic event, they were quite short. In either case, they could be comprehended as a whole. In practice, however, programs will often be large and complex, and will have to be *designed*. That is a plan will have to be made for their construction. We consider here two such programs – though, of course, they are still quite small.

6.1   Producing a table of dates for Summer-time

In many countries, especially in temperate areas, clocks are moved forward one hour during summer. It is traditional for the changes to take place at 2am on a Sunday. Thus a typical situation is (for the Southern Hemisphere): "*Clocks will be advanced by 1 hour on the last Sunday in October, and reset on the first Sunday in March*". Because it is important to know the precise dates of the changes, we will write a program that will write out, for a range of years, the dates of *Summer-time*, as this period is called. The results might be :

```
YEAR        END     START

1983     6 MAR    30 OCT
1984     4 MAR    28 OCT
1985     3 MAR    27 OCT
1986     2 MAR    26 OCT
1987     1 MAR    25 OCT
1988     6 MAR    30 OCT
1989     5 MAR    29 OCT


SOME SUMMER-TIME DATES
======================
```

Let us assume that the answers are wanted for some number of consecutive summers, so that the data will consist of just two integers, *tablesize*, specifying the number of years in the table, and *firstyear* specifying the year in which the table starts. The output above was produced from the data *7 1983*.

We have already written a program, which determines the day of the week on which a given date falls (using Zeller's Congruence), so let us assume that we can with a little work adapt that to find the two dates involved each year. We will return to the problem shortly. Even if we had not seen Zeller's Congruence this strategy of postponing consideration of details would still be a wise one to adopt.

Often, as here, the form of the output of a program determines its broad outline, and the first step is to sketch the output in some detail. In this case we already have the output in full detail, and this leads immediately to the outline program given in Prog 6.1, in which the English sentences represent the parts of the program we have yet to design. Six of these sentences are concerned with the details of producing the output, which consists of three columns, one holding a year, the other two holding dates, with gaps in between. Suppose we decide:

- the year column is 4 characters wide;

- the date columns are 6 characters wide;

- the gaps are 3 characters wide.

The total width of the table is 22 characters which is exactly the same as the number of characters in the title, so we can simply place it underneath. Given these decisions, it is now easy to fill out the parts of the outline dealing with output. Firstly *Announce the purpose of the program* can be implemented by the statement:

writeln('This program writes out a table of Summer-time dates.')

Prog 6.1 The outline of the Summer-time program

```
program SummerTime;
  var
    tablesize : 1..maxint;
    firstyear, year : 1583..maxint;
begin
  Announce the purpose of the program;
  Ask for and read tablesize and firstyear;
  Write out the column headings;
  for year := firstyear to firstyear + tablesize − 1 do
    begin
      Write year;
      Calculate summer-time finish-date;
      Write out the finish-date;
      Calculate summer-time start-date;
      Write out the start-date
    end;
  Write out the title
end.
```

Secondly *Write out the column headings* can be expressed:

```
writeln;
writeln('YEAR' : 4, '  ' : 3, 'END' : 6, '  ' : 3, 'START' : 6);
writeln
```

Finally *Write out the title* can be expressed:

```
writeln;
writeln('SOME SUMMER-TIME DATES');
writeln('======================')
```

The other output statements are in a loop. Let us assume that the two calculating statements within the loop set *endday* to the day in March on which summer-time ends, and *startday* to the day in October on which it starts. If we allow 2 places for the day part of the date, and 3 for the month part, leaving a one-character gap, then the loop can be expanded to:

```
write(year : 4);
...
write('  ' : 3, endday : 2, ' MAR');
...
write('  ' : 3, startday : 2, ' OCT');
writeln
```

All we have to do now is to fill in the pair of statements, represented by the three dots, which actually calculate the days on which Summer-time finishes and restarts! Let us concentrate on the first of the pair. We have to find the date of the first Sunday in March. The last date it could possibly be is the 7th. Let us find out what day of the week that is, and work our way back from there. We already have Zeller's Congruence, which, assuming the year starts in March, gives for the d th day of the mth month of year y the value:

$$(y + y \text{ div } 4 - y \text{ div } 100 + y \text{ div } 400 + (13*m-1) \text{ div } 5 + d) \text{ mod } 7$$

For 7 March of *year* we have $d = 7$, $m = 1$, $y = year$ and the formula reduces to:

$$(year + year \text{ div } 4 - year \text{ div } 100 + year \text{ div } 400 + 2) \text{ mod } 7$$

If this value is 0, then 7 March is a Sunday, and so is the first Sunday in March. If the value is 1, then 7 March is a Monday, and therefore the first Sunday in March is the day before, 6 March. It is clear that to get the date we subtract the result of the formula from 7:

$$7 - (year + year \text{ div } 4 - year \text{ div } 100 + year \text{ div } 400 + 2) \text{ mod } 7$$

A similar approach can now be applied to the last Sunday in October, which produces for *enddate*:

$$31 - (year + year\ \textbf{div}\ 4 - year\ \textbf{div}\ 100 + year\ \textbf{div}\ 400 + 2)\ \textbf{mod}\ 7$$

Once we have made the appropriate declarations for the variables, we have the complete program, which is given in Prog 6.2.

Prog 6.2 The Summer-time program

```
program SummerTime;
{This program produces a table of Summer-time dates.}
  var
      tablesize : 1..maxint;
      firstyear, year : 1583..maxint;
      startday : 25..31;
      endday : 1..7;
begin
    writeln('This program writes out a table of Summer-time dates.');
    write('For how many years do you want it to run? ');
    readln(tablesize);
    write('At what year should it start? ');
    readln(firstyear);
    writeln;
    writeln('YEAR' : 4, '  ' : 3, 'END' : 6, '  ' : 3, 'START' : 6);
    writeln;
    for year := firstyear to firstyear + tablesize - 1 do
      begin
        write(year : 4);
        endday := 7 - (year + year div 4 - year div 100 + year div 400
                                                              + 2) mod 7;
        write('  ' : 3, endday : 2, ' MAR');
        startday := 31 - (year + year div 4 - year div 100 + year div 400
                                                              + 2) mod 7;
        write('  ' : 3, startday : 2, ' OCT');
        writeln
      end; {of loop on "year"}
    writeln;
    writeln('SOME SUMMER-TIME DATES');
    writeln('======================')
end.
```

6.2   Drawing a board for Noughts-and-Crosses or Tic-Tac-Toe

For our second example we consider a program which is concerned almost exclusively with output. The following is an example of a board for placing the game known variously as Noughts-and-Crosses or Tic-Tac-Toe, drawn using writeln-statements as on the screen of a computer or on a lineprinter.

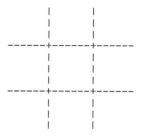

If your computer has graphics facilities, then you would be able to draw the board more accurately – and more easily.   However, many programs require some graphical content to otherwise purely alpha-numerical output so that this example can be quite rewarding.   We are going to design a program to draw one of these of a size determined by the data.   Let us define the size to be the number of "|" symbols used in drawing the side of one of the nine squares it contains.   Thus the board above is of size 3.   Notice that, because of the rectangular shape of a character position on most output devices, we have used twice as many "-" symbols for the horizontal lines as "|" symbols for vertical lines.

The problem we have to overcome in this program, and in any program which uses pictorial output, is the constraints of the output device.   When we draw a board by hand (or using graphics facilities) we draw two vertical lines and two horizontal lines – and that is all that is required.   However, the printer moves across a line from left to right, and down the page from top to bottom, and our program must be written accordingly.   A good way to visualize the problem is to cover up the example board above, and reveal it a line at a time.   This is the order in which the computer must draw it.   We see immediately that the board is composed of five *components*.   The first, third and fifth components are made up of the appropriate parts of the vertical lines.   Each of the second and fourth components consists entirely of a horizontal line.   We could construct an outline of the program based on the five components.   However, with the facilities we have so far introduced, a more structured program arises if we consider the board as composed of three sections, each, except the last, consisting of two of the com-

Fig 6.1   The sections of a Tic-Tac-Toe board

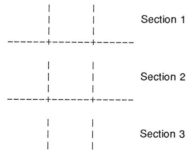

ponents referred to above, with the last consisting only of a part of the verticals. In Fig 6.1 we show the board split into these three sections. This enables us to write the program as a loop whose body is obeyed three times. The body consists of the drawing of two components, the first consisting of parts of the vertical lines, the second being a full horizontal line. On the last traverse, of course, only the vertical components are drawn. From these observations the outline of Prog 6.3, which assumes a maximum size of 10, follows.

Prog 6.3   An outline of the Tic-Tac-Toe program

```
program TicTacToe;
  var
    size : 1..10;
    section : 1..3;
begin
  Announce the purpose of the program;
  Ask for and read size;
  for section := 1 to 3 do
    begin
      Draw a part of the vertical lines;
      Draw a horizontal line unless this is the last section
    end {of loop on "section"}
end.
```

The first two statements *Announce the purpose of the program* and *Ask for and read size* we can immediately expand to:

```
writeln('This program writes out a board for playing');
writeln('Noughts-and-Crosses or Tic-Tac-Toe.');
write('How many lines deep would you like each square? ');
readln(size)
```

We now proceed to attack the part which draws a section. Fig 6.2 shows the two components of a section, which includes part of the vertical lines and a horizontal line. We consider first *Draw a part of the vertical lines*. This component must be drawn as *size* patterns, each consisting of the parts of the vertical lines, separated by the appropriate amount of space, and appearing on a separate line.

Fig 6.2   One of the sections of the board

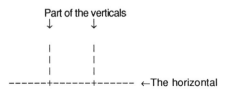

Thus we need a loop:

> **for** line := 1 **to** size **do**
> Draw the pattern of the verticals part

The pattern consists of two *blocks* each containing a single character of the vertical line, and 2*size blanks. (Remember that a horizontal line consists of twice as many characters as a vertical line to make allowance for the way characters are printed.) There is no need, of course, to explicitly write out the blanks to the right of the second line. Thus the whole of the top part of a section can be drawn by:

> **for** line := 1 **to** size **do**
>   **begin**
>   **for** block := 1 **to** 2 **do**
>   write(' ' : 2 * size, '|');
>   writeln
>   **end** {of loop on "line"}

Now for *Draw a horizontal line unless this is the last section.* Clearly this is a conditional statement and can be immediately written as:

> **if** section <> 3 **then**
> Draw a horizontal line

Because of the symmetry of the board, the horizontals can also be considered as being made of three sections. However, we will not do so. Instead we will regard a horizontal as consisting of a pair of blocks each containing a sequence of 2*size characters used to make up the horizontal line, followed by a character which represents the point at which horizontal and vertical lines cross, terminated by a block consisting just of 2*size horizontal characters. This can be simply programmed and with the appropriate variable-declarations, we can produce the complete program as shown in Prog 6.4.

Exercises

6.1 If you live in the northern hemisphere, and you have Summer-time, modify the program *SummerTime* for your own use.

Problems

6.1 Design a program to tabulate the dates of festivals such as Melbourne Cup Day (the first Tuesday in November), Thanksgiving Day (the fourth Thursday in November), and so on.

6.2 Design a program to tabulate fixed dates such as New Year's Day, May Day and Christmas Day.

6.3 We noted in section 6.2 that the Tic-Tac-Toe board could be considered as having five components instead of the three sections we chose to split it into. Design a program based on this five-component view. Compare it with the design given here.

6.4 Write a program which will ask the user for a date and write out a calen-

Prog 6.4   The Tic-Tac-Toe program

```
program TicTacToe;
{This program draws out a Tic-Tac-Toe board of a given size.}
  var
    size, line, col : 1..10;
    section : 1..3;
    block : 1..2;
begin
  writeln('This program writes out a board for playing');
  writeln('Noughts-and-Crosses or Tic-Tac-Toe.');
  write('How many lines deep would you like each square? ');
  readln(size);
  writeln;
  writeln;
  for section := 1 to 3 do
    begin
      {Draw a part of the verticals.}
      for line := 1 to size do
        begin
          for block := 1 to 2 do
            write(' ' : 2 * size, '|');
          writeln
        end; {of loop on "line"}
      {Draw the horizontal unless this is the last section.}
      if section <> 3 then
        begin
          for block := 1 to 2 do
            begin
              for col := 1 to size do
                write('--');
              write('+')
            end; {of loop on "block"}
          for col := 1 to size do
            write('--');
          writeln
        end {of drawing a horizontal}
    end {of loop on "section"}
end.
```

---

dar for that month. Thus for 1 January 1990 it will produce:

```
                   JANUARY 1990

     Sun   Mon   Tue   Wed   Thu   Fri   Sat

            1     2     3     4     5     6
      7     8     9    10    11    12    13
     14    15    16    17    18    19    20
     21    22    23    24    25    26    27
     28    29    30    31
```

7

Constants and types

With only a couple of exceptions, we have covered all the facilities that are *necessary* for writing Pascal programs. However, Pascal's great strength lies in the facilities it provides for making programs easy to write, to read and to adapt. These facilities allow us to produce programs which are *structured*. We have already seen structured-statements, such as the if-statement and the for-statement, and in later chapters, we will consider the structuring of data. In this chapter, we consider the important concepts of *constants* and *types*.

Let us return to the payroll program. Periodically, some of the parameters of the problem change. The normal working week might be reduced to 36¼ hours, for example, or the tax-free limit increased to $150. When this happens the program must be changed accordingly. This process is error-prone because we have to find all occurrences of the old value and change them, and only them, to the new value. As an example, look back at the Summer-time program of the last chapter, and find which *4*s need to be changed if the width of the year column were to be increased to 5. Note that some of the *4*s have nothing to do with the column width. Pascal's *constant* facility allows us to make such changes without this search-and-replace technique.

7.1   Constant-definitions

Consider the *constant-definition-part*:

```
const
    normal = 37.5;
    threshold = 100;
    taxrate = 0.20;
```

This defines *normal* to be synonymous with 37.5, *threshold* to be synonymous with 100, and *taxrate* to be synonymous with 0.20 throughout the program. Thus if we use the constant-definition, we can replace both occurrences of 37.5 with *normal*, both occurrences of 100 with *threshold*, and the one occurrence of 0.20 with *taxrate*. The result is shown in Prog 7.1.

Now if we have to change the program because, say, the working week is reduced to 36¼ hours, the tax-free limit is increased to $150 and the tax rate increased to 25%, then we simply change the value in the constant-definition thus:

```
const
  normal = 36.25;
  threshold = 150;
  taxrate = 0.25;
```

and run the program again. Note how the constant-definitions give names to the concepts that are important in the problem for which the program is being designed. For example, the idea of a normal working week is fundamental to the description of a wages system, and that of a threshold is equally fundamental to a taxation system. By using constants we include those concepts in the program.

Prog 7.1   The payroll with constants

```
program Payroll;
{This program calculates the payroll for all employees.}
  const
    normal = 37.5;
    threshold = 100;
    taxrate = 0.20;
  var
    code : 1000..9999;
    rate, hours, gross, overtime, tax, nett : real;
    employee, staffsize : 1..maxint;
begin
  writeln('This program calculates your employees" wages. ');
  write('How many staff do you have? ');
  readln(staffsize);
  writeln('For each in turn give me code number, basic rate ');
  writeln('and hours worked, on one line, separated by spaces.');
  for employee := 1 to staffsize do
    begin
      readln(code, rate, hours);
      if hours > normal then
        overtime := hours – normal
      else
        overtime := 0;
      gross := hours * rate + overtime * 0.5 * rate;
      if gross <= threshold then
        tax := 0
      else
        tax := taxrate * (gross – threshold);
      nett := gross – tax;
      writeln('Employee ', code : 4, "'s wage is $', gross : 6 : 2, '.');
      writeln('After tax of $', tax : 6 : 2,' this leaves $',nett : 6 : 2, '.')
    end {of loop on "employee"}
end.
```

The constant-definition-part is written just after the program-heading, before the variable-declaration-part. In Fig 7.1 we give its syntax. From the syntax diagrams we see that a constant can be defined as being equal to some previously-defined constant, or to the negative of some previously-defined constant. For example:

const
    size = 10;
    upper = size;
    lower = −upper;

This might be appropriate where some component of a problem has a *size*, which for the moment at least has the value 10; and where some other component has a value which is symmetric about 0 (so that *upper* and *lower* have the same absolute value but different signs); and where, again for the moment, the value of *upper* is the same as that of *size*. If during development of the program *size* changes to 15, but the relationships remain the same, we simply change the first definition to:

Fig 7.1 The syntax of *constant-definition-part*

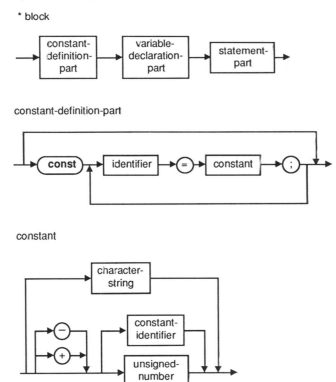

* block

constant-definition-part

constant

    size = 15

If the value of *upper* ceases to be related to *size*, we change the second definition. We have already seen one constant, *maxint*, which is the one *required constant* of Pascal. It has as its value the largest integer that the computer can hold. In advanced applications it can be used to enable a program to run on any computer regardless of its size. In this situation the definition:

    const
      minint = −maxint;

is often appropriate. One limitation of the constant facility is that the value of a constant cannot be expressed as a more complex expression, the sum of two other constants, for example.

    The syntax diagram also shows that constant can be defined to be a string. The following shows some examples:

    const
      margin = '   ';
      cross = '+';

In the above, *margin* is equal to a string of four spaces. It is intended to be used to keep output away from the left-hand margin of the paper on which it is printed. *Cross* is meant to represent some part of a diagram where two lines cross. Should it be decided, as the result of experience with the output, to change it to say a blank, or a dash, we simply change the constant-definition.

    There is another use for a constant, exemplified by this definition:

    const
      pi = 3.14159265;

We are unlikely ever to want to change the value of *pi*. We use the constant for two reasons. Firstly, *pi* is shorter than 3.14159265. Secondly, if we mistype it once as, say, *pu*, then the compiler will catch the error (unless *pu* is the name of a real variable), whereas a mistyping of 3.14159265 as 3.14195265 will be undetected.

7.2   Types

    The use of constants in a program provides two advantages. Firstly, as we said above, it makes a program more amenable to the sorts of changes a program goes through in its lifetime. Secondly, it highlights important concepts in a program by giving them names. In the payroll program the idea of a normal working week, a tax threshold and a tax rate are significant.

    This idea of giving significant concepts a name is an important aspect of Pascal. It extends, for example, to types. In the sum of the cubes of the digits problem we had the variable-declaration:

var
    h, t, u : 0..9;

The program is clearly about digits: indeed the the concept of a digit is central to the problem. Pascal enables us to recognize this by introducing the new type *digit*:

type
    digit = 0..9;

and then declare the variables to be of *digit* type:

var
    h, t, u : digit;

The *type-definition-part* appears immediately after the constant-definition-part in a program and has a similar syntax to it as shown in Fig 7.2.

We will use this facility quite extensively in the rest of the book. Two types which appear frequently are:

type
    natural = 0..maxint;
    posint = 1..maxint;

The first describes variables which will never be negative; the second describes those which will always be strictly positive. By way of a fuller example, let us write a program which will read in a number in the range 1 to 99 and write it out with its equivalent in Roman notation. The Roman system is based on the juxtaposition of the representations of the tens digit and the units digit. The representations are given overleaf.

Fig 7.2   The syntax of *type-definition-part*

* block

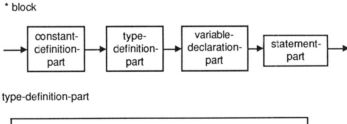

type-definition-part

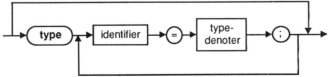

1	I	10	X
2	II	20	XX
3	III	30	XXX
4	IV	40	XL
5	V	50	L
6	VI	60	LX
7	VII	70	LXX
8	VIII	80	LXXX
9	IX	90	XC

Thus 47 in Roman is XLVII. Prog 7.2 gives an appropriate program.

7.3   Enumerated-types

A type-definition gives a name to a type-denoter. But what are the possible type-denoters? They can be some existing type, such as *integer* or *real*, in which case the appropriate identifier will be used, or they can be some *new-type*. These are divided into two classes: *simple-types* and *structured-types*. The simple-types include the required types, *integer* and *real* (and *char* and *Boolean*, to be introduced in later chapters) together with the new ones we are about to describe. In this collection the real-type is distinguished from the others, which are described as *ordinal-types*. The ordinal-types are represented accurately, whereas the real-type is an approximation.

Prog 7.2 A program to convert Arabic numerals to Roman

```
program ArabicToRoman;
{This program converts from Arabic notation to Roman.}
  const
    gap = ' ';
  type
    digit = 0..9;
  var
    count, number, arabic : 1..99;
    tens, units : digit;
begin
  writeln('This program will read in integers less than 100, ');
  writeln('and write them out in Roman.');
  write('How many numbers do you wish to convert? ');
  readln(number);
  writeln('Type the numbers one by one followed by a space.');
  for count := 1 to number do
    begin
      read(arabic);
      write(gap);
      tens := arabic div 10;
      units := arabic mod 10;
```

```pascal
      case tens of
        0 :
          ;{write nothing}
        1 :
          write('X');
        2 :
          write('XX');
        3 :
          write('XXX');
        4 :
          write('XL');
        5 :
          write('L');
        6 :
          write('LX');
        7 :
          write('LXX');
        8 :
          write('LXXX');
        9 :
          write('XC')
      end; {of cases on "tens"}
      case units of
        0 :
          ; {write nothing}
        1 :
          write('I');
        2 :
          write('II');
        3 :
          write('III');
        4 :
          write('IV');
        5 :
          write('V');
        6 :
          write('VI');
        7 :
          write('VII');
        8 :
          write('VIII');
        9 :
          write('IX')
      end; {of cases on "units"}
      writeln
    end {of loop on "count"}
end.
```

We consider now the *new-simple-types*. Firstly, the *enumerated-types*. One of the great misconceptions about computers is that they can process only numbers. This is not the case, and Pascal has facilities for dealing with non-numerical quantities. To take a local example, Australia has six states, and it is preferable to be able to refer to them by their names or by their accepted abbreviations, instead of by some arbitrarily assigned number. In Pascal we can define an *enumerated-type* whose constants are these names or abbreviations. For example:

type
statetype = (QLD, NSW, VIC, TAS, SA, WA);

Equally, if our program was about the European Community, we might define:

type
statetype = (Belgium, France, ...);

And, of course, if it were about the United States of America there would be 50 constants. However, these examples are a bit parochial and so we will use a couple of more general examples, even though they illustrate some of the weaknesses of the facilities provided. The examples are the months of the year, and marital status, for which we introduce the types:

type
monthtype = (Jan, Feb, Mar, Apr, May, Jun, Jul, Aug, Sep, Oct, Nov,
                                                                 Dec);

maritalstatus = (single, married, divorced, widowed);

and declare some variables of those types:

var
thismonth, startmonth, finishmonth : monthtype;
status : maritalstatus;

Note that *Jan, Feb, ... , Dec* do not *have* values: they *are* values. Indeed, they are the only values that variables of type *month* may have! Note that a type-definition declares not only the identifier of the type, but the identifiers of all the constants as well. The syntax is straight-forward and is given in Fig 7.3.

Fig 7.3 The syntax of *enumerated-type*

enumerated-type

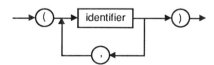

We will introduce a number of different types in subsequent chapters and for each we need to know the operations that are available with variables of the type. This is, of course, true for enumerated-types, and we now discuss these in turn.

(i) We can assign to variables. For example, using the variables declared above, we can write:

```
startmonth := thismonth;
finishmonth := Aug
```

The form of expression allowed on the right-hand side is quite simple: either a variable-access or a constant, as shown above, or a function-designator. There are two *required functions, succ* and *pred*. The successor of a value, *succ*, is the value which succeeds it in the enumeration of the constants. Thus:

```
succ(Jan) = Feb
succ(Jun) = Jul
```

Note that *succ(Dec)* is undefined, since *Dec* is the last constant in the enumeration. To set *nextmonth* to the month after *thismonth* we write:

```
if thismonth <> Dec then
  nextmonth := succ(thismonth)
else
  nextmonth := Jan
```

The required function *pred* gives the predecessor of a value, that is the value which precedes it in the enumeration of the constants. In the current example, *pred(Jan)* is not defined.

(ii) We can compare expressions of the same enumerated type. For example:

```
if (thismonth <> May) and (thismonth <> Jun)
                and (thismonth <> Jul) and (thismonth <> Aug) then
  writeln('It is safe to eat oysters.')
else
  writeln('It is not safe to eat oysters.')
```

expresses the dictum that it is safe to eat oysters only when there is an "r" in the month. All six relational-operators are available. Set notation is particularly appropriate with enumerated types, so that:

```
if thismonth in [Jan..Apr, Sep..Dec] then
  writeln('It is safe to eat oysters.')
else
  writeln('It is not safe to eat oysters.')
```

means the same thing.

(iii) There is a *transfer function, ord*, which converts a value of any ordinal-type to a value of integer-type. The constant-identifiers are assigned the values 0, 1, 2, ... in the order of their appearance in the type-denoter. Thus:

ord(Jan) = 0
ord(Dec) = 11

There is no transfer-function for converting from the integer value to a value of the enumerated-type. We have instead to use a case-statement as discussed below.

(iv) As Fig 7.4 shows, the control-variable, the initial-value and the final-value of a for-statement may be of an enumerated-type, indeed of any ordinal type. Thus we can write:

for status := single **to** widowed **do**

to control a loop in which *status* takes on all 4 of the values *single, married, divorced* and *widowed*. So, too, may the case-index and the case-constants of a case-statement. The syntax is given in Fig 7.5.

Fig 7.4 The correct syntax for *for-statement*

for-statement

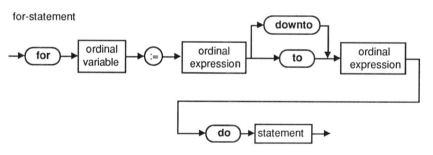

Fig 7.5 The correct syntax for *case-statement*

case-statement

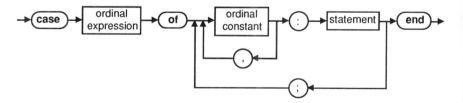

Thus we can write:

```
case status of
  single:
    ... ;
  married:
    ... ;
  divorced :
    ... ;
  widowed :
    ...
end {of cases on "status"}
```

to enable us to perform the appropriate statement, depending on the value of *status*.

(v) We cannot read variables of an enumerated-type, nor write expressions of one. These actions have to be simulated. We start with reading. There are two choices. Firstly, we can require the user to type the values in full, and write the program so that it reads them in character by character (though we have not yet considered how a program might read in characters). Alternatively, we give the values a coding which the user is obliged to type, read the coded values, and then convert them to the appropriate enumerated values. A sequence for reading a marital status is given below.

```
read(s);
case s of
  1:
    status := single;
  2:
    status := married;
  3:
    status := divorced;
  4:
    status := widowed
end {of cases on "s"}
```

This is, of course, a weakness of Pascal, which, in most cases, we must just live with, though some compilers have been extended to allow reading and writing of enumerated values. The weakness is not quite as serious as it first seems, because many enumerated-types are created purely for the internal workings of a program and have no external existence anyway. We use a similar technique for writing. Below is a sequence for writing out the value of *status*.

```
case status of
  single:
    write('single');
```

```
married:
  write('married');
divorced:
  write('divorced');
widowed:
  write('widowed')
end {of cases on "status"}
```

Generally speaking, we do not often want to write out values of enumerated-types using precisely the same identifiers as used in the program. With *month*, for example, we may wish to write out the name in full, or we may need to write it in a foreign language. Thus we would have to use a case-statement anyway.

7.4   Subrange-types

The other form of simple-type is the *subrange-type*, which we have used extensively already. As can be seen from the syntax diagram of Fig 7.6, this is not restricted to integers: we can have a subrange of any ordinal-type. For example, we can have types defined:

```
type
  secondQtype = Apr..Jun;
  notsingle = married..widowed;
```

Note that the range can be specified by any constant, not just one that appears in the definition of the original type. Thus we might have:

```
const
  start = Apr;
  finish = Jul;
type
  workmonth = start..finish;
```

Of course, this cannot appear within programs such as we have written so far, because to do so we must first define *monthtype*, then define the constants *start* and *finish*, and finally define the type *workmonth*, and Pascal specifically forbids this intermingling of type- and constant-definitions. However, we can have it within a procedure, the topic of the next chapter, if *monthtype* is declared in the program itself.

Fig 7.6 The syntax of *subrange-type*

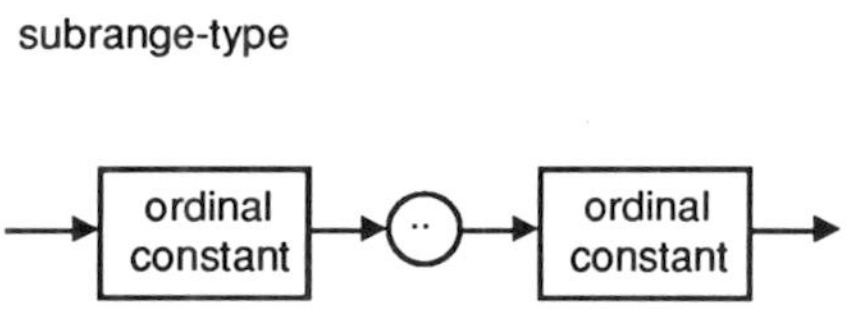

subrange-type

7.5   The ordinal-types

The classification of the types we have seen in this chapter is shown pictorially in Fig 7.7. As we have noted the significance of the ordinal-type is that it can be represented accurately. The required functions *ord*, *succ* and *pred* are applicable to all ordinal-types. Thus if *i* is of integer-type:

$$\text{ord}(i) = i \qquad \text{succ}(i) = i + 1 \qquad \text{pred}(i) = i - 1$$

though the functions are not often used with integers. It is because of the discrete nature of the values of ordinal-types that the case-statement and the for-statement are applicable to them.

Fig 7.7   A tree diagram of types

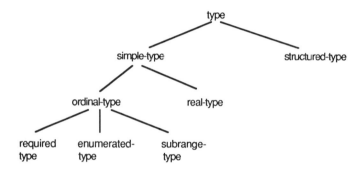

Exercises

7.1   Define enumerated-types appropriate for:

(i)   variables whose values range over the days of the week;
(ii)   variables whose values range over the subjects available to you in your course of study;
(iii)   variables whose values range over the four suits of a deck of playing cards;
(iv)   variables whose values range over the punctuation marks.

7.2   Modify the program *SummerTime*, designed in the last chapter, to use constants and types appropriately.

Problems

7.1   Modify your exam marks program to use constants and types appropriately.

7.2   Write a program which will read in a three-digit number, and write it out in English. That is if the data is 372, the program will write:

```
372 is three hundred and seventy-two.
```

7.3 Write a program which will read in a three-digit number and write it out as three words representing its digits. To use the example of Problem 7.2, for 372 the program will write:

```
372 is three seven two.
```

7.4 Write a program which will read in a time in the 24-hour clock convention and write it out in the usual English style. For example, it will respond to 1545 by:

```
1545 is a quarter to four.
```

8

Procedures and functions

The notion of structure is important in programming, as in any other complex activity. Pascal is particularly strong in this area, as we have noted before. In previous chapters we have introduced the idea of structured statements, such as the for-statement and the if-statement, which are built up from simpler statements, and which may in turn be used to build more complex statements, and in subsequent chapters we will use structured data, where quite complex data objects can be built up from the simple types such as *integer* and *real*. Before we do that though, we will consider, in this chapter, higher-level structures in the program: *procedures* and *functions*.

8.1 Structuring the payroll program with procedures

If we were to design the payroll program afresh along the lines of Chapter 6, we might come up with a broad strategy rather like that of Prog 8.1. We might then proceed by filling out each line with from one to a dozen statements. This obscures the outline making it hard to see the original design. If you refer back to the program of Prog 7.1, for example, it is not immediately obvious where the calculation of gross pay ends, and where the calculation of tax starts. It would be much better to retain the clarity of the outline within the pro-

Prog 8.1 An outline of the payroll program

---

begin
  Announce the purpose of the program;
  Find the staff size;
  Give instructions for the entry of data;
  for employee := 1 **to** staffsize **do**
    begin
      Read in the work details;
      Calculate the gross pay (from hours worked & pay rate);
      Calculate the tax payable (from gross pay);
      Calculate the nett pay (from gross pay & tax);
      Write out the wage details
    end {of loop on "employee"}
end.

---

gram itself, so that the program might look something like that given in Prog 8.2. We do this by using *procedures*. A procedure consists of two parts, a *procedure-declaration* (not shown in Prog 8.2), which defines the meaning of the procedure, and a *procedure-statement*, such as those in Prog 8.2, which invoke the procedure. As an example, consider the procedure *Announce*. Its procedure-declaration is:

```
procedure Announce;
begin
  writeln('This program calculates your employees" wages.')
end {of procedure "Announce"}
```

This procedure-declaration defines how the purpose of the program is *announced* to the user: simply by writing out the usual message. In many programs the announcement might be more expansive including, for example, the writer's logo and a copyright message. Note that a procedure-declaration *defines what is meant* by a procedure; it does not cause the procedure-body to be obeyed. What causes the body to be obeyed is the procedure-statement, often referred to as the *procedure-call*. Of course, the body may be obeyed any number of times in a program, though it must be defined only once.

In the army, drill lessons go something like this:

> When I say "stand-at-ease", you will lift your left foot smartly off the ground to a height of 6 inches and place it down firmly 15 inches to left. At the same time you will ...

Thereafter the command "STAND-AT-EASE" means that you lift your left foot

---

Prog 8.2   The main program if the payroll program is procedurized

---

```
program Payroll;

{The global const, type, var and procedure declarations}

begin
  Announce;
  FindStaffSize(staffsize);
  GiveInstructions;
  for employee := 1 to staffsize do
    begin
      ReadWorkDetails(code, rate, hours);
      CalculateGross(gross, rate, hours);
      CalculateTax(tax, gross);
      CalculateNett(nett, gross, tax);
      WriteWagesDetails(code, gross, tax, nett)
    end {of loop on "employee"}
end.
```

---

smartly off the ground to a height of 6 inches and place it down firmly 15 inches to left ... This is closely parallel to the situation with procedures. The procedure-declaration is the means by which the programmer tells the system what he means by some procedure; the procedure-statement is the means by which he asks the system to carry out that procedure.

The *Announce* procedure is very simple: it always does the same thing, and has no effect on the calculation being performed. More often, a procedure does affect the progress of the calculation, by setting some of the program's variables, or by writing their values as output. It does this by means of *parameters*. Consider the procedure-declaration *FindStaffSize*:

```
procedure FindStaffSize (var staffsize : posint);
begin
   write('How many staff do you have? ');
   readln(staffsize)
end {of procedure "FindStaffSize"}
```

Within the brackets we have the *formal-parameter*:

```
var staffsize : posint
```

The **var** indicates that this procedure will set (or change) the value of *staffsize*. A parameter of this class is said to be *called as a variable*. Note that the type of the formal-parameter must be specified, here *posint*. Where a procedure will *use* the value of a parameter, rather than calculate it, the **var** is omitted, and the parameter is said to be *called by value*. The two classes may be mixed in a procedure. For example, consider *CalculateNett*:

```
procedure CalculateNett (var nett : real;
                gross, tax : real);
begin
   nett := gross − tax
end {of procedure "CalculateNett"}
```

The procedure requires the values of both *gross* and *tax*, from which it calculates *nett*, so *gross* and *tax* are called by value and *nett* is called as a variable. Prog 8.3 gives a procedurized version of the payroll program.

8.2   Stylistic conventions

The choice of identifier for the name of the procedure is, as usual, a matter of personal taste. You may, for example, prefer a more fulsome name, such as *AnnounceThePurposeOfTheProgram*. Whatever you choose, it should describe the purpose of the procedure. In this book, we use long, descriptive names, with the initial letter of each word capitalized to help the eye read them. In a block, the procedure(-and-function)-declaration-part follows the variable-declaration-part and precedes the statement-part. Note that we have added a

Prog 8.3   The payroll program with procedures.

```
program Payroll;
{This program calculates the payroll using procedures.}
  type
    posint = 1..maxint;
    codetype = 1000..9999;
  var
    code : codetype;
    rate, hours, gross, tax, nett : real;
    employee, staffsize : posint;

  procedure Announce;
  begin
    writeln('This program calculates your employees" wages. ')
  end;{of procedure "Announce"}

  procedure FindStaffSize (var staffsize : posint);
  begin
    write('How many staff do you have? ');
    readln(staffsize)
  end;{of procedure "FindStaffSize"}

  procedure GiveInstructions;
  begin
    writeln('For each in turn give me code number, basic rate ');
    writeln('and hours worked, on one line, separated by spaces.')
  end;{of procedure "GiveInstructions"}

  procedure ReadWorkDetails (var code : codetype;
            var rate, hours : real);
  begin
    readln(code, rate, hours)
  end;{of procedure "ReadWorkDetails"}

  procedure CalculateGross (var gross : real;
            rate, hours : real);
    const
      normal = 37.5;
    var
      overtime : real;
  begin
    if hours > normal then
      overtime := hours − normal
    else
      overtime := 0;
    gross := hours * rate + overtime * 0.5 * rate
  end;{of procedure "CalculateGross"}
```

```
procedure CalculateTax (var tax : real;
            gross : real);
  const
    threshold = 100;
    taxrate = 0.20;
  begin
   if gross <= threshold then
     tax := 0
   else
     tax := taxrate * (gross – threshold)
  end;{of procedure "CalculateTax"}

procedure CalculateNett (var nett : real;
            gross, tax : real);
  begin
   nett := gross – tax
  end;{of procedure "CalculateNett"}

procedure WriteWagesDetails (code : codetype;
            gross, tax, nett : real);
  begin
   writeln('Employee ', code : 4, '''s wage is $', gross : 6 : 2, '.');
   writeln('After tax of $', tax : 6 : 2, ' this leaves $', nett : 6 : 2, '.')
  end;{of procedure "WriteWagesDetails"}

begin
  Announce;
  FindStaffSize(staffsize);
  GiveInstructions;
  for employee := 1 to staffsize do
    begin
      ReadWorkDetails(code, rate, hours);
      CalculateGross(gross, rate, hours);
      CalculateTax(tax, gross);
      CalculateNett(nett, gross, tax);
      WriteWagesDetails(code, gross, tax, nett)
    end {of loop on "employee"}
end.
```

comment to the end of each procedure giving its name. We will usually add a comment at the head of a procedure too explaining its purpose, just as we have done with programs. We take the liberty of omitting these comments with the payroll program to keep its size down – every reader will know the purpose of each procedure well enough! Note, too, that we have inserted a blank line before and after each procedure to give a visual clue to the reader of the structure of the program. Of course, these are not obligatory; they are just a convention which we will use throughout.

8.3   The relative independence of procedures

The program of Prog 8.3 is textually longer than the equivalent program without procedures (Prog 7.1) because of the procedure-headings and the procedure-statements, and it runs (a little) more slowly. However, we prefer the program with procedures since it has structure. This aids readability (we can look at the main program and see, almost at a glance, what the program does) and, providing the procedures are well chosen, it gives the program some degree of robustness.

The structure of the program of Prog 8.3 is a two-level one. At the top level (the *strategy* in military terms), we have the broad structure as expressed by the relationships between the calls of the procedures. At the bottom level we have the details of the workings of the individual procedures (the *tactics*), and significantly these are relatively independent. Thus the details of the tax calculation are quite independent of the details of announcing the purpose of the program. Furthermore the details of the tax calculation are quite independent of the broad strategy as well, so that, for example, the changes required to the program to be used in a batch-processing mode, would not affect the *CalculateTax* procedure. We said earlier that procedures give some degree of robustness to the program provided that they are relatively independent. Clearly then, we have to partition our programs into procedures so that changes to individual procedures have the minimal effect on other procedures and on the main program.

The relevant syntax diagrams are given in Fig 8.1 from which we see that the structure of a procedure-declaration, a procedure-heading followed by a procedure-block, is essentially the same as that of a program, which is, of course, a program-heading followed by a program-block. (Remember from Chapter 3 that we often precede syntactic variables, here "heading" and "block", by adjectives, here "procedure" and "program", to distinguish their uses.)

In particular, a procedure may have its own variables called *local variables.* Local variables are accessible only within the procedure in which they are declared; they cannot be accessed by the main program or by other procedures. This last sentence suggests that statements within a procedure may access the variables of the *main program* (the program-body) directly. And indeed they can. However, to increase the robustness of a program, we will restrict ourselves to accessing the local variables and the parameters only. Equally, procedures may have their own local constants and types. Consider the procedure *CalculateGross*. The variable *overtime* is declared within *CalculateGross* and may be accessed only within that procedure. This is how it should be: the variable exists purely to enable *CalculateGross* to do its job, and is of no concern to other procedures or to the main program. The same is true of the local constant *normal*. Its value is relevant to the calculation of the gross wage of an employee, and nothing else. Global quantities, however, may be accessed by all procedures and also by the main program. Finally a procedure may have its own local procedures, created to help it do its job. We give two illustrations of the importance of the relative independence of procedures.

Firstly, we modify a procedure without needing to change the main program. Consider the procedure *CalculateTax*: it uses the simple tax scheme of a 20% tax with a $100 tax threshold. Suppose we implement the scheme of Chapter 4.

Weekly wage	Base tax	% on excess over column 1
0	0	0
78	0.32	32
331	81.28	46
662	233.54	60

Fig 8.1   The syntax diagrams for procedure-declarations

* block

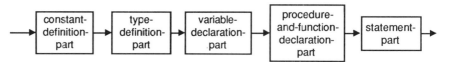

* procedure-and-function-declaration-part

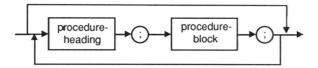

procedure-heading

* formal-parameter-list

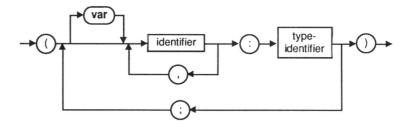

The procedure becomes:

```
procedure CalculateTax (var tax : real;
            gross : real);
  const
    threshold1= 78;
    threshold2= 331;
    threshold3= 662;
    base1= 0.32;
    base2= 81.28;
    base3= 233.54;
    taxrate1 = 0.32;
    taxrate2 = 0.46;
    taxrate3 = 0.60;
  begin
    if gross < threshold1 then
      tax := 0
    else if gross < threshold2 then
      tax := base1 + taxrate1 * (gross – threshold1)
    else if gross < threshold3 then
      tax := base2 + taxrate2 * (gross – threshold2)
    else
      tax := base3 + taxrate3 * (gross – threshold3)
  end {of procedure "CalculateTax"}
```

Secondly we modify the main program, without having to consider the procedures, by expanding it to calculate the total of the employees' nett wages, enabling the employer to have the right amount of money on pay day (Prog 8.4).

Prog 8.4   The main program when totals are accumulated

```
begin
    Announce;
    FindStaffSize(staffsize);
    GiveInstructions;
    InitializeTotal(totalnett);
    for employee := 1 to staffsize do
      begin
        ReadWorkDetails(code, rate, hours);
        CalculateGross(gross, rate, hours);
        CalculateTax(tax, gross);
        CalculateNett(nett, gross, tax);
        WriteWagesDetails(code, gross, tax, nett);
        UpdateTotal(nett, totalnett)
      end; {of loop on "employee"}
    WriteTotal(totalnett)
end.
```

We create three procedures, for initialization, updating and writing out the total, and expand the main program to include calls for these procedures. Prog 8.4 gives the statement-part of an appropriate main program, leaving to the reader the writing of the new procedures. Of course *totalnett* must be declared as a global variable.

Note the implication of all this, that we can discuss a procedure on its own, independently of the program which uses it. Hence we can even set up libraries of procedures which can be used in a variety of programs. Not all modifications can be handled so simply. Those that are essentially structural require changes to the structure of the program, and to the global variables. For example, if the tax laws were changed so that overtime was not taxed, then the *CalculateTax* procedure would need not just the gross wage but also a knowledge of how much of that was due to overtime.

It is to keep the structure fairly regular that we choose to use a procedure such as *CalculateNett*. Its body is a single assignment-statement and we could quite simply have left it in the main program. However, if we were to expand the program significantly, then we might have to handle all deductions (not just tax) in which case *CalculateNett* would become a significant procedure. The real challenge is to anticipate these developments and structure the program to minimize the changes necessary to accommodate them.

8.4 Storage allocation

In the early chapters of this book we drew diagrams of the store to illustrate the nature of variables. Using a similar, but more stylized sort of diagram, the storage allocation for the main payroll program is as shown below.

code	rate	hours	gross	tax	nett	employee	staffsize

How does the introduction of procedures affect this allocation? On entry to the program, the variables of the main program are allocated storage. Each procedure needs some space allocated to it, not only for its parameters and local variables but also for what are called *links*, the information required by the system to manipulate the storage. This storage is allocated when a procedure is called. The situation when the main program has called *CalculateGross* is:

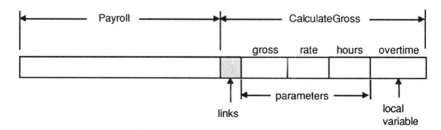

The allocated space is recovered when the procedure ends. This storage allocation scheme is called a *stack*, a word which has the connotation of orderliness in contrast to a *heap*, which we shall introduce later in the book. The layout of the storage as the payroll program progresses is shown in Fig 8.2, where the details of each individual procedure's storage has been suppressed. Thus it can be seen that the procedures share the same storage space, so that when a procedure is called a second time, the initial value of its local variables is unpredictable.

8.5   Formal-parameters and actual-parameters

As we noted earlier, there are two classes of formal-parameter. A *variable-parameter* is one for which the procedure calculates a value. It is indicated by **var** preceding its identifier. A *value-parameter* is one which has a value initially, and which the procedure uses in its operation. In this case the identifier is not preceded by any such indicator. We noted, too, that the type of the

Fig 8.2 The operation of the stack

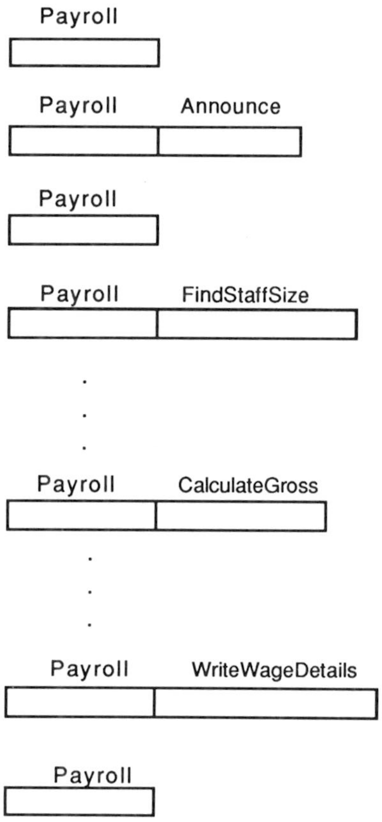

Payroll

Payroll   Announce

Payroll

Payroll   FindStaffSize

.
.
.

Payroll   CalculateGross

.
.
.

Payroll   WriteWageDetails

Payroll

parameter must be given, and that parameters of the same class and type can be grouped with the class and type given once, as with *rate* and *hours* above. When writing a procedure we choose the formal-parameters and write the procedure-body in terms of them. When the procedure is subsequently obeyed (as a result of the call) the actual-parameters are associated with the formal-parameters and then the body of the procedure obeyed.

The syntax diagrams are quite simple as Fig 8.3 shows. The form of association between an actual-parameter and its formal-parameter depends on the class of the formal-parameter. If the formal-parameter is called by value, then the actual-parameter may be any expression of the appropriate type. The formal-parameter acts just like a local variable, except that it is initialized to the value of the actual-parameter. All references to the formal-parameter within the procedure-body access this local value. If the formal-parameter is called as a variable, on the other hand, the actual parameter must be a variable-access. The formal-parameter acts as an indirect reference to the actual-parameter. All references to the formal-parameter within the procedure-body access the actual-parameter indirectly. Note that any change to the value of the formal-parameter means that the corresponding actual-parameter is changed.

We can illustrate the nature of the two classes of parameter by showing a diagram of the store for the payroll program, just as the procedure *CalculateGross* is called. Remember that it has one parameter, *gross*, called as a variable, and two, *rate* and *hours*, which are called by value. Assuming our usual data:

```
code = 2134;
hours = 42.75;
rate = 8.26
```

Fig 8.3   The syntax of procedure-statement

procedure-statement

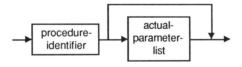

* actual-parameter-list

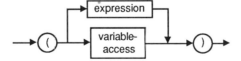

the store when the procedure is called, is as follows:

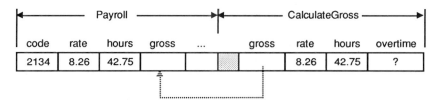

where the dotted line shows that the formal-parameter *gross,* indirectly refers to the actual parameter which is also called *gross.* The parameters called by value, *rate* and *hours*, are initialized to the values of the actual-parameters. If we had used *CalculateGross* in another program, then after the call:

CalculateGross(grosspay, payrate, hours)

the store would have been like this:

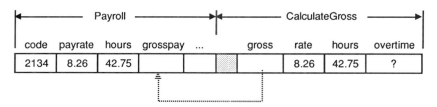

We return to our version of the payroll, rather than this hypothetical one. At the end of the body of *CalculateGross* , *overtime* will have been evaluated as 5.25, and *gross calculated* as 374.7975. Thus the store will look like this.

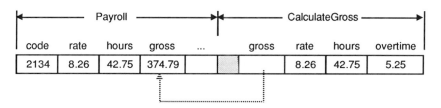

When control returns from *CalculateGross* the store is recovered so that the formal-parameters and the local variables go out of existence.

It should be noted that, since a value parameter acts like a local variable, its value may be changed during the execution of the procedure, without any effect on the value of the variables of the main program. As an example let us rewrite the procedure for *CalculateGross* so that it calculates the overtime payment first.

```
procedure CalculateGross (var gross : real;
              rate, hours : real);
  const
    normal = 37.5;
  var
    overtimepay : real;
  begin
    if hours > normal then
      begin
        overtimepay := (hours – normal) * 1.5 * rate;
        hours := normal
      end
    else
      overtimepay := 0;
    gross := hours * rate + overtimepay
  end;{of procedure "CalculateGross"}
```

Note that if overtime has been worked, the value of *hours* is changed within the procedure, but there is no effect on the actual parameter.

8.6   The design of procedures

We noted earlier that procedures can be written in isolation. We do so now. The strategy is quite straight-forward.

- Decide on the parameters, the quantities the procedure operates on.

- Decide on their types and modes.

- Thus write the heading.

- Write the body in terms of the heading.

As an example, consider the Cartesian plane shown in Fig 8.4.

Fig 8.4 The Cartesian plane

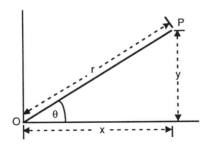

Let us design a procedure that converts from Cartesian co-ordinates of a point P to polar co-ordinates. Although this is a mathematical problem, the mathematics is trivial. The Cartesian coordinates (x,y) of the point P are just the distance East (x) and North (y) from the so-called origin O. The polar coordinates (r, θ) are the direct distance (r) from O, and the angle (θ) of the line above due East. The relationships between the coordinates are:

$$r = \sqrt{x^2 + y^2}$$
$$\theta = \tan^{-1} \frac{y}{x}$$

We now design the procedure using the strategy we outlined above.

- The parameters are *x* and *y*, the Cartesian co-ordinates, and *r* and *theta*, the polar co-ordinates.

- All are of real-type: *x* and *y* are called by value, since the procedure requires their values to do its calculations; *r* and *theta* are called as variables since they are to be calculated by the procedure.

- Thus the heading is:

```
procedure CartToPolar(x, y : real;
              var r, theta : real);
```

- From the formulae given above we might write the body as:

```
begin
  r := sqrt(sqr(x) + sqr(y));
  theta := arctan(y/x)
end
```

However, if P is on the y-axis, *x* = 0, and the division *y/x* would cause overflow. The correct value for *theta* is, of course, 90° or π/2 radians. We must program this explicitly:

```
begin
  r := sqrt(sqr(x) + sqr(y));
  if x = 0 then
    theta := pi/2
  else
    theta := arctan(y/x)
end
```

where *pi* is the constant we introduced in Chapter 7.

The procedures we have discussed so far have all had parameters of both modes. However this need not be the case. A procedure which is concerned purely with output, such as *WriteWagesDetails*, will not have parameters called as variables, because such a procedure will not be calculating values for the main program. If it calculates anything, it will be values to be output. Thus if such procedures have parameters they will be called by value. (There is an exception to this rule which will be discussed in Chapter 13.) Of course some, such as *Announce*, may have no parameters at all. Similarly, a procedure which is concerned purely with input, such as *ReadWorkDetails*, will not have parameters called by value.

8.7   Functions

There is one class of procedure which occurs so often that Pascal, and most other languages for that matter, deals with them specially. This class contains procedures that calculate precisely one value. They can be cast as *functions*. As the word "function" suggests, they closely resemble mathematical functions, and it is therefore not surprising that they are distinguished in this way. What characterizes a function from a programming point of view is that it is activated by a *function-designator*, which can be used as an operand in any expression, rather than by a procedure-statement. We have used function-designators already, of course. In Section 2.9 we gave a table of the required functions of Pascal, and we saw there that we could write function-designators such as:

```
log(x)
log(sin(x))
sqrt(sqr(x) + sqr(y))
```

We will illustrate how functions are written by considering (yet again) the procedure *CalculateGross* from the payroll program.

```
procedure CalculateGross (var gross : real;
            rate, hours : real);
  const
    normal = 37.5;
  var
    overtime : real;
  begin
    if hours > normal then
      overtime := hours – normal
    else
      overtime := 0;
    gross := hours * rate + overtime * 0.5 * rate
  end {of procedure "CalculateGross"}
```

It clearly calculates only one quantity, *gross* and so can be recast as a function:

```
function GrossWage (rate, hours : real) : real;
  const
    normal = 37.5;
  var
    overtime : real;
begin
  if hours > normal then
    overtime := hours − normal
  else
    overtime := 0;
  GrossWage := hours * rate + overtime * 0.5 * rate
end {of function "GrossWage"}
```

There are two significant differences between the procedure and the function. Firstly, the function has only two parameters, *rate* and *hours*. But it also *has* a value! We talk of the function "returning a value", or "yielding a value". The type of (the value returned by) a function is specified after the formal-parameter-list. Here, of course, it is the gross wage which is of real-type. As well, the heading also starts with **function** instead of **procedure.** Note that the function has been renamed as *GrossWage* to reflect the fact that it is a function, and therefore yields a value, rather than a procedure which causes some operation to take place. The syntax diagrams are given in Fig 8.5. Secondly, the value returned by the function is specified by means of a special assignment-statement in which the left-hand size consists not of a variable-access, but of the function-identifier. As we noted before, functions are invoked by means of a function-designator used as an operand in an expression. Therefore, if we replaced the procedure *CalculateGross* by the function *GrossWage* in the payroll program, then the pro-

Fig 8.5   The syntax of functions

procedure-and-function-declaration-part

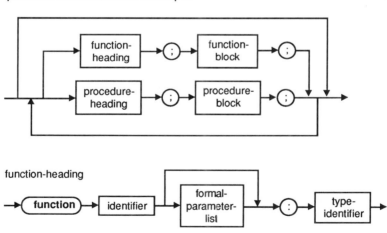

function-heading

cedure statement:

> CalculateGross(gross, rate, hours)

would have to be replaced by the assignment-statement:

> gross := GrossWage(rate, hours)

There does not appear to be much gain here, and indeed there isn't. But in general there is, because a function-designator can be used as an actual-parameter in some other function-designator. For example, if we had recast *CalculateTax* as a function *TaxPayable* then we could, perhaps in some other part of the program, calculate directly the tax payable for a given rate of pay and a given number of hours worked by:

> TaxPayable(GrossWage(rate,hours))

The value of the function must be stored somewhere between its assignment, and its subsequent use in the expression from which the function was invoked. In fact it is stored as one of the links. Returning to the situation where *GrossWage* was called directly from within the main program, the store looks something like this just before the end of the function:

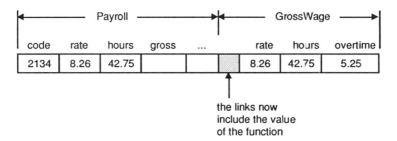

the links now
include the value
of the function

8.8   The design of procedures and functions

In section 8.6 we gave a strategy for writing procedures. We now extend it to cater for functions as well.

- Determine the quantities that the procedure operates on.

- Decide on their types and modes.

- If only one value is to be calculated, then a function is appropriate, otherwise a procedure. Thus write the heading.

- Write the body in terms of the heading.

- If it is a function, specify the value of the function by an assignment, on the left-hand side of which is the function-identifier.

Let us try this with a couple of simple examples. First we will design a function which will raise a real number to a power which is a natural number.

- The parameters are the real number x, the natural number n, and the real result.

- x is real-type, n is natural-type, and the result is also real-type.

- As there is only one result a function is needed, with the heading :

> **function** Power (x : real;
> n : natural) : real;

- In the body we simply initialize a local variable, p, to 1, and in a loop, multiply it by x a total of n times.

- We assign p to be the value of the function.

This results in the function of Prog 8.5.

Prog 8.5 A function for powering
***

```
function Power (x : real;
             n : natural) : real;
{This function returns the value of x^n.}
  var
    p : real;
    i : natural;
  begin
    p := 1;
    for i := 1 to n do
      p := p * x;
    Power := p
  end {of function "Power"}
```
***

As a second example, we will write a function which returns a value which is the factorial of its argument, n, which is a natural number. Using our strategy:

- The quantities involved are n , and the resultant factorial.

- Both quantities are natural numbers.

- As there is only one result an appropriate heading is:

function Fact (n : natural) : natural;

- In the body, a local variable, *p*, is initially set to 1, and in a loop is multiplied by 1, 2, ..., *n*.

- We assign *p* to be the value of the function.

This results in the function of Prog 8.6.

Prog 8.6 A factorial function

```
function Fact (n : natural) : natural;
{This function returns n!}
  var
    p, i : natural;
begin
  p := 1;
  for i := 1 to n do
    p := p * i;
  Fact := p
end {of function "Fact"}
```

Exercises

8.1 Recast *CalculateGross* so that it calculates *gross* directly, instead of using overtime. See Chapter 4.

8.2 Write a procedure with the heading:

procedure PolarToCart(r, theta : real;
var x, y : real)

which converts the Polar coordinates of a point into its Cartesian ones. This procedure is the inverse of the one given in Section 8.6.

8.3 Write a procedure with the heading:

procedure BlankLines(n : natural)

which leaves *n* blank lines on the output.

8.4 Write a function with the heading:

function Power (x : real;
n : integer) : real

which returns x^n where n is of integer-type (and might therefore be negative).

8.5 Write a function with the heading:

> **function** Median (a, b, c : natural) : natural

which returns the median (i.e. the middle value) of *a, b, c*.

Problems

8.1 Recast your exam marks program so that it uses procedures where appropriate.

8.2 Redesign the Tic-Tac-Toe program of the last chapter to use procedures. Be prepared to adopt a different structure than the one we chose there.

8.3 Modify the payroll program to accumulate the total of the nett wages, as outlined in Section 8.3, and extend it to accumulate as well the totals of the gross wages and the tax deducted.

9

Iteration and Booleans

In Chapter 5 we introduced one form of repetitive-statement, the for-statement. The characteristic of this statement is that the number of repetitions is known at the time the statement is about to be obeyed. We call such loops *deterministic*. There are many loops like this, of course, as all the programs we have written so far testify. However, there is another class of loops, probably larger, where the number of repetitions required is not known until the last one has been done. Naturally enough such loops are said to be *non-deterministic*. Most often the loops arise in the context of *iteration*.

9.1 Euclid's algorithm

Consider the problem of finding the greatest common divisor (GCD) of two natural numbers. Before we explain how to evaluate GCDs let us use the methodology of the last chapter to design the procedure-heading.

- The procedure involves three quantities, the two numbers, traditionally *p* and *q*, and the GCD.

- All three are of natural-type; *p* and *q* are called by value, and the GCD is the result. Therefore a function is appropriate.

- The function-heading is:

    function GCD (p, q : natural) : natural;

But how do we write the body in terms of the parameters? As it happens there is a simple algorithm due to Euclid for calculating the GCD of two natural numbers. It is:

- Divide *p* by *q* to give a remainder *r*,

- If $r = 0$ then the GCD is *q*,

- Otherwise repeat this procedure with *q* and *r* taking the place of *p* and *q*.

For example, given 366 and 150 as the numbers, the calculation proceeds as follows:

Dividend	Divisor	Remainder
366	150	66
150	66	18
66	18	12
18	12	6
12	6	0

giving the answer 6. Note that the number of repetitions is not known until the GCD has actually been found. The body of the loop is clearly:

```
begin
  p := q;
  q := r;
  r := p mod q
end
```

but how do we express the fact that the loop is to be obeyed, not some known number of times, but until *r* reaches 0?

9.2   The while-statement

The answer is by using another form of repetitive-statement, the *while-statement*, so that the loop becomes:

```
while r <> 0 do
  begin
    p := q;
    q := r;
    r := p mod q
  end {of loop "while r <> 0"}
```

The syntax of the statement is quite simple as Fig 9.1 illustrates. The meaning of the while-statement is quite simple, too. If the Boolean-expression initially has the value *true*, the statement is obeyed; then the Boolean-expression is re-evaluated and, if its value is still *true*, the statement is obeyed again; and so on

Fig 9.1 The syntax diagram for *while-statement*

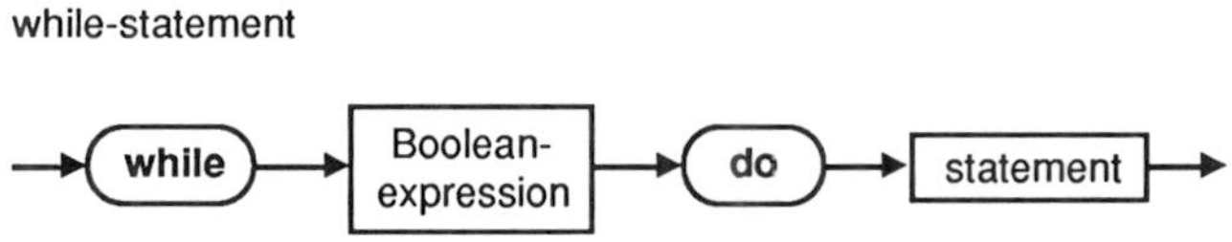

while-statement

until ultimately the Boolean-expression becomes *false*, and the while-statement terminates. In other words, while the Boolean-expression is true, the statement which is the body of the loop is repeatedly obeyed. Note that this means:

- The Boolean-expression is tested initially so that there may be no repetitions.

- Some initialization is necessary so that the Boolean-expression has a value initially.

- Within the loop, some statements must have the potential to change the value of the Boolean-expression.

In the GCD example, r is calculated within the loop, so that the Boolean-expression, $r <> 0$, will at some stage become *false*. It must be initialized before the loop so that we arrive at the function of Prog 9.1.

Prog 9.1 A function for the GCD of two natural numbers

```
function GCD (p, q : natural) : natural;
{This function returns the GCD of p and q.}
  var
    r : natural;
begin
  r := p mod q;
  while r <> 0 do
    begin
      p := q;
      q := r;
      r := p mod q
    end;{of loop "while r <> 0"}
  GCD := q
end {of function "GCD"}
```

9.3   The *Boolean-type*

Boolean-expressions do not exist in a vacuum to be used only in if-statements and while-statements. There is a third required type, *Boolean*, so that Boolean variables may be declared:

```
var
  p, q, disc, third, conj : Boolean;
```

Why would we wish to declare such variables? One answer is that they are often used as temporary variables to hold the result of some condition (Boolean-expression) for use later on, in the same way that arithmetic variables sometimes hold the result of some arithmetic calculations for subsequent use. They do, though, have an independent existence as we see later. It is usually the case with a new type that a programmer needs to ask only two questions: what values may variables of that type assume, and, as we saw with enumerated-types, what operations may be performed on the variables? With Booleans, the answer to the first question is simply that the variables may take one of only two values, *true* and *false*. These two values then are the constants of Boolean-type, and are represented by the identifiers:

> *true*   *false*

9.4   Operations on Booleans

The operations that can be performed are rather extensive, but not complete.

(i) Boolean values cannot be read. Inasmuch as most Boolean variables are temporary variables, and therefore of internal significance only, this does not really matter. If, however, truly Boolean data is required then an indirect approach must be used. The value could literally be entered as *true* or *false*, the characters which compose these values read in (as described in a later chapter), and after checking, converted to the Boolean values. A simpler approach would be to type *true* as 1 and *false* as 0. Each value could then be read, checked for consistency and converted to a Boolean value as follows:

```
read(n);
if n = 1 then
   p := true
else if n = 0 then
   p := false
else
   writeln('The data is not Boolean.')
```

Boolean values can, however, be written. The words *true* or *false* are written with leading spaces inserted, if necessary.

(ii) Boolean values may be assigned. Using the variables declared above we might have:

```
p := true;
p := q;
disc := sqr(b) >= 4*a*c;
third := (−pi/2 <= x) and (x <= pi/2);
p := p and q or r
```

The first simply sets *p* to *true* (often useful for initialization). The second sets *p* to the same value as *q*; and the third sets *disc* to *true* if $b^2 \geq 4ac$, and to *false* otherwise. The last two will be explained shortly. Note that for the third example:

disc := sqr(b) >= 4*a*c

is preferable to:

if sqr(b) >= 4*a*c **then**
   disc := true
else
   disc := false

since it is shorter, faster and expresses more clearly the meaning of assigning the value of a Boolean-expression to a variable. Fig 9.2 gives the full syntax of Boolean-expression. From the diagram we can make the following deductions:

- The order of precedence of the logical operators is **not**, which has the highest priority, followed by **and**, followed by **or**. Thus:

        not p **and** q   means   (**not** p) **and** q
        p **and** q **or** r   means   (p **and** q) **or** r.

As with arithmetic, brackets can be used to overcome precedence.

Fig 9.2 The syntax of *Boolean-expression*

Boolean-expression

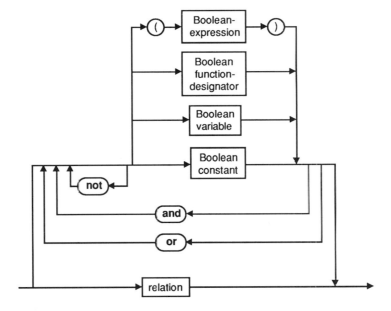

- **Not** is a unary operator which gives the value *true* if its operand is *false*, and vice versa. The fact that we can write **not not not** p is not not not very useful.

- If either operand of a logical operator is a relation of any type, including Boolean (defined below), then the relation must be enclosed in brackets. Thus:

> exhausted **or** found
> (sqr(trial) <= number) **or** found
> (sqr(trial) <= number) **or** (number **mod** trial = 0)

are all correct, and the brackets are non-redundant. This is a less restrictive statement than the one given in Chapter 4 (because at that point we had not considered Boolean variables).

(iii) Procedures may have parameters of Boolean-type, and functions may return Boolean values. In Prog 9.2, we give a function *Leap* which returns the value *true* if its parameter y is a leap year, and *false* otherwise. There is one required Boolean function, *odd*, which returns true if and only if its integer parameter is odd. Thus *odd(n)* is equivalent to n **mod** $2 = 1$.

Prog 9.2 A function which is true if its parameter is a leap year

---

function Leap (y : yeartype) : Boolean;
{This function returns true if and only if y is a leap year.}
begin
  Leap := (y **mod** 400 = 0) **or** (y **mod** 100 <> 0) **and** (y **mod** 4 = 0)
end {of function "Leap"}

(iv) We may compare Boolean variables for equality so that:

> p = q

may thankfully be written instead of:

> p **and** q **or not** p **and not** q

Similarly we can write:

> p := (a >= 0) = (b >= 0)

which sets *p* to *true* iff *a* and *b* are of the same sign. This is one example of a Boolean relation. All six relations are available and *false* is defined to be less than *true*. The syntax diagram is exactly the same as that for arithmetic relation, and so we do not give it. The relational-operators effectively have a lower priority than the Boolean operators. Thus:

p = q **and** disc   means   p = (q **and** disc)
disc **and** p = q   means   (disc **and** p) = q

As always, brackets can be used to over-ride the order of precedence as in:

(p = q) **and** disc

(v) The required functions *succ* and *pred* also apply to Booleans (as Boolean functions) but they are not very useful since although *succ(false)* = *true* and *pred(true)* = *false* both *succ(true)* and *pred (false)* are undefined.

(vi) We can use the transfer function *ord* to convert a Boolean value to the appropriate integer value, 0 for *false* and 1 for *true*. This is sometimes used to avoid the conditional incrementing of a variable. That is, instead of:

if n = 1 **then**
   p := p + 1

we could write:

p := p + ord(n = 1)

It would be fair to say that this use is not generally considered to be fashionable – even though the hardware of modern machines supports it directly. We will use it though in the next chapter. There is no reverse operation but the statement:

p := n = 1

will effectively transfer an integer in *n* to a Boolean in *p*. Note that this statement will assign *false* to *p* for all values of *n* not equal to 1.

(vii) We can cycle through both Boolean values in a for-statement:

for p := false **to** true **do** ...
for q := true **downto** false **do** ...

This is rarely used, but has some applications in problems dealing with logic.

(viii) We can use a case-statement with the Boolean constants as case-constants. Thus, in place of:

if p **then**
   "statement"
else
   "statement"

we can write:

```
case p of
   true:
     "statement";
   false:
     "statement"
end {of cases on "p"}
```

Note that this statement has the advantage that the appropriate condition (here just *true* or *false*) is attached to each of the two consequent statements.

9.5   Operator priorities

The interrelation between expressions and relations is quite subtle. For example, if *p* and *q* are of integer-type and *disc* is of Boolean-type, then:

p = q **and** disc

is not a Boolean-expression. To make it valid, brackets are required:

(p = q) **and** disc

Yet if *p* and *q* are of Boolean-type then it is valid and means:

p = (q **and** disc)

All this can be deduced from the syntax diagrams though it means looking at a number of such diagrams. Instead we can distill out the essence and create a table of the precedence of all Pascal operators. This is shown below:

not
  *, /, **div**, **mod**, **and**
  +, −, **or**
  =, <, >, <>, <=, >=, **in**

where **not** is of the highest priority, and the relational-operators are of the lowest. Note from this table that **and** is regarded as a multiplying-operator and **or** as an adding-operator.

If the application of this table to a Boolean-expression we are about to write produces nonsense (as it would if *p* and *q* were of integer-type in the above expression) or assigns the wrong interpretation (as it might if *p* and *q* were of Boolean-type), then brackets must be used to override the precedence.

9.6   The relationship between for- and while-statements

From the description it is clear that the while-statement can be used for deterministic loops, too. In general, the relationship can be illustrated:

```
                     i := 1;
for i := 1 to n do   while i <= n do
  begin                begin
    S₁;                  S₁;
    ...                  ...
    Sₖ                   Sₖ;
                         i := i + 1
  end                  end
```

The *Factorial* function of Chapter 8, can be recast to use the while-statement as shown in Prog 9.3.

Prog 9.3   The factorial function recast using the while-statement

---

```
function Fact (n : natural) : natural;
{This function returns n!}
  var
    p, i : natural;
  begin
  p := 1;
  i := 1;
  while i <= n do
    begin
      p := p * i;
      i := i + 1
    end;{of loop "while i <= n"}
  Fact := p
  end {of function "Fact"}
```

Many authors regard the while-statement as the fundamental loop statement, with the for-statement as simply syntactic sugar. We will take a more even-handed approach, always using the for-statement for deterministic loops, reserving the while-statement for non-deterministic loops. The reasons for this are:

- The for-statement is shorter and clearer, and all the appropriate information about the loop (control variable, initial value and final value) is given explicitly, whereas with the while-statement the information is spread over at least 3 statements.

- It is very easy to get the control statements wrong when using a while-statement. It is all too easy to type "<" instead of "<=", for example, or to increment the control variable at the head of the loop without making other appropriate adjustments.

- The control variable of the for-statement always remains within the range specified, whereas with the while-statement given above, the control variable is assigned one extra value. Thus the equivalent while-statement for:

for month := Jan **to** Dec **do**
     S

will fail as it tries to assign the successor of *Dec* to *month*. Of course, it is possible to modify the while-statement to avoid this problem, but that only makes it even longer and uglier than the for-statement!

- For-statements always terminate. Properly written while-statements terminate too, but it is all too easy to accidentally write infinite loops.

9.7   A strategy for writing loops

One strategy for designing loops proceeds in three stages.

- Determine what has to be done repeatedly, the body of the loop.

- Determine under what conditions it is to be repeated. This determines the type of loop, **for** or **while** or (see later) **repeat**, and the conditions for loop termination. It may also mean adding some incrementing instructions to the body of the loop.

- Decide on the initialization.

We illustrate this strategy by means of an example. Suppose we want a function which returns the smallest natural number whose factorial exceeds its argument, *limit*. First the function-heading! By now the strategy of the last chapter should be almost reflex, and so we quickly arrive at:

function FactorialFloor(limit : natural) : natural

Now for the body. The obvious strategy for determining the floor is to calculate in a loop, the factorials, *fact*, of all the natural numbers, *count*, from 1 up to the one whose factorial exceeds *limit*. We proceed to write the loop.

- Determine the body. The next factorial in the sequence is calculated from the previous one, which implies that *count* is incremented in the loop, thus:

count := count + 1;
fact := fact * count

- Determine the conditions under which the body is to be obeyed. Clearly the number of times the body is to be obeyed is not known so that a while-statement is appropriate. Further, the terminating criterion follows immediately from the discussion above.

```
while fact <= limit do
  begin
    count := count + 1;
    fact := fact * count
  end
```

• Initialize. We need to ensure both *count* and *fact* are initialized:

```
count := 0;
fact := 1
```

The complete function is given in Prog 9.4. In the factorial floor function, there is only a single terminating condition: *fact <= limit*. Such functions are usually very easy to write. Quite often, though, the terminating condition is more complex, involving two or more concepts.

Prog 9.4 The factorial floor of a natural number

```
function FactorialFloor (limit : natural) : natural;
{This function returns the smallest number whose factorial exceeds
limit.}
  var
    count, fact : natural;
begin
  count := 0;
  fact := 1;
  while fact <= limit do
    begin
      count := count + 1;
      fact := fact * count
    end; {of loop on "while fact <= limit"}
  FactorialFloor := count
end {of function "FactorialFloor"}
```

As a second example, consider a function which returns *true* if its argument, *number*, is a prime and *false* otherwise. The function heading is:

function Prime (number : natural) : Boolean

The simplest technique for determining whether *number* is prime is to divide *number* by all the integers from 2 up to and including the square root of *number*; if none divides exactly, then *number* is prime. Let us use a natural number, *trial*, for the successive integer divisors. The design of the function follows:

- Within the loop we must determine whether the current value of *trial* is a factor, and increment *trial* in anticipation of the next traverse of the loop. Since we will need to know why the loop terminated to determine whether *number* is prime, it will be convenient to have a local variable *factorfound* which is true iff the current value of *trial* is a factor. Thus:

      factorfound := number **mod** trial = 0;
      trial := trial + 1

- The loop is obeyed either until all integers ≤ √*number* have been tried, or until one of the integers is a factor. This is implemented:

      while (sqr(trial) <= number) **and not** factorfound **do**
        begin
        factorfound := number **mod** trial = 0;
        trial := trial + 1
        end

Note that we have compared the square of *trial* against *number*, rather than *trial* against the square root of *number*, since squaring is very much faster than square-rooting.

- We must initialize both *trial* (to 2) and *factorfound* (to *false*).

      trial := 2;
      factorfound := false

Thus we are lead to the function of Prog 9.5.

Prog 9.5 A prime function

---

function Prime (number : natural) : Boolean;
{This function returns true iff number is a prime number.}
  var
    trial : natural;
    factorfound : Boolean;
begin
  trial := 2;
  factorfound := false;
  while (sqr(trial) <= number) **and not** factorfound **do**
    begin
      factorfound := number **mod** trial = 0;
      trial := trial + 1
    end;
  Prime := **not** factorfound
end {of function "Prime"}

9.8   The repeat-statement

It is clear from the description of the meaning of the while-statement, that the body may never be obeyed. There are many programming situations in which the body will always be obeyed at least once. A closely related statement, the *repeat-statement*, is provided. Fig 9.3 gives the syntax. Note that because **repeat** and **until** effectively act as brackets, there is no need to turn the body of the loop into a single statement by using **begin** and **end**.

As with the while-statement, the body must contain statements which will alter the value of the Boolean-expression so that it becomes (initially or subsequently) true.   Since the Boolean expression is tested at the end of the loop, the initialization required is small, if not actually nil. So which, the while-statement or the repeat-statement, should we use in a given situation? We said earlier that the for-statement should be used in preference to the while-statement in situations where the number of traverses of the loop was known on entry to the loop. With the while- and the repeat-statement it is more difficult to classify situations which are appropriate to each construct. We can make some general observations though.

- The while-statement is sufficient and any repeat-statement can be rephrased in terms of it. To give complete equivalences is not very rewarding so we merely comment that the transformation may be trivial; or it may require a copy of part of the body to be placed before the while-statement; or it may require phony initialization to give values to the variables of the Boolean-expression.

- The body of a repeat-statement will always be obeyed once where that of a while-statement may not be obeyed at all. This, of course, classifies some situations as inappropriate for the repeat-statement.

- The while-statement is more rugged in the sense that it handles the special case of traversing the loop no times.

- The repeat-statement is marginally more efficient since there is no initial test on entering the loop.

- With the repeat-statement, there is likely to be less initialization (or even none) of the variables associated with loop control. One indication that the repeat-statement is the correct one to use is where the initialization

Fig 9.3 The syntax of the *repeat-statement*

repeat-statement

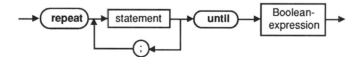

of the while-statement becomes 'unnatural'.

Perhaps the real solution to the problem is to sketch out both the while sequence and the repeat sequence and then choose the better one. More importantly there are situations where neither is particularly appropriate (yet one must be chosen). The classical situation is where, instead of wanting to obey the loop *n* times, we want to obey part of it *n* times and the rest *n–1* times. Clearly part of the body of the loop must appear outside the loop as well. As an example, suppose that we have a list of positive numbers in our data, and that instead of preceding them by the number of numbers, as we have done so far, we terminate them by a special distinguishable number, say, –1. If we wish to read them and write out their sum, we have to read one more number (the –1) than we add, so a read statement will appear both inside and outside the loop. See program 9.6.

Prog 9.6   A program to sum some numbers terminated by –1

```
program FindSum;
{This program reads in some numbers and writes out their sum.}
  var
    sum, next : real;
begin
  writeln('This program will sum a string of numbers.');
  writeln('Give them to me one to a line, with –1 to terminate.');
  sum := 0;
  readln(next);
  while next <> –1 do
    begin
      sum := sum + next;
      readln(next)
    end; {of loop "while next <> –1"}
  writeln('Their sum is', sum : 6 : 2)
end.
```

9.9   State variables

There is a style of programming in which the repeat-statement is fundamental. Consider once again the *Prime* function. If we think of the way the function works we can see that at any point it is in one of three states:

• a factor has just been found,

• all trial values have been considered,

• tests are continuing.

Accordingly, we can introduce an enumerated variable, describing the state of the calculation, called a *state* variable:

> state : (testing, factorfound, trialsexhausted)

Assuming that *state* is initialized to *testing*, the body of the loop is concerned with determining the new state, and, if appropriate, updating *trial*. Thus the body is:

> **if** sqr(trial) > number **then**
> state := trialsexhausted
> **else if** number **mod** trial = 0 **then**
> state := factorfound
> **else**
> trial := trial + 1

This is repeated until *state* is in the set {factorfound, trialsexhausted}. The complete function is given in Prog 9.7.

Prog 9.7   A prime function, using a state variable

```
function Prime (number : natural) : Boolean;
{This function returns true iff number is a prime number.}
  var
    trial : natural;
    state : (testing, factorfound, trialsexhausted);
begin
  trial := 2;
  state := testing;
  repeat
    if sqr(trial) > number then
      state := trialsexhausted
    else if number mod trial = 0 then
      state := factorfound
    else
      trial := trial + 1
  until state in [factorfound, trialsexhausted];
  Prime := state = trialsexhausted
end {of function "Prime"}
```

Exercises

9.1   Write a function with the heading;

> **function** Digits (number : natural) : natural

which returns the number of decimal digits in *number*.

9.2 Write a function with the heading;

function Digits (number, base : natural) : natural

which returns the number of digits in the base *base* expansion of *number.*

9.3 Write a function with the heading;

function IntegerSqrt (number : natural) : natural

which returns the largest natural number which is less than or equal to the square root of *number.*

9.4 Write a function with the heading;

function IntegerLog (number : natural) : natural

which returns the largest natural number which is less than or equal to the logarithm to the base 2 of *number.* Thus if *number* = 15, the function returns 3, and if *number* = 16, it returns 4.

9.5 Write a function with the heading;

function LS1 (number : natural) : natural

which returns the position of the least significant 1 in the binary expansion of *number.* Thus if *number* = 48, the function returns 4, and if *number* = 49, it returns 0.

9.6 Replace the following conditional-statement, where *sign* is of an enumerated-type, by an assignment-statement:

```
if sign = minus then
   characters := digits + 1
else
   characters := digits
```

9.7 Assuming that *n* is a positive integer, replace the following for-statement by a conditional-statement:

```
for i := 1 to n do
   p := not  p
```

Problems

9.1 Vieta's formula for π is given by:

$$\frac{2}{\pi} = \frac{\sqrt{2}}{2} \times \frac{\sqrt{2+\sqrt{2}}}{2} \times \frac{\sqrt{2+\sqrt{2+\sqrt{2}}}}{2} \quad \cdots$$

Write a function with the heading:

function Pi (e : real) : real

which returns the value of π to an accuracy e using this formula. The calculation should terminate when the next product falls short of 1 by less than $e/2$.

9.2 Write a program which will print out a table of the prime factors of a range of natural numbers. A sample output is:

```
NUMBER         FACTORS
    2          2
    3          3
    4          2,2
    5          5
    6          2,3
    7          7
    8          2,2,2
    9          3,3
   10          2,5
```

9.3 The age of the first author of this book is a prime number. Next year his age will be twice a prime number. Write a program to determine and write out his age.

10

Program design with procedures

The procedure facility of Pascal fits naturally into the top-down design strategy we used in Chapter 6. As we progressively refine a program outline, the individual components can be expressed as procedures. In this chapter we consider a couple of examples.

10.1   Writing out PIN numbers

Most readers will be familiar with automatic teller machines (ATMs), and with the personal identification number (PIN) that the user must key in to the ATM in order to be identified as the legitimate owner of the ATM card. These numbers are invariably of four digits, and when one is sent to a user it is given both as a 4-digit number, and as the four digits spelled out. For example *1572* would be spelt out as *one five seven two*. What is useful in real life is the *procedure* that actually deals with a single number, but in this chapter, we will write a program in which the user is asked to type numbers one by one until he has dealt with them all. Rather than have him count the number of numbers, as we have done in the past, we allow him to type the numbers as they come and terminate them by typing an integer that is not a 4-digit one. A sample output is shown below:

```
This program will print out the English spelling
digit-by-digit of the PIN numbers you type in.
Type each number in turn followed by a return.
Terminate by an integer outside the range 1000-9999.

1234
one two three four
5678
five six seven eight
9012
nine zero one two
0
```

This is clearly a case for the use of the while-loop. The number of numbers to be written is not known until the last is typed, so that the body of the loop must be obeyed until a number which is not a PIN number is typed. Thus whenever a number is read it might be a PIN number, but equally it may be a number acting purely as a terminator. We introduce a procedure *ReadNumber* which will return two values, a Boolean *isaPINnumber*, which is true iff the number typed was a PIN number, and *PINnumber*, which is its value if it were a PIN number. Note that there must be a call for *ReadNumber* before the loop, for initialization purposes, and another inside the loop. This technique for reading data, and variants of it, are very frequently used in programs. Clearly it will be useful to declare:

type
    PINtype = 1000..9999;

to describe PIN numbers.

Because we are using procedures we will not use the semi-formal outline as we did earlier, but go straight to the main program with its procedure calls:

```
begin
    Announce;
    GiveInstructions;
    ReadNumber(isaPINnumber, PINnumber);
    while isaPINnumber do
      begin
        WritePINNumber(PINnumber);
        writeln;
        ReadNumber(isaPINnumber, PINnumber)
      end {of loop on while "isaPINnumber"}
end.
```

We now consider writing the four procedures of the program. *Announce* and *GiveInstructions* are trivial, and we consider them no further.

As we noted before, the procedure *ReadNumber* returns two values, a Boolean *isaPINnumber*, which is true iff the number typed was a PIN number, and the PIN number itself, *PINnumber,* where applicable. Thus the procedure must have a local variable, *number,* which holds the number actually typed by the user. Since the user may legitimately type any integer, *number* must be of integer-type. Of course, any valid PIN number entered will be of *PINtype*. The procedure tests the number typed and determines whether or not it is a PIN number, setting *isaPINnumber* appropriately. If it is a PIN number, *PINnumber* is assigned the value of *number*. This strategy of reading data using a variable of a general type, and, after testing it for validity, assigning it to a variable of the appropriately constrained type is much used. In this program all possible integers are valid, but usually only a subset of integer values are valid and this strategy enables a program to repeatedly ask the user for a value until a valid one is typed. Of course, if the user types letters or punctuation marks, the program will fail, and for really rugged programs the data must be read character by character, with the program doing the conversion, as we shall see in the next chapter.

The procedure is quite straight-forward:

```
procedure ReadNumber (var isaPINnumber : Boolean;
        var PINnumber : PINtype);
var
  number : integer;
begin
  readln(number);
  isaPINnumber := (number >= 1000) and (number <= 9999);
  if isaPINnumber then
    PINnumber := number
end {of procedure "ReadNumber"}
```

Note that we do not use the set facilities for testing whether number is in the range 1000 to 9999. The reason is one of efficiency. Many compilers forbid sets of that size, 9000 elements, and those that do not forbid them compile rather poor code for such a test. As a general rule, we will use the set facilities only where the size of the sets is, say, between 1 and 32.

WritePINNumber writes out the digits of the PIN number. Its action is straightforward. It must decompose *PINnumber* into thousands (*th*), hundreds (*h*), tens (*t*) and units (*u*); then it must write out each of the four digits in turn. This leads to the following procedure.

```
procedure WritePINNumber(PINnumber:PINtype);
begin
  DetermineTheDigits(th, h, t, u, PINnumber);
  WriteDigit(th);
  write(space);
  WriteDigit(h);
  write(space);
  WriteDigit(t);
  write(space);
  WriteDigit(u)
end {of procedure "WritePINNumber"}
```

To write out a digit involves a simple case-statement as we saw in Chapter 7. To decompose a number into its digits is an old friend too, so that the procedures *WriteDigit* and *DetermineTheDigits* are straight-forward.

The complete program is given in Prog 10.1.

Prog 10.1   The PIN numbers program

---

program PINNumbers;
{This program reads in a series of PIN numbers, in the range 1000..9999, and for each writes out the English spelling of its four digits. The series is terminated by any natural number outside the range of PIN numbers.}
  type
    PINtype = 1000..9999;

```pascal
var
  PINnumber : PINtype;
  isaPINnumber : Boolean;

procedure Announce;
begin
  writeln('This program will print out the English spelling');
  writeln('digit-by-digit of the PIN numbers you type in.')
end;{of procedure "Announce"}

procedure GiveInstructions;
begin
  writeln('Type each number in turn followed by a return.');
  writeln('Terminate by an integer outside the range 1000-9999.');
  writeln
end;{of procedure "GiveInstructions"}

procedure ReadNumber (var isaPINnumber : Boolean;
          var PINnumber : PINtype);
  var
    number : integer;
begin
  readln(number);
  isaPINnumber := (number >= 1000) and (number <= 9999);
  if isaPINnumber then
    PINnumber := number
end;{of procedure "ReadNumber"}

procedure WritePINNumber (PINnumber : PINtype);
  const
    space = ' ';
  type
    digit = 0..9;
  var
    th, h, t, u : digit;

  procedure DetermineTheDigits (var th, h, t, u : digit;
            PINnumber : PINtype);
  begin
    th := PINnumber div 1000;
    h := PINnumber mod 1000 div 100;
    t := PINnumber mod 100 div 10;
    u := PINnumber mod 10
  end;{of procedure "DetermineTheDigits"}

  procedure WriteDigit (d : digit);
  begin
    case d of
```

```
    0 :
      write('zero');
    1 :
      write('one');
    2 :
      write('two');
    3 :
      write('three');
    4 :
      write('four');
    5 :
      write('five');
    6 :
      write('six');
    7 :
      write('seven');
    8 :
      write('eight');
    9 :
      write('nine')
    end {of cases on "d"}
  end;{of procedure "WriteDigit"}

begin
  DetermineTheDigits(th, h, t, u, PINnumber);
  WriteDigit(th);
  write(space);
  WriteDigit(h);
  write(space);
  WriteDigit(t);
  write(space);
  WriteDigit(u)
end; {of procedure "WritePINNumber"}

begin
  Announce;
  GiveInstructions;
  ReadNumber(isaPINnumber, PINnumber);
  while isaPINnumber do
    begin
      WritePINNumber(PINnumber);
      writeln;
      ReadNumber(isaPINnumber, PINnumber);
    end {of loop on while "isaPINnumber"}
end.
```

10.2   Easter day

Easter, as the book of Common Prayer says, is a "moveable feast". That is, the date on which Easter Day falls varies from year to year. It is important, in Christian countries at least, that the date for a given year be known well in advance, for social and educational reasons, as well as for religious ones. In this section we will write a program which will write out a table of Easter dates like that given below.

```
This program prints a table of up to 20 Easter dates.
How many years should it cover? 10
Starting from when? 1988


                  EASTER
     YEAR           DAY

     1988       3 April
     1989      26 March
     1990      15 April
     1991      31 March
     1992      19 April
     1993      11 April
     1994       3 April
     1995      16 April
     1996       7 April
     1997      30 March
```

This program is of itself useful, but the procedure for determining the Easter date is even more so. It is clear from the output that the program first asks questions of the user to determine the range of years involved, and then for each year determines and writes out the date. Thus the main program is:

```
begin
  Announce;
  DetermineYearsInvolved(startyear, finishyear);
  WriteHeading;
  for year := startyear to finishyear do
    begin
      CalculateDateOfEaster(day, month, year);
      WriteDateOfEaster(day, month, year)
    end {of loop on "year"}
end.
```

As usual, most of the procedures are trivial, and we will not expand on them in the text. The interesting procedure is *CalculateDateOfEaster*, and many readers will be wondering how indeed Easter is determined. Technically, Easter Day is the first Sunday after the first full moon on or after the vernal equinox (21ˢᵗ March). Clavius, the originator of the Gregorian calendar, tabulated the dates for 5000 years, and mathematicians, including Gauss, gave algorithms for its calculation. The algorithm we are going to use is due to O'Beirne. It is defined as in the following table taken straight from his paper.

Step	Dividend	Divisor	Quotient	Remainder
(1)	x	19	-	a
(2)	x	100	b	c
(3)	b	4	d	e
(4)	8b + 13	25	g	-
(5)	11(b–d–g) – 4	30	θ	-
(6)	7a + θ + 6	11	ϕ	-
(7)	19a + (b–d–g) + 15 – ϕ	29	-	ψ
(8)	c	4	i	k
(9)	(32+2e) + 2i – k – ψ	7	-	λ
(10)	90 + (ψ+λ)	25	n	-
(11)	19 + (ψ+λ) + n	32	-	p

In the year x AD of the Gregorian calendar, Easter Sunday is the pth day of the nth month.

With the aid of the **div** and **mod** functions the procedure follows almost immediately. However there are some minor programming details to be considered. First, the identifiers. The algorithm contains Greek letters, θ, ϕ, ψ and λ, but of course Pascal allows only Roman letters in identifiers. We choose as identifiers the English names of the letters *theta*, *phi*, *psi* and *lambda* respectively. What about the other letters in the algorithm? They can hardly be called mnemonic, since they are just random letters. However, the algorithm gives no hint of the physical significance of the quantities, so we cannot use mnemonic identifiers. In any event it would be wise to use the same names as used in the algorithm. Second, the types of the identifiers. Note that for many variables, all those in the *Remainder* column, the types can be precisely defined as a subrange whose lower bound is 0. For example, a is in the range 0..18, since it is the remainder of a division by 19. The others though have a range which is harder to define. Should we declare each of the variables of the first class to be of the appropriate subrange, and declare the others as being of type natural? This solution would almost double the size of the procedure, and we would run the risk of making mistakes in defining the types. On the other hand, when coding the algorithm the most common error comes from typing **mod** for **div** and vice versa. On balance, and with some misgivings, we choose to declare all variables as being of natural type. This leads to the following procedure:

```
procedure CalculateDateOfEaster (var p : daytype;
            var n : monthtype;
            x : Gregorian);
  type
    natural = 0..maxint;
  var
    a, b, c, d, e, g, theta, phi, psi, i, k, lambda : natural;
  begin
    a := x mod 19;
    b := x div 100;
    c := x mod 100;
    d := b div 4;
    e := b mod 4;
    g := (8 * b + 13) div 25;
    theta := (11 * (b − d − g) − 4) div 30;
    phi := (7 * a + theta + 6) div 11;
    psi := (19 * a + (b − d − g) + 15 − phi) mod 29;
    i := c div 4;
    k := c mod 4;
    lambda := ((32 + 2 * e) + 2 * i − k − psi) mod 7;
    n := (90 + (psi + lambda)) div 25;
    p := (19 + (psi + lambda) + n) mod 32
  end {of procedure "CalculateDateOfEaster"}
```

DetermineYearsInvolved can be interesting, too, if we write it so as to check that the user enters sensible data. We use the idea described in the last section. We check the user's responses, and if the number read is not valid, we ask him to try again. A sample of the dialogue produced by the author's being awkward is given below:

```
This program prints a table of up to 20 Easter dates.
How many years should it cover? 25
The table must be between 1 and 20 in size.
Please try again.  How many years should it cover? 5
Starting from when? 1066
The table must start after 1583.
Please try again.  Starting from when? 1900


                  EASTER
         YEAR      DAY

         1900   15 April
         1901    7 April
         1902   30 March
         1903   12 April
         1904    3 April
```

The strategy for programming this is as follows. First the program asks its question. Then in a loop it reads the user's answers in turn into an integer variable until a valid one is given. If an invalid one is given, the user is told and the question repeated. When a valid answer is given it is assigned to the appropriate variable, and of course the loop terminates. The following sequence reads the number of years in the table:

```
write('How many years should it cover? ');
repeat
  readln(number);
  if number in [1..maxdates] then
    noyears := number
  else
    begin
      writeln('The table must be between 1 and ', maxdates:1, ' in size.');
      write('Please try again.  How many years should it cover? ')
    end
until number in [1..maxdates]
```

Note that because there must be at least one answer from the user, the loop will be traversed at least once, and so a repeat-loop is required. There is a similar sequence to find the starting date. The complete program is given in Prog 10.2.

Prog 10.2   The Easter program

```
program Easter;
{This program prints out a table of dates for Easter Day.  The algorithm,
due to O'Beirne, is described in Chapter 10 of "Programming via
Pascal".}
  const
    maxdates = 20;
    yearwidth = 5;
    gap = '   ';
    datewidth = 8;
  type
    Gregorian = 1583..maxint;
    daytype = 1..31;
    monthtype = 3..4;
  var
    year, startyear, finishyear : Gregorian;
    day : daytype;
    month : monthtype;

  procedure Announce;
  begin
    writeln('This program will print a table of up to ', maxdates : 1,
                                      ' Easter dates.')
  end;{of procedure "Announce"}
```

```
procedure DetermineYearsInvolved (var startyear,
        finishyear : Gregorian);
var
  number : integer;
  noyears : 1..maxdates;
begin
  write('How many years should it cover? ');
  repeat
    readln(number);
    if number in [1..maxdates] then
      noyears := number
    else
      begin
        writeln('The table must be between 1 and ', maxdates : 1, ' in
                                                          size.');
        write('Please try again. How many years should it cover? ')
      end
  until number in [1..maxdates];
  write('Starting from when? ');
  repeat
    readln(number);
    if number >= 1583 then
      startyear := number
    else
      begin
        writeln('The table must start after 1583.');
        write('Please try again.  Starting from when? ')
      end
  until number >= 1583;
  finishyear := startyear + noyears − 1
end;{of procedure "DetermineYearsInvolved"}


procedure WriteHeading;
begin
  writeln;
  writeln;
  writeln(' ' : yearwidth, gap, 'EASTER' : datewidth);
  writeln('YEAR' : yearwidth, gap, 'DAY' : datewidth);
  writeln
end;{of procedure "WriteHeading"}


procedure CalculateDateOfEaster (var p : daytype;
        var n : monthtype;
        x : Gregorian);
type
  natural = 0..maxint;
var
  a, b, c, d, e, g, theta, phi, psi, i, k, lambda : natural;
```

```
begin
  a := x mod 19;
  b := x div 100;
  c := x mod 100;
  d := b div 4;
  e := b mod 4;
  g := (8 * b + 13) div 25;
  theta := (11 * (b − d − g) − 4) div 30;
  phi := (7 * a + theta + 6) div 11;
  psi := (19 * a + (b − d − g) + 15 − phi) mod 29;
  i := c div 4;
  k := c mod 4;
  lambda := ((32 + 2 * e) + 2 * i − k − psi) mod 7;
  n := (90 + (psi + lambda)) div 25;
  p := (19 + (psi + lambda) + n) mod 32
end;{of procedure "CalculateDateOfEaster"}

procedure WriteDateOfEaster (day : daytype;
            month : monthtype;
            year : Gregorian);
begin
  case month of
    3 :
      writeln(year:yearwidth, gap, day : 2, 'March' : datewidth − 2);
    4 :
      writeln(year:yearwidth, gap, day : 2, 'April' : datewidth − 2)
  end {of cases on "month"}
end;{of "WriteDateOfEaster"}

begin
  Announce;
  DetermineYearsInvolved(startyear, finishyear);
  WriteHeading;
  for year := startyear to finishyear do
    begin
      CalculateDateOfEaster(day, month, year);
      WriteDateOfEaster(day, month, year)
    end {of loop on "year"}
end.
```

Problems

10.1 Write a procedure which will write out the value of its argument, a natural number, in the full English form. For example, the number *1572* would be written as *one thousand, five hundred and seventy-two*. (This is how it is written in Britain and Australia. If your country adopts a different style, do likewise.) Use the procedure in a program rather like the PIN program.

10.2 Easter Day must fall between 22 March and 25 April. Using the procedure *CalculateDateOfEaster* write a program which will determine the next year in which Easter will fall on a date provided by the user.

10.3 O'Beirne has also given a restricted algorithm, which is appropriate only to years, *y*, between 1900 and 2099. It is defined as in the following table taken from his paper.

Subtract 1900 from *y* to find *n*, such that $0 \le n \le 199$; then use *n* as indicated below.

Step	Dividend	Divisor	Quotient	Remainder
(1)	n	19	-	a
(2)	7a + 1	19	b	-
(3)	(11a + 4) − b	29	-	m
(4)	n	4	q	-
(5)	n + q + (31 − m)	7	-	w

Between the years 1900 and 2099 inclusive, Easter Sunday is the April $(25 - m - w)$: with an obvious interpretation of data from April 0 to April (−9), inclusive.

Write a procedure to implement this algorithm and use it in place of *CalculateDateOfEaster* of Prog 10.2.

11

Program development

A program which does not work is useless. So, too, is one which seems to work but in whose workings we have no real confidence: we would not care to use it when it really matters. So the question arises: how can we ensure that a program we design is correct? It is unfortunately true that the only way we can be completely sure of a program's correctness is by proving it to be so. This is a very difficult activity, and although we are making some progress in being able to prove programs correct by mathematical means, it is by no means a practical approach yet. For the present, we must concern ourselves with *testing* programs on carefully selected data. If our tests show the program to be incorrect, we must correct it, an activity called *debugging*.

11.1   Testing the programs we designed earlier

Before we go into details, let us see first how we might test the programs we designed in the earlier design chapters.

(i) *Drawing a board for noughts-and-crosses or Tic-Tac-Toe.*
This class of problem is one of the easiest to test, since the output is purely visual. Running the program twice for two different sizes, say *3* and *4*, followed by a visual inspection is probably adequate. Why two sizes? Why not one, say *3*? The answer is simple. If in the program the constant *3* appeared, even once, in place of the variable *size*, then the program would be wrong, but would give the correct output for the chosen data; and of course this can easily happen, since *3* appears in the program in another context – as the number of sections into which we decomposed the board. With two different values this possibility is eliminated.

(ii) *Producing a table of dates for Summer-time.*
This problem is more complex, because it involves some calculation. (The Tic-Tac-Toe program had none at all, except for the doubling of the number of horizontal characters.) Running it for one year will certainly not do. We must make sure that it operates correctly for leap years, and that it always produces dates that are the first or the last such days of the month. Caution suggests that we choose years just before and just after leap years too. Leaving aside century years, a suitable series of test data is from 1989 to 2000. But how do we know what the correct answer is? For the next year or two we can use a calendar. For later years, we may have access to a perpetual calendar. If not we must work it out by hand from the previous year, taking special care with leap years.

(iii) *Writing out PIN numbers.*

There is one fool-proof set of test data – all 9000 PIN numbers. The weakness of this approach is that the labour of checking them is simply too great. In any event, since the problem is structured, and the program is structured, we should be able to test it in a structured way. We have to ensure two things: that the program writes out each digit correctly, and that it decomposes a number into its four digits correctly. We leave the details as an exercise.

(iv) *Easter Day*

This is really difficult. The expressions required by the algorithm are obscure, and there is no apparent structure to them. Furthermore it is quite difficult to find the correct dates of Easter more than a few years into the future. In fact they can be obtained from tables in the *Book of Common Prayer*, but that is not immediately available to all of us. We will delay full testing of this procedure till Chapter 17.

11.2   The philosophy of testing

Note that where large computer systems are involved, there are two types of testing. Programmers test their programs during development, and a separate group of people tests them again before they are made available to the public. These two groups test the programs from different points of view. Programmers are concerned generally with testing the actual code written; the product testers are more concerned that the program conforms to its specifications. Therefore their tests will generally consider the problem, rather than the program.

It should be noted, too, that testing cannot demonstrate the absence of bugs, only their presence. That is, after all tests, it is possible that errors still exist in the program. The tests may not include some case, or some combination of cases, which may cause the program to fail. The only complete solution to this problem lies in the proof of programs. However, we must not allow this disturbing fact to depress us; rather, we must ensure that our tests are as comprehensive as possible. It is an interesting, and humbling, exercise to determine minimal changes to a program, which will make it faulty, but will still allow it to pass the tests. It is for this reason that the external tests to be applied to a program should never be made available to the programmer, since it is a trivial task to write a program to pass a known test: the program simply reads the (known) data, ignores it, and writes out the (known) results!

Just as we have structured our programs, so too we should structure our tests. We start with the simple statements, in particular with the assignment-statement.

11.3   Testing assignment-statements

For example, consider the mortgage repayment formula of Problem 5.5:

$$p = \frac{A * \dfrac{r}{100} * (1 + \dfrac{r}{100})^n}{(1 + \dfrac{r}{100})^n - 1}$$

To test (the program containing) it we would have to run it with selected values of A, r and n; do the calculation by hand or calculator; and compare the two. Clearly a typical choice:

> $A = 50000$
> $r = 14.75$
> $n = 27$

(typical at least in Australia during the late 1980s) would make the hand calculation tedious and error-prone. A better choice would be:

> $A = 1000$
> $r = 10$
> $n = 2$

Note that the test data should not include the identities of algebra, 0 and 1. For example, a choice of $n = 1$ would allow a program which was coded incorrectly according to the formula:

$$p = \frac{A * \dfrac{r}{100} * (1 + \dfrac{r}{100})}{(1 + \dfrac{r}{100})^n - 1}$$

to produce the correct answer. The relationship between the variables can be quite subtle. For example, a choice of $r = 50$, $n = 2$ would not catch the mistypings below:

$$p = \frac{A * \dfrac{r}{100} * (1 + \dfrac{r}{100})^n}{(1 - \dfrac{r}{100})^n + 1}$$

We must also be sure that the data values for A, r and n are different from each other. For example, if r and n had the same values, then execution of the program would not disclose the error of an instance of n being mistyped as r.

The operators **div** and **mod** are a ripe source of errors, because they are discontinuous. The test data should ensure that they are discontinuous at the correct places. For example, the following is an adaptation of Zeller's Congruence for finding the day on which New Year's Day falls in a given year, y.

> first := $(y + (y - 1)$ **div** $4 - (y - 1)$ **div** $100 + (y - 1)$ **div** $400)$ **mod** 7

We may think of this formula as taking Sunday, 1 Jan 0, as a base, with New Year's Day advancing by one day every year, with a further day advance after each leap year. The leap year effect is produced by adding one day each 4 years, subtracting one day every 100 years and adding it back again every 400 years. We need to make sure that the three **div** operations are correct, so that their value increases at the appropriate value of *y*, not before and not after. Below is an appropriate set of test data:

```
1985   1986   1987   1988   1989
1999   2000   2001   2099   2100   2101
2199   2200   2201   2299   2300   2301
2399   2400   2401   2499   2500   2501
```

11.4 Testing compound-statements

A compound-statement is simply a sequence of statements considered as a group. These statements either co-operate to produce a single value; or relatively independently, they produce a series of values. The implication is that to test a compound-statement we must test its components. We give no examples here: they will be found as part of subsequent examples.

11.5 Testing conditional-statements

In a conditional-statement one of a number of statements is obeyed depending on a condition (or, in the extended **else** case, a sequence of conditions). Our tests must ensure that the conditions are correct and that each of the statements is correct. As an example, consider the sequence for calculating the tax payable on a given gross income, *gross*, used many times already:

```
begin
  if gross <= threshold1 then
    tax := 0
  else if gross <= threshold2 then
    tax := base1 + taxrate1 * (gross – threshold1)
  else if gross <= threshold3 then
    tax := base2 + taxrate2 * (gross – threshold2)
  else
    tax := base3 + taxrate3 * (gross – threshold3)
end {of procedure "CalculateTax"}
```

To check that each assignment-statement is correct we proceed along the lines of the earlier section. These are quite simple assignments, only one variable is involved in each expression, so that the test is straight-forward. To test that the conditions are correct we must ensure that the assignments are obeyed for the appropriate values of *gross*. What can go wrong with the conditions? Firstly, one of the constants could have been typed incorrectly. With the sequence above that is all too easy: we have simply to mistype a digit! Secondly, we could mistype one of the relational-operators. The solution to this is to test values on both sides of the test criterion value. Thus, appropriate test data is:

```
77      78      79
330     331     332
661     662     663
```

Testing a case-statement is generally clear: there is only one condition, though the alternatives tend to be more extensive. They must all be tested. Thus the following sequence, which writes out the name of the day *first* in English, requires seven tests.

```
case first of
  0 :
    writeln('Sunday.');
  1 :
    writeln('Monday.');
  2 :
    writeln('Tuesday.');
  3 :
    writeln('Wednesday.');
  4 :
    writeln('Thursday.');
  5 :
    writeln('Friday.');
  6 :
    writeln('Saturday.')
end {of cases on "first"}
```

Consider testing a program for writing out the day on which New Year's Day occurs for years read as data. This will contain both the case-statement above and the assignment-statement which determines the day, given in an earlier section. Testing this as a complete program is more complicated than testing the two sequences separately, because the calculation of *first* for the appropriate test data may not give all of the seven values for *first* that are required for testing the case-statement!

11.6   Testing repetitive-statements

A repetitive statement consists of a (compound-) statement which must be obeyed a number (possibly zero) of times. Thus we must ensure that the body is correct and that it is obeyed the correct number of times. When considering the number of times the loop is obeyed there are two quite distinct situations. In one, the incorrect number of loop traverses produces incorrect results; in the other, the incorrect number of loop traverses produces the correct result, but in an inefficient manner. We consider this last case in a subsequent section.

Testing loops responsible for output is usually very easy: the results are there to see, and in a very visual form. For example the loop producing the horizontal lines in the *Tic-Tac-Toe* program:

```
for col := 1 to size do
  write('--')
```

can be seen to work the correct number of times just by looking at the output, provided, of course, that we have ensured that *size* is correctly assigned! As we noted earlier, this program is easy to test because it is all output.

Generally, the problem is more subtle. Consider the sequence below derived from the Olympic Scores program of Chapter 5 by eliminating all the dialogue and calculating the average score rather than the total. Note that the readln-statement has been replaced by a read-statement, so that all the marks can be on one line.

```
totalmark := 0;
bestmark := 0;
worstmark := 10;
for judge := 1 to panelsize do
  begin
    read(nextmark);
    totalmark := totalmark + nextmark;
    if nextmark > bestmark then
      bestmark := nextmark;
    if nextmark < worstmark then
      worstmark := nextmark
  end; {of loop on "judge"}
score := (totalmark – bestmark – worstmark) / panelsize
```

Before we consider testing that the loop is obeyed the correct number of times, we must ensure that the body of the loop is tested adequately. There are four statements:

- The read-statement tests itself.

- To ensure that the assignment is tested, we must ensure that at least one of the marks assigned to *nextmark* is non-zero.

- To test the first if-statement we must ensure both that the assignment to *bestmark* is correct, and that it is obeyed at the correct places. For the first part we must ensure that at least one mark is non-zero; for the second, we must ensure that the best mark is not the last one.

- Testing the second if-statement is quite similar.

Now to the loop itself. We must ensure that the body is obeyed the correct number of times. That is we must ensure that the last mark must affect the solution. So we could make it the best mark or the worst mark. Certainly it must not be the average! Thus a set of data might be:

    9.5   9.7   9.2   9.1   9.9

Note that there are some loops that it is impossible to test. Consider the following sequence from the "sum of the cubes of the digits" problem of Chapter 5.

```
for h := 0 to 9 do
  for t := 0 to 9 do
    for u := 0 to 9 do
      if h * h * h + t * t * t + u * u * u = 100 * h + 10 * t + u then
        writeln(100 * h + 10 * t + u : 3)
```

The sequence has no data, and so there is no way we can use the data to check that the loops are correct. This is true of all *exploratory* programs, that is programs that are searching for solutions. What we can do is to modify the program so that it writes out values which enable us to check the ranges of the values of the control variables of the loop. This is, of course, a different program and there are problems with ensuring that the insertion of these statements, and their subsequent deletion, do not introduce errors into the program.

11.7   Other considerations

    An analysis like those given above is quite complicated, and certainly not foolproof, since it ignores compensating errors. Indeed it can be more difficult than the design of the program itself. Consequently, if we cannot trust our program design ability, we would be foolish to trust our test data analysis. In practice we perform the analysis and run the program with test data but we also run with other test data. This might be random; it might be data used previously for testing alternative versions; it might be data created by considering the problem rather than the program; it might be some standard test data.
    Consider the sequence below for reading in pairs of numbers and calculating their GCD.

```
r := p mod q;
while r <> 0 do
  begin
    p := q;
    q := r;
    r := p mod q
  end; {of loop "while r <> 0"}
GCD := q
```

A simple analysis shows that only two sets of data are required, one in which the loop is never obeyed ($p = 144$, $q = 24$) and one in which the loop is obeyed at least once ($p = 144$, $q = 30$). Consideration of the problem might lead us to try a pair which are relatively prime ($p = 144$, $q = 35$) and a pair in which the smaller number comes first ($p = 30$, $q = 144$). As mentioned earlier, this is the approach taken by what we have called product testers.

11.8 Checking that the algorithm is implemented

So far we have considered only functional correctness, that is we have checked only that the program gives correct results. This is certainly necessary and for most of the programs we have written up to now it is generally sufficient, too. However, this is not always the case, and we often need to check that the program implements the desired algorithm and does not do unnecessary computation. If we have a good idea of how long the program should take we could run it with a large set of data and check the time. Where this is not possible, or thought to be lacking in finesse, then we have no alternative but to put extra write-statements in the program which print out sufficient information to enable us to be sure that the program went through the correct path. We might write out the values of certain variables; we might write out textual remarks to indicate which loops have been entered, and how many times they have been traversed; and so on. Note the implication: it is possible for a loop to be incorrect and yet for the right answers to be produced.

In some programs a print of the numbers of arithmetic and logical operations, the number of loop entries, the number of loop traverses, the number of comparisons, the number of assignments and the number of procedure calls can be a useful aid in the analysis of the algorithm. This means that having tested the program for certain sets of data we can analyse its performance (that is, speed) and so can estimate its performance on other data without actually having to execute the program using that data. This is the concept of *algorithm analysis*, which is the subject in many second courses in programming.

11.9 A testing strategy

For convenience, we have considered only fragments of programs until now. In practice, we have to test programs, which are composed of procedures. Consider the stylized program skeleton of Prog 11.1, which has been deliberately kept simple. Our program design strategy has been top-down. It makes sense, therefore, for our testing strategy to be top-down, too. That is we can test our program progressively as we refine it. To do this we use what are called *stubs*. These are simple replacements for procedures which are not yet written. To take an extreme example, we could replace all three procedures in Prog 11.1 with stubs and run it, thereby testing the main program – what little there is of it. A stub is quite simple. It may, for example, just write out a message indicating that it had been successfully called:

```
procedure Process;
begin
    writeln('The Process procedure has not yet been written!')
end
```

As we refine a procedure we replace its stub, and maybe change other stubs to accommodate the new procedure. For example, at some point we may be refining the *OutputResults* procedure, which means of course that the variables it is processing should have some appropriate values. An appropriate stub for a

Process procedure then might look like this:

```
procedure Process;
begin
  {SOME SIMPLE ASSIGNMENTS}
end
```

It is important to develop and test procedures in a planned sequence rather than at random. The *OutputResults* procedure should be developed first, using stubs like those described above. Of course this will not be a rigourous test, being constrained by the need to write assignments in the stub. However, a careful choice of values, perhaps requiring a number of runs with different stubs, will give us some confidence in its correctness. Next we can develop the *InputData* procedure, using the *OutputResults* procedure to write out what the *InputData* procedure has read. The stub for the *Process* procedure can return

Prog 11.1   A program skeleton

```
program OpusMagnum;

  {DECLARATIONS VARIOUS}

  procedure InputData;
  begin
    .
    .
    .
  end; {of procedure "InputData"}

  procedure Process;
  begin
    .
    .
    .
  end; {of procedure "Process"}

  procedure OutputResults;
  begin
    .
    .
    .
  end; {of procedure "OutputResults"}

begin
  .
  .
  .
end.
```

---

to null. Once the input appears to work for simple data, more rigourous tests can be applied to both *InputData* and *OutputResults* procedures. Finally we can develop *Process*, in the confidence that *ReadInput* will safely deliver data to it, and that *OutputResults* will faithfully write out the values calculated.

11.10   Correcting the program that is found to be faulty

Now we have a strategy for testing, what do we do when the tests indicate that the program is faulty? This will become manifest in three ways:

(i) The compiler may detect syntactical and semantic errors. Most Pascal compilers perform very well in this respect, pointing to the part of the program where a symptom was detected and writing out a message describing the symptom. After some experience, it is generally a simple matter to diagnose the fault from the symptoms. All that is required is a little (lateral?) thinking.

(ii) The program may fail at run-time (because it tried to assign a value that is out of a variable's range, or tried to take the square root of a negative number, for example). Again most Pascal systems are helpful in that, when the symptoms are found, facilities are often provided for the programmer to access the values of the program. In batch systems, this is generally done automatically in what is called a *post-mortem dump*.

(iii) The program may just give the wrong answers.

In the last two cases, we have to deduce the fault from the information available. Consider the program of Prog 11.2, which is meant to write out a table for New Year's Day. In fact it has an error in it, and produces the following output:

```
This program writes out a table for New Year's Day.
For how many years do you want it to run? 10
At what year should it start? 1985

YEAR      DAY

1985    Wednesday
1986    Friday
1987    Sunday
1988    Tuesday
1989    Sunday
1990    Tuesday
1991    Thursday
1992    Saturday
1993    Thursday
1994    Saturday

NEW YEAR'S DAY
==============
```

How do we go about finding out what is wrong? We could of course just look closely at the program to see if we can discover the problem — and sometimes

Prog 11.2 A faulty program for New Year's Day

```
program NewYearsDay;
{A program which produces a table for New Year's Day.}
  var
    tablesize : 1..maxint;
    firstyear, y : 1583..maxint;
    day : 0..6;
begin
  writeln('This program writes out a table for New Year"s Day. ');
  write('For how many years do you want it to run? ');
  readln(tablesize);
  write('At what year should it start? ');
  readln(firstyear);
  writeln;
  writeln('YEAR' : 4, ' ' : 3, 'DAY' : 6);
  writeln;
  for y := firstyear to firstyear + tablesize − 1 do
    begin
      write(y : 4, '' : 3);
      day := (y + (y−1) mod 4 − (y−1) mod 100 + (y−1) mod 400)
                                                            mod 7;
      case day of
        0 :
          write('Sunday');
        1 :
          write('Monday');
        2 :
          write('Tuesday');
        3 :
          write('Wednesday');
        4 :
          write('Thursday');
        5 :
          write('Friday');
        6 :
          write('Saturday')
      end; {of cases on "day"}
      writeln
    end; {of loop on "year"}
  writeln;
  writeln('NEW YEAR"S DAY');
  writeln('===============')
end.
```

this works. More often it does not, so what then? A good way to start is to write
out the correct answers beside the ones the program produced.

YEAR	DAY (Computer)	DAY (Correct)
1985	Wednesday	Tuesday
1986	Friday	Wednesday
1987	Sunday	Thursday
1988	Tuesday	Friday
1989	Sunday	Sunday
1990	Tuesday	Monday
1991	Thursday	Tuesday
1992	Saturday	Wednesday
1993	Thursday	Friday
1994	Saturday	Saturday

Now we endeavour to find a pattern in the results. This will show us what the
program actually does, and with luck the relationship between what it does and
what it is supposed to do will guide us to the error. To return to the *New Year's
Day* problem, the correct answers confirm the observation in an earlier section
that the day advances by one, except for the year after a leap year, when it
advances by two. The program, on the other hand, produces results in which the
day advances by two, for three years out of four, and retreats by two on the fourth.
Why? Let us look at the expression which calculates *day*:

$$\text{day} := (y + (y - 1) \bmod 4 - (y - 1) \bmod 100 + (y - 1) \bmod 400) \bmod 7$$

It is clear that the term *y* causes the day to advance by one. The other three
terms in combination are supposed to advance a further day after a leap year,
but, since the data does not cover a century year, we can concentrate on the
second term. It should cause an advance every fourth year. Clearly it causes an
advance every year except the fourth, so it must be wrong! And it is: we have
used **mod** instead of **div**!

We now must make sure that this error explains the results. Our changes will
increase the value of the expression by:

$$((y - 1) \textbf{ div } 4 - (y - 1) \bmod 4) \bmod 7$$

which, for 1985, is unfortunately zero. Therefore, there must be another error.
We may try to deduce it too, or we may wish to make the correction, run the
program and repeat the whole process. We leave the finding of the other error(s)
as an exercise.

11.10   If all else fails: debug printing

Sometimes a program may give incorrect results and the nature of the
problem may be such that it is very difficult to discover exactly what is going

wrong. In these situations we have to resort to *debug printing,* which simply means that we have to insert write-statements into the program in appropriate places so that we can more easily deduce the cause or causes of the problem. We may print textual remarks to indicate which loops have been entered, which conditions have been satisfied and so on. We may write out the values of variables at appropriate places. We must, of course, make sure that the write-statements give us sufficient information. That is, it would be senseless to write out values of variables at various places in the program without including some text to indicate from which variables these values came and from which part of the program the information was written.

Many computer systems provide tools which help to automate this process. They enable the programmer to insert *stop-points* in the program, which cause the computer to stop when it reaches any such point, and to investigate, and even change the values of variables when stopped at those points. It is very wise to investigate thoroughly the facilities available on your system.

11.12   A caveat

We have already noted that logically it is impossible to test any program. Therefore even tests designed along the lines described here may not be sufficient. Even so testing is important – in practical terms, it is all we have. This chapter has not done justice to the subject. We have not considered the idea of *bottom-up testing,* for example; nor the idea that even within the top-down testing strategy, it is sometimes useful to take out a procedure, and run it separately using a *driver program,* whose sole purpose is to test it thoroughly. The reader may care to look at the companion book in this series, *Writing Pascal programs,* by the first author of the current book, in which 15 programs are designed, developed, and rigorously tested.

Problems

11.1   Using the analytical method described above, design some suitable test data for Prog 10.1, the PIN number program.

11.2   For any two programs you have written as solutions to problems given in recent chapters consider how well you tested them. If you think, in the light of this chapter, that your previous testing was less than adequate, test them more thoroughly.

11.3   Find the remaining error(s) in the New Year's Day program of Prog 11.2.

11.4   Prog 11.3 gives an incorrect program for writing out a table of the prime factors of consecutive integers. It operates as follows. For each number it divides by a sequence of trial factors, which it determines by incrementing the previous one until it reaches one that is prime. If a trial factor is a factor, then it is written out, appropriate arrangements being made to separate the factors by commas. The number is divided

Prog 11.3 A faulty program for a Prime Factor Table

```
program Factors;
{This program writes out a table of the prime factors of the numbers
between limits specified by the user.}
  type
    natural = 0..maxint;
  var
    min, max, number, residue, trialfactor : natural;

  function Prime (n : natural) : Boolean;
  {This function returns true iff n is a prime number.}
    var
      trial : natural;
      state : (testing, factorfound, trialsexhausted);
  begin
    trial := 2;
    state := testing;
    repeat
      if sqr(trial) > n then
        state := trialsexhausted
      else if n mod trial = 0 then
        state := factorfound
      else
        trial := trial + 1
    until state in [factorfound, trialsexhausted];
    Prime := state = trialsexhausted
  end; {of function "Prime"}

begin
  writeln('This program produces a table of prime factors.');
  write('Type in the limits of the table. ');
  readln(min, max);
  writeln;
  writeln('NUMBER', ' ' : 6, 'FACTORS');
  for number := min to max do
    begin
      write(number : 6, ' ' : 6);
      residue := number;
      trialfactor := 2;
      while sqr(trialfactor) < residue do
        begin
          while residue mod trialfactor = 0 do
            begin
              if residue <> number then
                write(',');
              write(trialfactor : 1);
```

```
            residue := residue div trialfactor
          end;
        repeat
          trialfactor := trialfactor + 1
        until Prime(trialfactor)
      end;
    if residue <> 1 then
      begin
        if residue <> number then
          write(',');
        write(residue : 1)
      end;
    writeln
  end
end.
```

_____

by the factor, though a variable, *residue*, is used for this purpose. The division process repeats until the next trial is greater than the square root of the residue. The final residue is also a factor, unless it is 1. The program produced the following results:

```
This program produces a table of prime factors.
Type in the limits of the table. 2 20

NUMBER        FACTORS
    2         2
    3         3
    4         4
    5         5
    6         2,3
    7         7
    8         2,2,2
    9         9
   10         2,5
   11         11
   12         2,2,3
   13         13
   14         2,7
   15         3,5
   16         2,2,2,2
   17         17
   18         2,9
   19         19
   20         2,2,5
```

Deduce the error.

12

Characters

The reader cannot have failed to have noticed a certain asymmetry in our programs: while they have written out both numbers and alphabetic information, they have read and processed only numbers! Almost all programs perform some arithmetic calculations, of course. This is especially true of scientific programs, but it is also true of those classed as data processing (such as payroll, stock control and public authority billing). Equally almost all programs process alphabetic information (names, addresses, part descriptions and so on). Our payroll program, for example, might be expanded to include an address and we might also replace the employee's personal number by his name.

12.1 The required type *char*

Pascal has as its fourth (and last) required type the *char* (short, of course, for character). Variables of this type are declared for example:

var
ch1, ch2 : char;

A variable of *char-type* can have as its value any of the characters of the character set of the computer. These values are assumed to be ordered. Character sets vary from machine to machine, unfortunately, so that all that we can assume of this character set is that:

- The digits *0–9* are numerically ordered and contiguous,

- The upper-case Latin letters *A–Z*, if available, are alphabetically ordered but not necessarily contiguous,

- The lower-case Latin letters *a–z*, if available, are alphabetically ordered but not necessarily contiguous.

Many programs assume that both sets of letters are contiguous as well as ordered, and for computers using the ASCII code for representing characters this assumption is perfectly correct. Constants of char-type are represented by enclosing the character in quotes, for example:

'0'   '9'   '+'   'A'

12.2   Operations on characters

What operations are relevant to characters?

(i) Procedures may have parameters of char-type, as subsequent examples will show, and functions may return values of char-type.

(ii) We can read and write them. The read-statement:

read(ch1, ch2)

for example, will cause the next two characters to be read into *ch1* and *ch2* respectively. It is important to note that reading a character is a very simple operation indeed. Only the next character, which may well be the blank character, is read so that processing characters requires great attention to detail. In Prog 12.1 we give a procedure for reading the first subsequent non-blank character.

Prog 12.1   A procedure which reads the first non-blank character

---

procedure ReadFirstNonBlank (**var** ch : char);
{This procedure sets ch to the first non-blank character.}
begin
  repeat
    read(ch)
  until ch <> ' '
end {of procedure "ReadFirstNonBlank"}

We can always *look at*, as distinct from reading, the next character by accessing the *file-buffer variable*, as it is called, *input^*. Prog 12.2 gives a procedure which reads and ignores all blank characters, if any, before the next visible character. Each line of data has a special blank character, corresponding to the change to a new line, inserted at the end. If this special character is read, in a read-statement, it appears just as a normal space. However, it can be detect-

Prog 12.2   A procedure to skip over blanks

---

procedure SkipBlanks;
{This procedure reads the blanks up to the next non-blank character.}
  var
    ch : char;
begin
  while input^ = ' ' **do**
    read(ch)
end {of procedure "SkipBlanks"}

---

ed, because, when the last character of a line is read, and *input^* is therefore this special space, *eoln* becomes *true*. *Eoln* is a required Boolean function, whose identifier comes from <u>e</u>nd <u>o</u>f <u>li</u>ne.

Now for writing. When a character variable is included in the parameters of a write-statement, it is written as you would expect. The default is to use one position but this can be over-ridden by specifying an appropriate field width. Thus *write ("*":m)* will print an asterisk preceded by *m*–1 spaces. An interesting use is in, for example, *write(' ' : 25)* which produces 25 blanks.

(iii) We can assign to them:

ch1 := ch2
ch2 := 'E'

As the examples suggest, the form of a character expression is quite simple: it is either a character constant, a character expression or a character function-designator. There are no character operations!

(iv) We can compare characters thus:

ch1 = 'A'

is *true* if *ch1* has the value *'A'* and *false* otherwise. All six relations are available so that:

(ch >= '0') **and** (ch <= '9')

is true if *ch* is at least as high up the character set as '0' and at the same time at least as low down as '9'. In other words, if it is a digit (since the digits are numerically ordered and contiguous). An alternative is:

ch **in** ['0'..'9']

In Prog 12.3 we give a function which returns *true* if its parameter is a vowel.

(v) The required functions *succ* and *pred* also apply to characters. Thus:

ch1 := succ(ch1)

Prog 12.3 A function which tests for a vowel

---

function IsAVowel (ch : char) : Boolean;
{This function returns true if and only if ch is a vowel.}
begin
  IsAVowel := ch **in** ['A', 'E', 'I', 'O', 'U', 'a', 'e', 'i', 'o', 'u']
end { of function "IsAVowel"}

---

would be the essential incrementing instruction in a loop which was processing forwards through (part of) the character set. Similarly:

ch2 := pred(ch2)

would be relevant when moving backwards. Note that these functions must be used with care since they may be undefined in situations where the character set has holes in it, and at both ends.

(vi) We can convert the character to an appropriate integer and back again by means of the transfer functions *ord* and *chr*. For example:

i := ord(ch1)

sets *i* to a machine-dependent integer which represents *ch1* called the *ordinal number* of *ch1*. Similarly,

ch := chr(i)

sets *ch* to the character whose ordinal number is *i* (if such a character exists!). It is clear that *chr(ord(ch1))* = *ch1* and *ord(chr(i))* = *i*, provided *chr (i)* exists.

It is important to note that the ordinal value of a digit will not generally have the same value as the integer composed of that digit. That is, for example:

ord('3') $\neq$ 3

However, digits are numerically ordered and contiguous so that:

ord('3') $-$ ord('0') = 3

This is a relation that we shall use in the examples later in this chapter. Prog 12.4 gives a function which, given a character returns the same character unless it happened to be a lower-case letter, in which case it is converted to the corresponding upper-case letter. It simulates the action of the CAPS LOCK key on many keyboards.

Prog 12.4   A function which converts to upper case

```
function UpperCaseOf (ch : char) : char;
{This function returns the upper case version of ch if ch is a
lower-case letter, and ch otherwise.}
begin
  if ch in ['a'..'z'] then
    ch := chr(ord(ch) − ord('a') + ord('A'));
  UpperCaseOf := ch
end {of function "UpperCaseOf"}
```

(vii) Similarly, the control variable of a for-statement can be a character variable with character expressions as the initial value and the final value. We can progress through a sequence of characters in a for-statement:

for ch1 := 'A' **to** 'Z' **do**

...

(viii) Finally, the selector of a case-statement may be a character expression with character constants as case-labels.

12.3   Slightly more realistic employee code numbers

So far, the employee code number has always been an integer in the mathematical sense of the word. That is, it consists of digits, and nothing else. In the real world, "number" means something more general. Such numbers often start with letters (look at your next bill from any public utility), and in general may consist of a mixture of letters and digits. Furthermore, a point we shall follow up in a later chapter, quite often what is called a "check digit" is added to the end of a number as a means of reducing the likelihood of typing errors. This digit is quite likely to be a letter! We can modify the payroll program to allow the code number to consist of 4 characters, which may or may not be digits. The declaration for *code* becomes:

var
    c1, c2, c3, c4 : char;

The procedures which deal with the code number, *ReadWorkDetails* and *WriteWagesDetails*, are modified by extending their parameter lists, and processing the characters individually:

```
procedure ReadWorkDetails (var c1, c2, c3, c4 : char;
            var rate, hours : real);
begin
  readln(c1, c2, c3, c4, rate, hours)
end; {of procedure "ReadWorkDetails"}

procedure WriteWagesDetails (c1, c2, c3, c4 : char;
            gross, tax, nett : real);
begin
  writeln('Employee ', c1, c2, c3, c4, "'s wage is $', gross : 6 : 2, '.');
  writeln('After tax of $', tax : 6 : 2, ' this leaves $', nett : 6 : 2, '.')
end {of procedure "WriteWagesDetails"}
```

and their calls in the main program become:

```
ReadWorkDetails(c1, c2, c3, c4, rate, hours);
WriteWagesDetails(c1, c2, c3, c4, gross, tax, nett)
```

It seems heavy-handed to use 4 parameters for a number of 4 digits – and in the next chapter we will consider how to handle any number of characters as a single entity.

12.4   Two examples

We conclude with two examples which simply reproduce facilities that exist in Pascal. They are to that extent useless. However, they illustrate most of the facilities relating to characters; and related input-output procedures such as one for processing numbers in some mixed-radix system such as the 24-hour clock can be easily based upon them. Furthermore, they act as a good model if we require an input procedure to do something about data errors rather than have the program terminated automatically.

Consider first a procedure which will write the integer *n* with a field width of *m* in the same format as Pascal's *write(n:m)*. It is much easier to calculate the digits of a positive number than a negative one, so the first action is to determine the sign of *n*, and replace *n* by its absolute value. In this procedure *m* acts as if it were *TotalWidth*, so that if the number of digits in *n*, plus 1 for the sign if *n* is negative, is less than *m*, the appropriate number of spaces must be written out first. Thus we must determine the number of digits in *n*. We do this by determining successive powers of 10, until the next one would exceed *n*. We are now in a position to decide whether leading spaces are to be written out. After these, if any, comes the sign, if any. Now for the digits. Dividing *n* by the power of 10 used earlier in determining the number of digits gives the most significant digit, which can be converted to a character and written out. The remainder of this division gives a number consisting of the rest of the digits. If the power of 10 is reduced by dividing by 10, then the next digit can be extracted and written out. Clearly a loop can be used to write them all out. The procedure is given in Prog 12.5.

The second procedure reads an integer *n* typed in the same format as is accepted by Pascal's *read(n)*. It first skips over any leading spaces, using the procedure *ReadFirstNonBlank* of Prog 12.1, reading the first non-blank-character, which should be either a plus sign, a minus sign or a digit. If it is a sign, it is remembered and the next character, which should be a digit, is read; if it is a digit then the sign is set to a plus. The last character read should have been a digit, and further digits may follow. The program reads all subsequent digits and accumulates the number by multiplying the number composed of the earlier digits by 10 and adding the value of the current one. Finally, the value is negated if the sign were negative. The procedure is given in Prog 12.6.

Input procedures are more difficult to write than output procedures because they have to handle faulty data. Notice in the description the continual use of the word "should" when describing the character being read. In Prog 12.6 we have simply written out a message, and not even given the parameter a value. In practice, something more positive should happen. The program might be terminated or restarted at a point determined by the programmer.

Prog 12.5 A procedure which writes integers as in Pascal's *write*

---

procedure WriteInteger (n : integer;
        m : posint);
{This procedure writes n using a minimum of m characters. If necessary, leading spaces are written. The sign is suppressed if n is positive, and immediately precedes the first significant character if n is negative.}
  var
    sign : char;
    characters, i : posint;
    power, digits : natural;
begin
{First determine the sign, and replace n by |n|.}
  if n < 0 **then**
    begin
      sign := '–';
      n := –n
    end
  else
    sign := '+';
  {Determine the number of digits in n,}
  {and hence the number of characters to be written.}
  digits := 1;
  power := 1;
  while power <= n **div** 10 **do**
    begin
      digits := digits + 1;
      power := power * 10
    end;
  characters := digits + ord(sign = '–');
  {Write out any leading spaces.}
  if m > characters **then**
    write(' ' : m – characters);
  {Write the sign if negative.}
  if sign = '–' **then**
    write(sign);
  {Now write all the digits.}
  for i := digits **downto** 1 **do**
    begin
      write(chr(n **div** power + ord('0')));
      n := n **mod** power;
      power := power **div** 10
    end
end {of procedure "WriteInteger"}

Prog 12.6   A procedure which reads an integer as in Pascal's *read*

```
procedure ReadInteger (var n : integer);
{This procedure reads an integer, which may be signed, into n, skipping
over all leading spaces, and stopping just before the first non-digit.}
  var
    ch, sign : char;
begin
  {First skip over leading spaces.}
  ReadFirstNonBlank(ch);
  {If there is a sign, remember it and read the next character.}
  if ch in ['+', '–'] then
    begin
      sign := ch;
      read(ch)
    end
  else
    sign := '+';
  {Digits should follow.}
  if not (ch in ['0'..'9']) then
    writeln('There are no digits.')
  else
    begin
      n := ord(ch) – ord('0');
      {Now read all the digits and accumulate the integer.}
      while input^ in ['0'..'9'] do
        begin
          read(ch);
          n := 10 * n + ord(ch) – ord('0')
        end;
      {Take account of the sign.}
      if sign = '–' then
        n := –n
    end
end {of procedure "ReadInteger"}
```

Exercises

12.1   Write functions with the headings:

(i) **function** IsADigit (ch : char) : Boolean;

which returns the value *true* if and only if its argument is a decimal digit.

(ii) **function** IsAnOctalDigit (ch : char) : Boolean;

which returns the value *true* if and only if its argument is an octal digit.

12.2 In hexadecimal (base 16) notation, the decimal digits *1 .. 9* are augmented by *A, B, C, D, E* and *F*, these having the values 10 .. 15 respectively. Thus *12A* has the decimal value:

$$1^*16^2 + 2^*16 + 10 = 298.$$

Modify the procedures of Section 12.4 to read and write hexadecimal numbers.

12.3 In Chapter 7, we described the Roman notation for numbers. Note that, while this notation is not a positional one, it nevertheless has structure. Numbers less than 10 are composed of the letters *I, V, X*, meaning 1, 5 and 10 respectively. Multiples of 10 are composed of the letters *X, L, C*, meaning 10, 50 and 100 respectively. Similarly, multiples of 100 are composed of *C, D* and *M*. These letters are combined in exactly the same way in all three cases. Write a procedure with the heading:

> **procedure** WriteRomanDigit (d : digit;
> one, five, ten : char)

which will write out the Roman equivalent of a decimal digit, *d,* given the appropriate letters. Thus the pair of calls:

> WriteRomanDigit (7, 'X', 'L', 'C');
> WriteRomanDigit (4, 'I', 'V', 'X')

will cause *LXXIV* to be printed.

Problems

12.1 Write a procedure of the heading:

> **procedure** WriteRoman (n : number);

which will print out its argument, *n*. It should use the procedure of Exercise 12.3.

12.2 Write a program which will read a number in Roman notation and write it in both Roman and Arabic.

12.3 Write a program which reads in a (variable length) string of characters and produces the Soundex Code equivalent as a (fixed length) string of characters. This code was developed by Remington Rand and its aim is to standardize names (of people or places) using phonetic coding. The algorithm is as follows:

- Select and store the first letter of the name.

- Replace double letters by single letters.

- Ignore the letters A,E,I,O,U,W,H,Y.

- Replace the first three remaining letters by digits according to the following table:

B,F,P,V	1
C,G,J,K,Q,S,X,Z	2
D,T	3
L	4
M,N	5
R	6

- For short names pad with zeroes.

Some examples are:

ELIOT, ELIOTT, ELLIOT, ELLIOTT	E430
ROHL, ROLE, ROLL, RHOL	R400
CALLENDER, CALLANDER, CALLENDAR	C453

12.4 In real estate advertisements it is common for the descriptions to be shortened by dropping vowels, so that "4 bedrooms, 2 bathrooms, lounge" becomes "4 bdrms, 2 bthrms, lng". Write a program which will read in a sentence (terminated by a full stop) and write out the abbreviated form.

13

Records and arrays

We have already seen that the statement-part of a Pascal program is highly structured. Though the examples we have been using have been chosen on the grounds that their data is quite simple, data, too, can be structured. There is an example in the payroll program. We have been using 6 separate variables, *code*, *rate*, *hours*, *gross*, *tax* and *nett* to describe the components of the "payslip details", or "pay details", a phrase we have used as part of the name of the writing procedure. Since we have a name for the collection of variables in the problem domain, this should be reflected in the program domain. This is a simple example of course, and in this chapter we explore how quite complex structures can be built up from simple components.

13.1   Records

We can define a *record-type*, *sliptype*, to define the collection of 6 *fields* representing the 6 quantities above:

```
type
  sliptype = record
       code : codetype;
       rate, hours, gross, tax, nett : real
     end;
```

Then we can declare a single variable:

```
var
  payslip : sliptype;
```

The variable *payslip* consists of 6 fields, each of which is accessed by what we call "dot notation". For example *payslip.code* refers to the *code* field of *payslip*.

What is the advantage of doing this? Why define a structure when accessing its components involves the extra typing of the dot notation? As we shall shortly see, there is a means of factoring out the variable name, so that the burden is less severe that it appears now. However, there are positive reasons for using the record facility freely. First of all, the definition of a type announces to the reader of the program that this is an important concept in the problem, and in the program which finds its solution. This is, of course, the reason which supports all structuring in programs. Secondly, we can assign one variable of a record type to another, either directly, in an assignment-statement, or indirectly as a parameter. Thus all the procedures of the payroll program which deal with the payroll proper can be recast to have a single parameter, the payslip. The main program becomes:

```
begin
  Announce;
  FindStaffSize(staffsize);
  GiveInstructions;
  for employee := 1 to staffsize do
    begin
      ReadWorkDetails(payslip);
      CalculateGross(payslip);
      CalculateTax(payslip);
      CalculateNett(payslip);
      WriteWagesDetails(payslip)
    end {of loop on "employee"}
end
```

The procedures themselves will access the individual fields of the *payslip* record using the dot notation. For example:

```
procedure CalculateGross (var payslip : sliptype);
  const
    normal = 37.5;
  var
    overtime : real;
  begin
    if payslip.hours > normal then
      overtime := payslip.hours − normal
    else
      overtime := 0;
    payslip.gross := payslip.hours * payslip.rate + overtime * 0.5 *
                                                    payslip.rate
  end {of procedure "CalculateGross"}
```

Note that the parameter, *payslip*, is called as a variable, because the procedure will change it, by changing one of its fields. This will be true of all the procedures except for *WriteWagesDetails* which simply writes out parts of the record.

The syntax of the record is quite simple, as Fig 13.1 shows, though it does not yet include records with variant-parts, which we will cover in a later section. Note that fields of the same type may be grouped together, and that the type of a field need not have an explicit name.

It is very important in programming to be able to recognize structure in the data, and to define the appropriate types in your program, and we give now a couple of examples of a more general nature. A complex number consists of two components, called the real and imaginary parts, each of which is of real-type. Traditionally, the real part is abbreviated to *re*, and the imaginary part to *im*, so an appropriate definition is:

```
type
  complex = record
      re, im : real
    end;
```

We can then declare variables such as:

```
var
    voltage, current : complex;
```

Such variables can be assigned values using pairs of assignment statements:

```
voltage.re := 10.5;
voltage.im := 0.02
```

More importantly, we can define procedures for operations on complex variables. For example, the following sets *c1* to the complex sum of *c2* and *c3*:

```
procedure ComplexAdd (var c1 : complex;
          c2, c3 : complex);
begin
  c1.re := c2.re + c3.re;
  c1.im := c2.im + c3.im
end {of procedure "ComplexAdd"}
```

Fig 13.1 The syntax of records

record-type

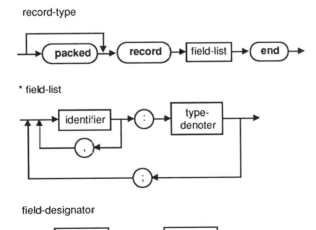

* field-list

field-designator

As a second example, we define a type appropriate to the Gregorian calendar:

type
    date = **record**
        day : 1..31;
        month : monthtype;
        year : 1583 .. maxint
    end;

To assign a value to a variable of this type requires three assignment-statements, though to modify it may take only one. Prog 13.1 gives a procedure which advances a date by 1 day. It assumes the existence of a function, *DaysInMonth*, which, given a month and a year, returns the number of days in that month.

Prog 13.1   **A procedure for advancing 1 day.**

```
procedure Advance1Day(var d : date);
{This procedure advances the date in d by 1 day, taking due care
of leap years.}
begin
  if d.day < DaysInMonth(d.month, d.year) then
    d.day := succ(d.day)
  else
    begin
      d.day := 1;
      if d.month < Dec then
        d.month := succ(d.month)
      else
        begin
          d.month := Jan;
          d.year := succ(d.year)
        end
    end
end {of procedure "Advance1Day"}
```

13.2   Records of records

Note from the syntax diagram that the type of a field-designator is any type-denoter, including any other record-type. This is, of course, very important. In the same way that structured-statements are built up from other structured-statements, so data structures are built up from other data structures. For example, suppose that a given electrical device is described by three quantities, its impedance (a complex quantity), the tolerance on that measurement (a percentage, and therefore a real) and its power rating (a real). Then given the existence of the type *complex*, defined earlier, an appropriate type definition is:

```
type
  device = record
      impedance : complex;
      tolerance, powerrating : real
  end;
```

How do we access the fields of the *impedance*, which is itself a field? We use two instances of the dot notation. Suppose we have the declaration:

```
var
    inductor : device;
```

then *inductor* refers to the whole record and is of type *device*; *inductor.impedance* refers to the first field of *inductor* and is of type *complex*; *inductor.impedance.re* refers to the first field of *inductor.impedance* and is of real-type. That is each dot selects a field of the record so far selected. Thus to set the impedance of *inductor* we write:

```
inductor.impedance.re := 10.5;
inductor.impedance.im := 0.02
```

The full power of this facility will be manifest in a couple of sections when we consider arrays. It is important to notice that even the intermediate fields of a record can be accessed as variables. Thus we could multiply *current* by the *impedance* field of *inductor* to get a *voltage*. Assuming a procedure for complex multiplication, we would write:

```
ComplexMultiply(voltage, current, inductor.impedance)
```

13.3   Storage of records

Fig 13.2 shows the store for the declaration:

```
var
    inductor : device;
```

Fig 13.2   The storage of records

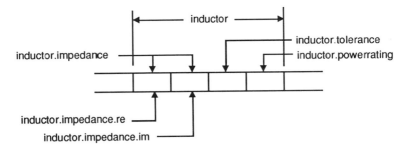

It is simply a sequence of the fields of the record. Because all the fields are in a fixed position with respect to the start of the record, accessing a field of a record is just as fast as accessing a variable of the same type as the field. That is, there is no cost associated with the dot operator.

13.4   Arrays

Records are essentially non-homogeneous structures. In general the fields are of different types, and have different operations applied to them. Even where the fields are of the same type, as in *payslip*, the operations applied to fields will in general be different.   There are, however, situations where components are of precisely the same type and have precisely the same operations applied to them. For example, if data for the payroll program included the number of hours worked each day, rather than the total number worked during the week, then we would wish to do the same things to these seven numbers. We would read them in the same way, and we would wish to add them together to find the total hours worked. Another example consists of the payslips of all the employees. At present each payslip is created, processed and written using the same record as the previous one. Should we wish to process all the records in some way, by sorting them for example, we would need to store them all, and the processing applied to each would be the same. For this Pascal provides a second structured-type, the *array*. To return to the hours example of this paragraph, we could declare:

> **type**
>   hourstype : **array** [daytype] **of** real;
> **var**
>   hours, dailyhours : hourstype;

where *daytype* is the enumerated-type used in earlier chapters. This defines *hours* to be a seven-component array whose elements, called *indexed-variables*, are

> hours[Sun]   hours[Mon]   hours[Tue]   hours[Wed]
> hours[Thu]   hours[Fri]   hours[Sat]

Note that the name of the array is followed by an *index* in square brackets. To find the total number of hours worked we could write:

> totalhours := hours[Sun] + hours[Mon] + hours[Tue] + hours[Wed] +
>   hours[Thu] + hours[Fri] + hours[Sat]

This is, however, not very fruitful. It is no advance over a record of seven fields. However, the index can be any expression. That is, we can write *hours[day]*, and this refers to *hours[Sun]* if *day = Sun*, *hours[Mon]* if *day = Mon*, and so on.   Thus we have a means of referring to any component of an array, and, combined with a for-statement, a means of referring to all elements of the array. A more appropriate way of finding *totalhours* is:

    totalhours := 0;
    for day := Sun **to** Sat **do**
        totalhours := totalhours + hours[day]

There is a strong relationship here with the dummy variable notion of mathematics. In mathematics we would have written:

$$\text{Total hours} = \sum_{day = Sun}^{Sat} \text{hours}_{day}$$

though mathematicians have a preference for *i* as a dummy variable!

The syntax of array-type and indexed-variable is given in Fig 13.3. Look closely at the syntax diagram for array-type; there's a great deal of power in it. For example, the subscript may be any ordinal-type. Most often it will be a subrange of the integer-type, but there are many cases where it will be an enumerated-type like *daytype* in the example above, or a subrange of such a type. The component-type may be any type-denoter, including all the simple-types. Thus the following are all valid:

    type
        hourstype : **array** [daytype] **of** real;
        codetype : **array** [1..6] **of** char;
        salestype : **array** [monthtype] **of** natural;
        leavetype : **array** [codetype] **of** monthtype;

There are three other observations which we shall consider in separate sections. First, the component may be a structured-type, including a record-type or another array-type. Second, the arrays may have more than one dimension. Finally, the arrays may be packed.

Fig 13.3 The syntax of arrays

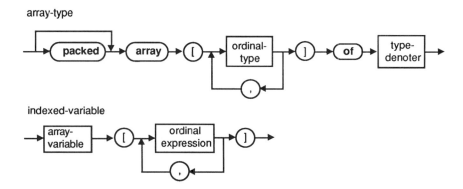

13.5   Strings

Packing is discussed fully in Section 13.14, but we will consider here one specific use, *strings*. We have already used strings such as *'employee'* and *'gross'* in write-statements. A string of *n* characters is actually a constant of the anonymous type:

packed array [1..n] **of** char

We can declare corresponding types and variables:

type
  string10 = **packed array**[1..10] **of** char;
var
  language : string10;

and then assign (remembering that the arrays must be of identical types)

language := 'Pascal   '

There are precisely four spaces before the closing quotation mark. We can, as well, compare operands of the identical packed character array-types, the comparison being in terms of the ordinal numbers of the characters and taking place from the first character. Thus:

'time   ' > 'tide   '

13.6   Arrays of records, records of arrays

As we have already noted, the components of an array-variable may be records whose components may be arrays of records, and so on. That is, we can build up structures of almost arbitrary complexity. For example, if in the payroll program we replace the code number of an employee by his name, introducing the definition of *nametype*, then the payslip can be defined:

type
  nametype = **packed array** [1..20] **of** char;
  sliptype = **record**
      name : nametype;
      rate : real ;
      hours : **array** [daytype] **of** real;
      gross, tax, nett : real
    end;
var
  payslip : sliptype;

To access a component of a variable such as *payslip* we must work our way through the structure using the dot and the square bracket notation to refer to the components on the way. Thus

payslip	is the whole record
payslip.name	is the *name* field of *payslip*
payslip.name[1]	is the first component of the *name* field of *payslip*

In many programs determining the data structure is the most important part of the design. Once it is done, the structure that the program must take becomes clear. As an example, consider the table below:

Name	Innings	Not Outs	Highest Score	Aggregate	Average
A.R.Morris	9	1	196	696	87.00
S.G.Barnes	6	2	141	332	83.00
D.G.Bradman	9	2	173 *	508	72.75
R.N.Harvey	3	1	112	133	66.50
E.R.H.Toshack	4	3	20	51	51.00
S.J.E.Loxton	3	0	93	144	48.00
A.L.Hassett	8	1	137	310	44.29
R.R.Lindwall	6	0	77	191	31.83
D.Tallon	4	0	53	112	28.00
K.R.Miller	7	0	74	184	26.29
W.A.Brown	3	0	32	73	24.33
W.A.Johnstone	5	2	29	62	20.67
I.R.Johnson	6	1	21	51	10.20

For those who know nothing of cricket, a few words are in order. Each *player* plays in a number of matches, in the course of which he has one or two *innings*. His object is to *score* the maximum number of *runs*. In an innings a player may be given *out* for a number of reasons, or may remain *not out*. Traditionally an asterisk or the abbreviation *n.o.* are used to indicate that the player was not out. The table above summarizes the performance of the members of a team during a series of games. (For the connoisseur, the table represents the complete performance in Test matches of the 1948 Australian team in England.) We can easily define a type for the innings:

```
type
  innings = record
    runs : natural;
    out : Boolean
  end;
```

From which we can easily define a record describing a player's performance:

```
type
  playerrecord = record
    name : nametype;
    noinnings, nonotouts : natural;
    highest : innings;
    aggregate : natural;
    average : real
  end;
```

Now let us consider defining a record describing the whole team's performance. Clearly we need an array. But how big should it be? Let us assume that the programs which maintain such a structure are intended to be run a number of times as the series of games progresses. As it is possible to add a new member to the team during this time, we cannot tell how big it should be. Therefore, we have to make it big enough to cover all eventualities. We introduce:

```
type
  playerrange = 1 .. playermax;
```

where *playermax* is an appropriate constant. We need to know the actual numbers of players in the table. Therefore, we need a record structure, with one field holding the number of players, and another holding the players' records:

```
teamrecord = record
  noofplayers : playerrange;
  player : array [playerrange] of playerrecord
end;
```

Note that we have introduced a number of named types, rather than declaring one monolithic type. This is because these intermediate types are of significance in the problem, and there may be variables of that type. Consider Prog 13.2.

Prog 13.2   A procedure for finding the highest scorer

```
function HighestScorer(var team : teamrecord) : playerrange;
  var
    p : playerrange;
    bestscore : natural;
begin
  bestscore := 0;
  for p := 1 to team.noofplayers do
    if team.player[p].highest.runs > bestscore then
      begin
        HighestScorer := p;
        bestscore := team.player[p].highest.runs
      end
end {of function "HighestScorer"}
```

The function *HighestScorer* returns the position in the table of the highest-scoring player.

We conclude this section with an alternative to the *string* type for representing names where the length is restricted to a maximum of *namemax* characters:

type
    nametype = **packed array** [1..namemax] **of** char;

Assigning variables of this type means assigning all *namemax* elements, including all the elements after the end of the characters of the name. Traditionally they are assigned as spaces. This can be an irritation. Furthermore when we write variables of *nametype* all *namemax* elements are written. While this is excellent if we require tabular output, it is not so good if we want flowing text, because it is difficult to test whether a given space occurs within a name or is one of the trailing spaces added at the end of the array. An alternative is to use:

type
    namerange = 1 .. namemax;
    nametype = **record**
        size : namerange;
        characters : **packed array** [namerange] **of** char
    end;

Here only the actual characters of the name are stored, the other elements of the array being left undefined. This makes reading names easy, but writing and comparing must be done character by character, rather than by using the string facilities, because of the undefined elements. Note the similarity with the definition of *teamrecord* used above. Almost all uses of arrays are like this: the array is declared as large as will ever be required, and is then paired in a record with a simple variable giving the size of the portion actually in use.

13.7 Storage of arrays

Fig 13.4 shows the store allocation for a variable *hours* of *hourstype* referred to earlier.

Fig 13.4 The storage of arrays

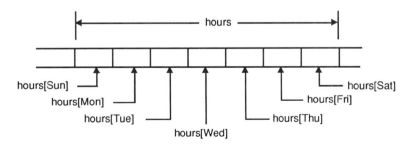

It consists simply of a sequence of the components of the array. Although all the components are in a fixed position with respect to the start of the array, we usually access indexed-variables with an index which is an expression. Therefore the indexed-variable referred to is at a variable distance from the start of the array, and has to be calculated, so there is a cost associated with the indexing operation. The cost though is not great, about the same as addition.

13.8   Entire- and component-variables

We can expand the tree diagram of types, as we left it in Chapter 7, to include the record-type and the array-type. This is given in Fig 13.5.

Fig 13.5   The tree diagram of types

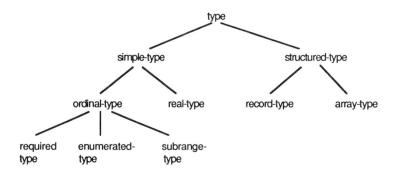

Notice that all the operations we have used on record-variables and array-variables have taken place on their components. Thus we have two concepts, an *entire-variable*, such as *voltage*, and the *component-variable*, such as *voltage.re* and *voltage.im*. As we mentioned earlier, the component-variables of a record are called field-designators, and those of an array are called indexed-variables. These ideas are illustrated in Fig 13.6. The operations available on a component-variable are precisely those available to all variables of that type. However, there is one operation that is available to entire record-variables and entire array-variables, assignment. Thus we can write:

Fig 13.6   A tree-diagram of variables

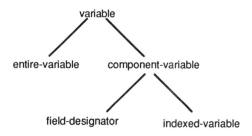

currentdate := startdate

and all three components of *currentdate* will be set to the value of the corresponding components of *startdate*. Similarly, if we write:

daily := hours

all seven components will be assigned. For array assignment, both arrays must be of *the same type*. The meaning of this phrase was not clear when many Pascal compilers were written, but it is safe to define it to mean "provided that they are declared by using the same type-identifier".

More often the assignment will be implicit, when an actual-parameter is assigned to a formal parameter. Unfortunately, functions may return neither record nor array values, and procedures must be used instead.

13.9   The with-statement

Accessing the fields of a complex record requires a good understanding of the dot notation, and we have used it fully in the examples we have given to encourage that understanding. However, it is quite painful to write, and obscures a program by its prolixity as the following procedure, for calculating the average column in the batting statistics table, shows:

```
procedure CalculateAverages(var team : teamrecord);
{This procedure calculates the averages for each batsman in the table
from the runs scored, and the number of completed innings.}
  var
    p : playerrange;
begin
  for p := 1 to team.noofplayers do
    team.player[p].average := team.player[p].aggregate /
                  (team.player[p].noinnings – team.player[p]. nonotouts)
  end {of procedure "CalculateAverages"}
```

Pascal provides a statement, the *with-statement*, to alleviate this problem, by allowing us to factor out the record involved. The previous procedure becomes:

```
procedure CalculateAverages(var team : teamrecord);
{This procedure calculates the averages for each batsman in the table
from the runs scored, and the number of completed innings.}
  var
    p : playerrange;
begin
  for p := 1 to team.noofplayers do
    with team.player[p] do
      average := aggregate / (noinnings – nonotouts)
  end {of procedure "CalculateAverages"}
```

The syntax of the with-statement is straight-forward as Fig 13.7 shows. Note that it is a record-variable, in the above *team.player[p]*, that is factored out.

Fig 13.7   The syntax of the *with-statement*

with-statement

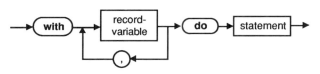

There is a restriction that if the record-variable is an indexed-variable, then nothing in the qualified statement may alter the subscript of the record-variable. Thus a with-statement is usually within a loop, rather than outside it as in the procedure *CalculateAverages* above. It is helpful to regard a with-statement as isolating a record-variable so that its fields may be accessed in the body of the statement. Accordingly, the code produced by a compiler may well be more efficient if a with-statement is used (especially if an array of structures is being processed) though we tend to lose some of the program's robustness. Further, where we are accessing two or more variables of the same type then only one may use the factoring facility. A with-statement may qualify another with-statement so that the *CalculateAverages* can be rewritten as in Prog 13.3.

Prog 13.3   A procedure to calculate team averages

---

procedure CalculateAverages(**var** team : teamrecord);
{This procedure calculates the averages for each batsman in the table
from the runs scored, and the number of completed innings.}
  var
    p : playerrange;
begin
  with team **do**
    for p := 1 **to** noofplayers **do**
      with player[p] **do**
        average := aggregate / (noinnings - nonotouts)
end {of procedure "CalculateAverages"}

13.10   The payroll program with sorted output

Let us expand the payroll program so that it writes out the payroll sorted alphabetically on the employee's name. To do this the program will need to hold the details for all the employees, since they cannot be sorted until the last one is available. Thus we must introduce an array to hold them all in what we call a *paysheet*. Its type definition is:

```
type
    sheettype = record
        staffsize : staffrange;
        payslip : array[staffrange] of sliptype
    end;
```

The main program needs to be re-organized to remove the writing of the individual payslips from the loop, to sort the slips and to write them all out after sorting. It also needs minor changes to access the elements of the paysheet:

```
begin
    Announce;
    FindStaffSize(paysheet.staffsize);
    GiveInstructions;
    for employee := 1 to paysheet.staffsize do
        with paysheet do
            begin
                ReadWorkDetails(payslip[employee]);
                CalculateGross(payslip[employee]);
                CalculateTax(payslip[employee]);
                CalculateNett(payslip[employee])
            end; {of loop on "employee"}
    SortPaySheet(paysheet);
    WriteWagesDetails(paysheet)
end
```

Note that we have not changed the bodies of the procedures within the loop: they still process a single payslip. The actual parameter in each case is the appropriate element of the paysheet.

How do we sort the elements of paysheet alphabetically? The sorting technique is not a particularly practical one where the number of items to be sorted is large but is very simple to understand and implement. We scan the *payslip* array from the first element to the last, looking for the name which occurs earliest in the alphabet and interchange it with the first; then we start at the second element looking, amongst those left, for the name which occurs earliest in the alphabet and interchange it with the second; and so on. Clearly a nest of two loops is required. The inner one will organize the scan so that the alphabetically earliest element in the relevant part of *paysheet* is found. The outer loop ensures that the appropriate number of passes is done, and that the interchanging takes place. The function of the inner segment of code is not so much to find the alphabetically earliest, but to find where it is so that it can be interchanged. We will remember where the (alphabetically) earliest one is by remembering its subscript which we will call *earliest*. The loop operates by initializing *earliest* to be the subscript of the first element in the part of paysheet under consideration, and then by comparing the name at *earliest* with each element in turn, intermittently updating *earliest* to refer, at any point in the scan, to "the earliest so far encountered". For the comparison it is convenient to use a string to hold the name. Thus we introduce the definitions:

```
const
  staffmax = 1000;
type
  staffrange = 1..staffmax;
  nametype = packed array[1..20] of char;
```

Then *name[i]* is alphabetically earlier than *name[j]* if *name[i] < name[j]*. Bearing in mind that on a given pass, we start the search from the element whose subscript is the same as the number of the pass, we can code the inner loop searching for the earliest name:

```
earliest := pass;
for next := pass + 1 to staffsize do
  if payslip[next].name < payslip[earliest].name then
    earliest := next
```

The interchanging sequence is quite simple but requires the use of a temporary variable:

```
tempslip := payslip[pass];
payslip[pass] := payslip[earliest];
payslip[earliest] := tempslip
```

If the element at the front of the part of the *payslip* array is the minimum element there is no point in doing the interchanging sequence. The sequence certainly works but it just interchanges one element with itself. We could therefore make the interchanging sequence conditional.

```
if earliest <> pass then
  begin
    tempslip := payslip[pass];
    payslip[pass] := payslip[earliest];
    payslip[earliest] := tempslip
  end
```

In practice this is never done for the following reason. The test takes computer time just like the assignments do. In this case the test takes about 30% of the time of the interchange. Thus if the test succeeds (and we avoid doing the interchange) we win by 70%. On the other hand, if the test fails (and we still have to do the interchange) we lose by 30%. If we do the appropriate sums we find that the test would have to succeed on at least 30% of the occasions if we were to win overall. With random data this is unlikely and so the simple solution – the one which always does the interchanging – is preferred. The complete program is given in Prog 13.4.

Prog 13.4 The payroll program with sorted output

```pascal
program Payroll;
{This program calculates and sorts the payroll.}
  const
    staffmax = 1000;
  type
    staffrange = 1..staffmax;
    nametype = packed array[1..20] of char;
    sliptype = record
        name : nametype;
        rate, hours, gross, tax, nett : real
      end;
    sheettype = record
        staffsize : staffrange;
        payslip : array[staffrange] of sliptype
      end;
  var
    paysheet : sheettype;
    employee : staffrange;

  procedure Announce;
  begin
    writeln('This program calculates your employees" wages.')
  end;{of procedure "Announce"}

  procedure FindStaffSize (var staffsize : staffrange);
  begin
    write('How many staff do you have? ');
    readln(staffsize)
  end;{of procedure "FindStaffSize"}

  procedure GiveInstructions;
  begin
    writeln('For each in turn give me name (terminated by a /), ');
    writeln('basic rate and hours worked, on one line, separated
                                          by spaces.')
  end;{of procedure "GiveInstructions"}

  procedure ReadWorkDetails (var payslip : sliptype);

    procedure ReadName (var name : nametype);
      var
        count : 0..20;
    begin
      count := 0;
      repeat
```

```
      count := count + 1;
      read(name[count])
    until name[count] = '/';
    for count := count to 20 do
      name[count] := ' '
  end;{of procedure "ReadName"}

begin
  with payslip do
    begin
      ReadName(name);
      readln(rate, hours)
    end
end;{of procedure "ReadWorkDetails"}

procedure CalculateGross (var payslip : sliptype);
  const
    normal = 37.5;
  var
    overtime : real;
begin
  with payslip do
    begin
      if hours > normal then
        overtime := hours – normal
      else
      overtime := 0;
      gross := hours * rate + overtime * 0.5 * rate
    end
end;{of procedure "CalculateGross"}

procedure CalculateTax (var payslip : sliptype);
  const
    threshold = 100;
    taxrate = 0.20;
begin
  with payslip do
    if gross <= threshold then
      tax := 0
    else
    tax := taxrate * (gross – threshold)
end;{of procedure "CalculateTax"}

procedure CalculateNett (var payslip : sliptype);
begin
  with payslip do
    nett := gross – tax
end;{of procedure "CalculateNett"}
```

```
procedure SortPaySheet (var paysheet : sheettype);
  var
    pass, next, earliest : staffrange;
    tempslip : sliptype;
  begin
   with paysheet do
     for pass := 1 to staffsize – 1 do
       begin
         earliest := pass;
         for next := pass + 1 to staffsize do
           if payslip[next].name < payslip[earliest].name then
             earliest := next;
         tempslip := payslip[pass];
         payslip[pass] := payslip[earliest];
         payslip[earliest] := tempslip
       end
 end;{of procedure "SortPaySheet"}


procedure WriteWagesDetails (var paysheet : sheettype);
  var
    employee : staffrange;

  procedure WriteName (var name : nametype);
    var
      count : 0..20;
  begin
   count := 0;
   for count := count + 1 to 20 do
     write(name[count])
  end;{of procedure "WriteName"}

  begin
   writeln('Employee Name     ' : 20, 'Gross' : 8, 'Tax' : 8, 'Nett' : 8);
   with paysheet do
     for employee := 1 to staffsize do
       with payslip[employee] do
         begin
           WriteName(name);
           writeln(gross : 8 : 2, tax : 8 : 2, nett : 8 : 2)
         end
 end;{of procedure "WriteWagesDetails"}

begin
 Announce;
 FindStaffSize(paysheet.staffsize);
 GiveInstructions;
 for employee := 1 to paysheet.staffsize do
   with paysheet do
```

```
    begin
      ReadWorkDetails(payslip[employee]);
      CalculateGross(payslip[employee]);
      CalculateTax(payslip[employee]);
      CalculateNett(payslip[employee])
    end; {of loop on "employee"}
  SortPaySheet(paysheet);
  WriteWagesDetails(paysheet)
end.
```

13.11   Multi-dimensional arrays

As we noted from the syntax diagram, we can have arrays of arrays. Consider the definition:

```
type
  line = array [1..pagewidth] of char;
```

which describes a line of a page of output. We could define a type *page*, in terms of *line* in a straightforward way:

```
    page = array [1..pagelength] of line
```

Given the declarations:

```
var
  lastchar, thischar : char;
  lastline, thisline : line;
  lastpage, thispage : page;
```

then, just as *thisline[j]* is a variable of char-type, which could be assigned to *thischar*; so *thispage[i]* is a variable of *line* type, which could be assigned to *thisline*, and *thispage[i][j]* is a variable of char-type. This concept is illustrated below in which we give three ways of copying *thispage* to *lastpage*.

- lastpage := thispage

- **for** i := 1 **to** pagelength **do**
  lastpage[i] := thispage[i]

- **for** i := 1 **to** pagelength **do**
  for j := 1 **to** pagewidth **do**
  lastpage[i][j] := thispage[i][j]

The first is, of course, preferred. The syntax also shows that an array may have more than one dimension, so that we might have defined a page as a two-dimensional array:

type
 page = **array**[1..pagelength,1..pagewidth] **of** char;

and accessed individual characters of *thispage* by *thispage[i,j]*. The two definitions, and the two methods of accessing, are exactly equivalent in Pascal. So which is better? For this example, the structured version is because it more closely reflects the traditional structure of a page composed of lines, and we are likely to want the definition of a line anyhow. For measurements of, say, temperatures at points on a rectangular grid or for matrices, the two-dimensional array definition is preferable because it reflects the data as simply a matrix of numbers.

13.12   Variant-records

Consider a program for, say, maintaining a small personal library. We ignore the details of the maintenance to concentrate on the data involved. The library might consist of monographs and journals. Appropriate type-definitions for these two classes might be:

type
 monograph = **record**
    title : titletype;
    publisher : publishertype;
    author : authortype;
    publicationdate : date
   end;
 abbreviation = (CACM,CompJ,JACM,TOMS...);
 journal = **record**
    name : abbreviation;
    publisher : publishertype;
    vol, no : natural;
    publicationdate : date
   end;

Clearly the data will consist of a sequence of variables of these types. In some situations we might be happy to have two arrays (or, as we shall see later, two files), one for each class. In others it might be preferable to have a single sequence containing both classes. Pascal allows *variant-records*. The following definition of *booktype* describes both a monograph and a journal.

type
 classtype = (monograph, journal);
 booktype = **record**
    publisher : publishertype;
    publicationdate : date;
      case class : classtype **of**
     monograph : (
        title : titletype;

```
            author : authortype
        );
        journal : (
            name : abbreviation;
            vol, no : natural
        )
    end;
```

The syntax of this construct leaves a lot to be desired and it is difficult to indent with any elegance, but it is clear that to each record is added an extra field, the *tag-field* (here *class*) whose value (here *monograph* or *journal*) specifies which of the variants is assumed by that record. The part that the variants have in common, the *fixed-part* (which may be null) precedes the variant-part. Fig 13.8 gives the expanded syntax of field-list. Note that all field identifiers, even those in different variants, must be distinct. This is because the tag itself does not appear in a field-designator. Thus, in a program administering books on loan held in:

```
        var
        onloan : array [1..maxloan] of booktype;
```

we might, in determining whether complete issues of *CACM* are out on loan (by setting the appropriate elements of the Boolean-array *out*) write:

```
        for i := 1 to noonloan do
          with onloan[i] do
            if class = journal then
              if name = CACM then
                out[vol, no] := true
```

Which variant of a record is assumed by a variable is not known until run-time (in-

Fig 13.8 The syntax of *field-list*

field-list

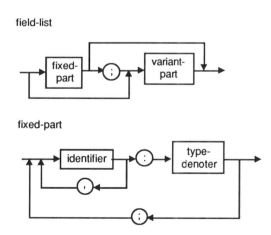

fixed-part

deed may well alter at run time), so that it is impossible for a compiler to check that a variable-access such as:

out[vol, no] := true

is valid. Such checking can only be done at run time by checking that *class = journal*. Since such assignments always occur (in correct programs) with a statement which explicitly tests that *class = journal*, and since almost all references to fields of the variant-part would require a test, it is rarely done. Thus extra care is required when writing sequences to deal with variants.

Note, too, that the tag-field can be absent, though the variants must still be labelled with constants of the type specified. This facility is useful where the variant is implied by the value of some field in the fixed part.

13.13   Structures as parameters

The difference between the two ways of calling parameters suggests that the decision on whether any parameter should be called by value or called by variable is straight-forward. This is the case for simple-types, and the rule is:

(i) If a parameter is to be assigned a value within the procedure (or if it is to be changed) then it *must* be called as a variable.

(ii) Otherwise (i.e. if it serves only to communicate a value to the procedure) it *should* be called by value.

For structured variables the rules are more complicated. Most procedures access the components of a structure at most once in any call. For example, in *WriteWagesDetails* we access the *gross* field of each element of *paysheet* in succession. In this case the time spent on the indirect access, if *paysheet* were called as a variable, is less than the time spent in assigning the whole record to the formal parameter if it is called by value. However, if the elements of a structure are accessed several times then the time spent on the indirect accesses, if the parameter is called as a variable, is greater than the time spent in assigning the array to the formal parameter if it is called by value. For structures, then, we have the following rule:

(i) If a parameter is to be assigned a value within the procedure (or if it is to be changed) then it *must* be called as a variable; if it serves to communicate a structured value whose components are accessed only once or twice, it *should* be called as a variable.

(ii) If it serves to communicate a structured value whose components are accessed many times, it *should* be called by value; if a local copy is required for the procedure's use, it *must* be called by value.

Remember that call by value implies that storage is allocated for a local copy of the whole structure (instead of for just a reference to the structure) so that call by variable is more economical in storage. This may be a factor affecting our decision when large structures are involved, especially when we are using recursion.

13.14   Packed arrays and records

We have already noted that arrays may be packed, and discussed a very important use of packing in the definition of strings. However, packing is a more general concept. Arrays and records (and arrays of records etc.) may have many components; and since, in the normal operation of a compiler, each component is allocated at least one word of store, the storage requirements can be quite large. If all the components are of an ordinal-type with relatively few possible values, significant space savings can be made by packing.

Note that the compiler may simply ignore **packed** and use the full amount of storage anyway. Further, if it does indeed pack, then the time taken to access the components may be considerably increased. If we have an array of packed arrays, or more likely a file of packed arrays (see the next chapter) we can achieve a compromise by *unpacking* a whole row at a time. Two procedures are provided. Given the declarations:

> **var**
>   u : **array** [u1 .. u2] **of** T;
>   p : **packed array** [p1 .. p2] **of** T;

where *T* is any type and where the size of $u \geq$ the size of *p*, the statement:

>   pack(u, offset, p)

means:

> **for** j := p1 **to** p2 **do**
>   p[j] := u[j − p1 + offset]

and:

>   unpack(p, u, offset)

means:

> **for** j := p1 **to** p2 **do**
>   u[j − p1 + offset] := p[j]

where j is an integer not occurring anywhere else in the program. Note:

- The erratic order of the parameters,

- The fact that the unpacked array must have at least as many elements as the packed one,

- That it is the packed array which specifies the number of elements packed or unpacked,

- That the elements may be in the middle of the unpacked array.

This facility is useful where we have an array packed for space-saving reasons and where we can usefully process individual rows. For example, given the declarations:

var
  u : **array** [0..width] **of** Boolean;
  p : **array** [0..depth] **of packed array** [0..width] **of** Boolean;

it might be convenient to unpack a row at a time by:

  unpack(p[i], u, 0)

in a loop (controlled by *i*) in which the row is processed.

Exercises

13.1 Define record-types suitable for:

    (i) student records held by a university or college,
    (ii) football league tables (or baseball or whatever),
    (iii) consumer records held by, say, your local energy authority,
    (iv) used car catalogue for a large dealer.

13.2 Consider the simple definition of *nametype* given in Section 13.6:

    type
      nametype = **packed array** [1 .. namemax] **of** char;

where we assume that spaces are stored in all elements after the characters of the name. Write a function with the heading:

    function Length (name : nametype) : natural;

which returns the number of characters in its parameter.

13.3 Rewrite the function *HighestScorer* of Prog 13.2 to use the with-statement to the full.

13.4 The *playerrecord*, as defined in Section 13.6, contains only a summary: it does not include the actual scores in any of the innings. Assuming that no player has more than *inningsmax* innings, expand the definition to include all the scores. Write functions to determine for each player:

    (i)   the number of not outs,
   (ii) the highest score,
  (iii) the aggregate,
  (iv) the average.

Problems

13.1   Modify your exam marks program so that it produces the output sorted on the final marks. Start by defining the data structure to hold all the data.

13.2   Add a procedure to your exam marks program to draw a histogram of the final marks.

13.3   A message in Morse code is typed one word per line, with the letters of the word separated by a single space. Write a program to read the message, decode it and write it out. Below is a table of the Morse Code for the letters of the alphabet.

```
A .-      J .---   S ...
B -...    K -.-    T -
C -.-.    L .-..   U ..-
D -..     M --     V ...-
E .       N -.     W .--
F ..-.    O ---     X -..-
G --.     P .--.    Y -.--
H ....    Q --.-    Z --..
I ..      R .-.
```

13.4   Write a program to print out Pascal's triangle in the form given below, choosing an appropriate maximum size.

```
            1
          1   1
        1   2   1
      1   3   3   1
    1   4   6   4   1
  1   5  10  10   5   1
```

Notice that the edges of the triangle are occupied by the digit 1 and that each number is the sum of the two numbers immediately above it.

13.5   A magic square of order *n* is found by arranging the numbers 1 to *n* in the form of a square so that the sum of the numbers in every row, every column and in each diagonal is the same. For example, the following is a magic square of order 5:

```
17  24   1   8  15
23   5   7  14  16
 4   6  13  20  22
10  12  19  21   3
11  18  25   2   9
```

If *n* is odd (as here) the magic square can be constructed as follows:

(i) The number 1 is placed in the middle of the top row. The next *n*–1 numbers are then placed in their natural order in a diagonal line which slopes upwards to the right except that:

- When the top row is reached, the next number is written in the bottom row as if it came immediately above the top row.

- When the right-hand column is reached, the next number is written in the left-hand column as if it immediately succeeded the right-hand column.

(ii) The next number, *n*+1, is placed immediately under the preceding number *n* and the next *n*–1 numbers are placed in their natural order on a diagonal line sloping upwards.

(iii) This procedure is then repeated a further *n*–2 times.

The above example has been constructed in this way. Write a program to read in an odd integer and write out a magic square of that order.

14

Sets

We are used to the idea that sets are of fundamental importance in mathematics: they are important in computing too. The definition:

type
    monthtype=(Jan, Feb, Mar, Apr, May, Jun, Jul, Aug, Sep, Oct, Nov,
                                                                Dec);

says that the value of a variable of *month* type must be a member of the set *{Jan, Feb, ..., Dec}*. There are many situations where we want a variable which has as its value a *set* of values. For example, given that the local energy authority sends out bills every three months, and that its billing is staggered so that different customers receive their bills at different times, it might be convenient, in a program which tries to control a personal budget, to have a variable whose value is, for example, the set *{Mar, Jun, Sep, Dec}*.

14.1   The set-types

The *set-type*, whose syntax is given in Fig 14.1, allows the definitions:

type
    author = (Aho, Hopcroft, Ullman);
    authorset = **set of** author;

which define a type, *authorset*, whose values are:

{ }	{Aho}	{Hopcroft}	{Ullman}
{Aho,Hopcroft}		{Aho,Ullman}	
{Hopcroft,Ullman}		{Aho,Hopcroft,Ullman}	

Fig 14.1 The syntax of *set-type*

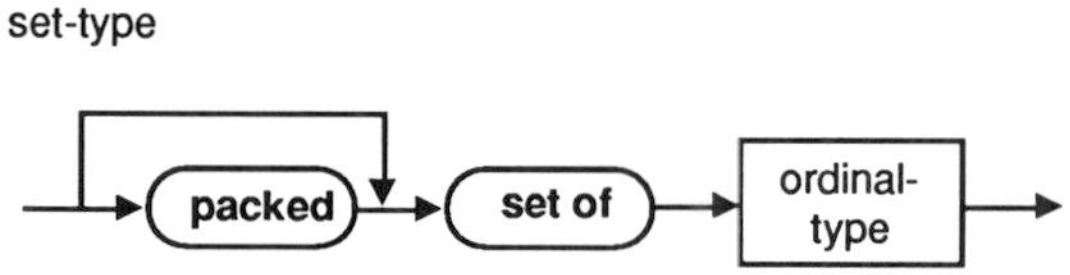

set-type

The type of the elements comprising the set is called the *base-type*. The base-type of *authorset* above is *author*. Note that the base-type must be an ordinal-type, so that we might have definitions such as:

type
    monthset = **set of** month;
    digitset = **set of** digit;
    charset = **set of** char;
    UCletterset = **set of** 'A'..'Z';
    floorset = **set of** 1..23;

Note that the fact that the base-type must be an ordinal-type is quite restrictive. We cannot, for example, define a type corresponding to a punctuation mark:

type
    punctuation = **set of** (',', '.', ';', ':', '?', '!');

We must instead use variables of *charset* type, and subsequently test they contain only punctuation marks. In fact, in a program processing characters, this is probably exactly what is required, since a given character will be recognized as a punctuation mark only after it has been read. Further, in most implementations the size of the base-type is restricted, often to a size of 64 or 128; and for a subrange-type, if the size is *n*, the values must be within the first *n* elements of the associated type. These restrictions on size are to enable very efficient implementation of the set facilities using the logical operations on words in the machine, though, of course, a competent compiler will achieve the same efficiency for small base-types without insisting on the total banning of larger bases.

14.2 Operations on sets

Although the set is a structured-type, it has a great deal in common with the required simple-types and so we will use the same framework for discussing it as we did for Booleans and characters. If we assume the declaration:

var
    Energy, Telephone, somebills, nobills, onebill, twobills : monthset;

then the operations available are as follows.

(i) We can neither read nor write sets.

(ii) We can assign a set expression to a set-variable. The syntax of set-expression is given in Fig 14.2. Note that there are no set-functions. There are no set-constants either: instead there is a more powerful facility for constructing sets. (Since the braces { and } are used for comments, Pascal requires square brackets [and] in their place for sets.) The elements may be specified by enum-

Fig 14.2 The syntax of *set-expression*

set-expression

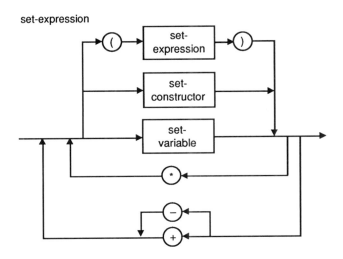

eration, or by using a subrange, or by a combination of both. The following are
set-constructors which define sets of type *monthtype*:

[ ]	{the null set}
[Jan]	{a singleton set}
[Mar, Jun, Sep, Dec]	{a set of 4 elements}
[Jan .. Mar, Oct .. Dec]	{a set of 6 elements}
[Jan .. Dec]	{the universal set}

Fig 14.3 gives the syntax of set-constructor. So far the notion of set-constructor
could with equanimity be called a set-constant. But note that the components can
be set-expressions. Thus we can write set-constructors whose elements, and
indeed whose size, are determined at run time.

Fig 14.3 The syntax of *set-constructor*

set-constructor

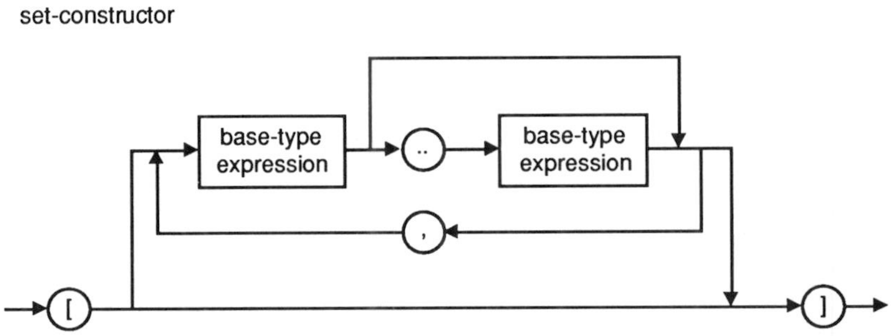

Examples are:

> [startmonth .. finishmonth]
> [Jan .. pred(startmonth), succ(startmonth) .. Dec]

Note that if *startmonth* > *finishmonth*, then the first example is equivalent to the null set.

As Fig 14.2 shows, the operations available over sets are + for *set union* (which is usually written ∪), * for *set intersection* (usually written ∩), and − for *set difference*. For completeness we give their definition.

- Union (+). The union of two sets *A* and *B* consists of elements which are members of *A* or of *B* (or of both). Thus:

  somebills := Energy + Telephone

  assigns to *somebills* a set consisting of those months when the Energy bill, the Telephone bill or both will arrive.

- Intersection (*). The intersection of two sets *A* and *B* consists of elements which are members of both *A* and *B*. Thus

  twobills := Energy * Telephone

  assigns to *twobills* a set consisting of those months when both Energy and Telephone bills arrive.

- Difference (−). The difference between sets *A* and *B* consists of elements which are members of *A* but not of *B*. Thus:

  onebill := somebills − twobills

  assigns to *onebill* a set consisting of those months when precisely one bill arrives. We use the set difference operation to form the complement of a set since that operation is not provided. Thus:

  nobills := [Jan..Dec] − somebills

The usual precedence rules hold:

- * is of higher precedence than + and −;

- operators of equal precedence are applied from left to right; and they may as usual be overruled by brackets.

(iii) We can compare sets. The usual relations are equality (=), inequality (≠), inclusion (⊇, ⊆) and membership (∈). We consider these below.

- Equality. Two sets are equal if they consist of precisely the same elements. In Pascal = is used for equality. Thus:

      onebill = somebills
      twobills = [ ]

are both true if Energy bills arrive in different months from the Telephone bills.

- Inequality. Two sets are unequal if they do not consist of precisely the same elements. In Pascal, of course, <> is used for ≠.

- Inclusion. The set *A* is included in *B* (or is a subset of *B*) if all the elements of *A* are also elements of *B*. This can be written in two ways *A* ⊆ *B*, and *B* ⊇ *A*. In Pascal we use <= for ⊆ and >= for ⊇. Thus:

      [Jan,Dec] <= nobills

is true if no bills arrive over the Christmas–New Year period.

- Membership. This is the fundamental operation between a value of the base-type and a set. We represent ∈ by **in**. Thus:

      (Jan **in** nobills) **and** (Dec **in** nobills)

is equivalent to:

      [Jan, Dec] <= nobills

Note that the membership predicate is redundant because, for example,

      Jan **in** onebill
      [Jan] <= onebill

are precisely equivalent. Nevertheless there are occasions where the membership relation is the more natural. We have been using it throughout this book in testing the value of ordinal-type variables in expressions such as:

      ch **in** ['A', 'E', 'I', 'O', 'U']

which tests whether *ch* is a vowel. Referring back to the punctuation example of the last section, to test whether *ch* is a punctuation mark we write:

      ch **in** [',', '.', ';', ':', '"', '?', '!']

or if *punctuation* is declared as a *variable* of *charset* type, we can assign it:

punctuation := [',', '.', ';', ':', '''', '?', '!']

and then write:

ch **in** punctuation

In Fig 14.4 we give the syntax of set-relation.

Fig 14.4 The syntax of *set-relation*

set-relation

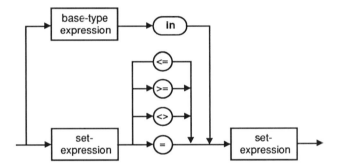

(iv) The sets are unordered. Thus we cannot get from one set to "the next", even though there are appropriate mathematical conventions.

(v) There are no transfer functions from a set to either its base-type or to the integer-type. Thus if we wish to process in some way each element of a set we must search through all possible elements looking for those present:

for month := Jan **to** Dec **do**
if month **in** nobills **then**...
{month is the next element in nobills}

(vi) A set may be passed as a parameter either by value or as a variable.

(vii) Set functions do not exist.

14.3   Examples

As our first example, we give a procedure which is explicitly concerned with sets, and which, therefore, uses the facilities to the full. Consider a graph such as the one in Fig 14.5.

A set of nodes each of which is joined to all the others is called a *clique*. In fact we are interested only in maximal cliques, that is cliques which do not contain any other cliques. Thus in Fig 14.5 the cliques are:

{1}
{2, 3}
{3, 4, 5}
{4, 6, 7}
{3, 4, 7, 8}

Note that a graph is fully specified by its cliques, so that, given appropriate values for *nodesmax* (the maximum number of nodes) and *cliquesmax* (the maximum number of cliques) the following defines a graph:

```
type
  node = 1 .. nodesmax;
  nodeset = set of node;
  graph = record
     nocliques : natural;
     cliques : array [1..cliquesmax] of nodeset
  end;
```

We consider now the problem of the changes to the cliques of a graph when an edge, say *m-n*, is deleted. We can easily verify that if a clique contains *m* and *n*, then the deletion of edge *m-n* will cause the clique to decompose into two smaller cliques. These pairs have the following properties:

• Each member is different from each member of any other pair created;

• No member can contain any of the original cliques;

Fig 14.5 An arbitrary graph

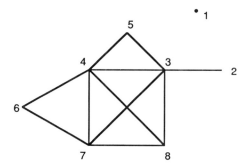

- Each member may be contained in one (or more) of the original cliques which did not include edge *m-n*.

Prog 14.1 gives a procedure for implementing this algorithm.

Prog 14.1 A procedure to replace the cliques of a given graph with the cliques obtained by deleting a given edge

---

procedure DeleteEdge (**var** gr : graph;
           m, n : node);
{This procedure replaces the cliques of the current graph held in the structure gr of graph type by the cliques of the graph obtained by deleting edge m-n.}
  var
    tempgr : graph;
    thisclique : nodeset;
    i, j, oldnocliques, buffer : natural;
  begin
    oldnocliques := gr.nocliques;
    gr.nocliques := 0;
    tempgr.nocliques := 0;

    {1.Scan through the cliques of the current graph held in gr. For each clique containing the edge m-n, store in tempgr the two (possibly redundant) cliques obtained by deleting each node of the edge.
    Copy each clique not containing the edge back to gr as a clique of the new graph.}
    for i := 1 **to** oldnocliques **do**
      begin
        thisclique := gr.cliques[i];
        if [m, n] <= thisclique **then**
          with tempgr **do**
            begin
              nocliques := nocliques + 1;
              cliques[nocliques] := thisclique − [m];
              nocliques := nocliques + 1;
              cliques[nocliques] := thisclique − [n]
            end {of saving the 2 cliques after the edge is removed}
        else
          with gr **do**
            begin
          nocliques := nocliques + 1;
          cliques[nocliques] := thisclique
          end {of saving the clique not containing the edge}
      end;{of loop on "i"}

    {2. Compare each clique in tempgr with those directly placed in gr. If it is a subset of any clique in gr it is ignored, otherwise it is added to gr. The searching process uses a variation of the sentinel technique of adding the item sought to the end of the sequence being searched to simplify the loop termination. Here, since gr is being extended but the searching takes place only over the initial part of gr, a buffer is left at the interface to be filled in just before exit.}

```
with gr do
  begin
    nocliques := nocliques + 1;
    buffer := nocliques;
    for i := 1 to tempgr.nocliques do
      begin
        thisclique := tempgr.cliques[i];
        cliques[buffer] := thisclique;
        j := 1;
        while not (thisclique <= cliques[j]) do
          j := j + 1;
        if j = buffer then
          begin
            nocliques := nocliques + 1;
            cliques[nocliques] := thisclique
          end {of adding the new clique to gr}
      end;{of loop on "i"}
    cliques[buffer] := cliques[nocliques];
    nocliques := nocliques − 1
  end {of "with gr do"}
end {of procedure "DeleteEdge"}
```

More often sets are created by programmers in the development of an algorithm. For example, suppose we are given the following types:

```
type
  length = 1..max;
  digit = '0'..'9';
  display = array[length] of digit;
```

and we want a function, *Valid*, which returns the value *true* iff all the digits in its parameter, which is of *display* type, are different. Clearly each element of the array must be tested to see whether it occurs in the earlier digits. If the elements were of integer-type, we would need two nested loops, with the inner loop comparing the current element against the elements previously considered. However, the elements of the array are of *digit* type. Therefore we can keep a set, *earlier*, containing the digits so far encountered. Then the inner loop can be replaced by a simple test of the current element against *earlier*. Prog 14.2 gives an appropriate procedure, which uses the state variable technique to control the outer (now only) loop.

**Prog 14.2   A function which returns true iff the digits in an array are
all different**

---

function Valid (d : display;
         ndigits : length) : Boolean;
{This function returns true iff all the digits in display are different.}
  var
      state : (repeating, alldifferent, unknown);
      earlier : **set of** digit;
      i : length;
  begin
    earlier := [ ];
    i := 1;
    state := unknown;
    repeat
      if d[i] **in** earlier **then**
        state := repeating
      else if i = ndigits **then**
        state := alldifferent
      else
        begin
          earlier := earlier + [d[i]];
          i := i + 1
        end
    until state **in** [repeating, alldifferent];
    Valid := state = alldifferent
  end {of function "Valid"}

Exercises

14.1 Write set-constructors of *charset* type which consist of:

        (i)   all lower-case letters;
        (ii) all letters;
        (iii) all letters and digits;
        (iv) all characters which have descenders;
        (v)   all characters which have ascenders.

14.2 Write a sequence for finding the cardinality of a set (i.e. the number of
     elements in it) of the type:

             type
                monthset = **set of** month;

14.3 Write a function with the heading:

> **function** NotIn (b : base;
>   s : setofbase) : Boolean

which returns true iff $b \notin s$.

14.4 Rewrite the function Valid of Prog 14.2 without using sets.

Problems

14.1 Write a program to read in some text and print out a frequency count of the occurrences of pairs of consecutive vowels: *aa, ae ... uo, uu*.

14.2 Write a procedure, *AddEdge*, which determines the changes to the cliques of a graph when an edge, say *m-n*, is added.

14.3 Consider the old computer games called *Moo* or *Bulls and Cows*. In this game the computer chooses a 4-digit number all of whose digits are different and the user (whom we shall call the player from now on) has to guess what it is. The computer provides clues to the number by responding to each guess. Any digit of the player's guess that is correct and in the correct position is described as a *bull*, and any digit that is correct but in the wrong position is called a *cow*. Thus if the target number is 2357, the computer will respond with 0 bulls and 4 cows to the guess 5723 and 2 bulls and 1 cow to the guess 2567. The player may make any number of guesses up to some maximum, *maxguesses*. (The reader will undoubtedly recognise the commercial game *MasterMind* in the description.) Write a program to play this game.

15

Files

The array is a ubiquitous data structure finding use in a variety of situations. We have used it for holding a sequence of hours (which had to be processed serially). We can use it to hold a table of tax details (which has to be searched), or a table of values of a function (which will be accessed at random). One aim of a second course in programming is to characterize these different applications, and consider *abstract data structures*, for which one implementation is the array.

15.1 File definitions

We will, in this chapter, consider one such abstract data structure: the *sequence*. The characteristic of the sequence is that elements can be accessed only on a strictly sequential basis (that is, one element after another). Thus the sequence might adequately represent the sequence of hours worked or the table of tax details, but would be quite inadequate for the table of values of a function. Pascal provides a sequence facility by means of the *file-type*. The syntax diagram is given in Fig 15.1, so that we might have definitions such as those below, where, again, we leave some types undefined.

```
type
  realfile = file of real;
  customerfile = file of
     record
       name : nametype;
       address : addresstype;
       lastreading : natural;
       readingdate : date;
       tariff : tarifftype
     end;
```

Fig 15.1 The syntax of *file-type*

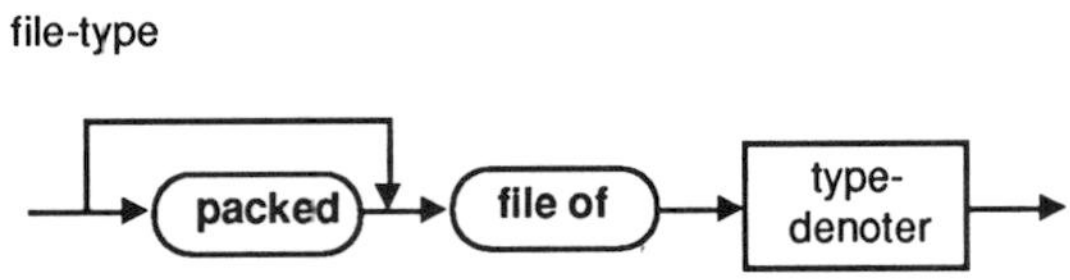

file-type

Note that we can have files of almost any type. In particular we can have files of records of arbitrary complexity. There is one constraint though: the component-type may not be another file-type, nor a structure whose own components include a file-type. This is the last of the structured-types, so it is a good time to give an expanded version of the tree of types (Fig 15.2).

Fig 15.2   The tree of types

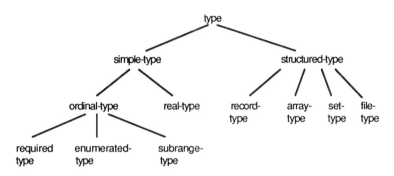

We shall see later that files may pre-exist and be accessed by a program or may be created by a program and continue to exist after the program has run. For the moment though we consider files created by the program and subsequently accessed by it. Consider, for example, the form of the payroll program in which the data included the hours worked on each of the seven days of the week. In Chapter 13 we stored the values in an array. We might instead create a file in *ReadData* and process it in *CalculateGross*. (This is an unlikely strategy, which we will pursue no further, using instead some abstract examples before returning to the payroll program with a more appropriate use of files.)

A file consists of an indefinitely long sequence of components (possibly records) which can be accessed only serially. Accessing an element of a file *f* is through a *window* with which is associated a *buffer-variable*, *f^*, though in many situations, as we shall see in later examples, this detail can be ignored. In Fig 15.3 we add this new form of variable-access.

Fig 15.3   The tree of variables

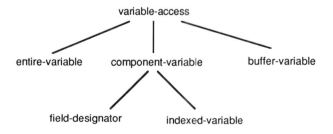

15.2   Creating a file

The following operations are available:

(i) *rewrite(f)*. This resets the window to the start of an empty file. Should *f* have previously been written, the old file will disappear.

(ii) *write(f, x)*. This appends the value of *x* to the file *f*. Thus assuming the type *realfile* defined earlier, and the declarations:

```
var
  i, size : natural;
  f : realfile;
  next : real;
```

the following sequence will create a file of numbers from data entered by a user:

```
rewrite(f);
for i := 1 to size do
  begin
    readln(next);
    write(f, next)
  end
```

(iii) *put(f)*. This appends the value of the buffer-variable *f^* to the file via the window, advances the window and makes *f^* undefined. Clearly a call for *put* must be preceded by an assignment to *f^*. The call *write(f, x)*, which we generally use, is simply a shorthand for *f^ := x; put(f)*.

We can illustrate the action of the file creation sequence pictorially. Below we give a diagram of the file immediately after *rewrite(f)*. The window is shown shaded. This is where the next value will be placed after a *write* or a *put*.

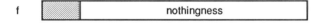

After the first time that *write(f, next)* is obeyed, assuming that 3.54 has been input by the user, this is how it looks:

And after the second time, with 2.10 input:

and the last time, with –3.00 input:

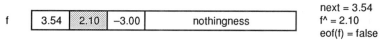

f | 3.54 | 2.10 | –3.00 | | nothingness | f^ undefined

15.3   Accessing a file

The following operations are available:

(i) *reset(f)*. This resets the window to the start of the file for reading.

(ii) *read(f, x)*. This accesses the next component of the file *f*, assigns it to *x* and moves the window on to the next component.

(iii) *eof(f)*. This function returns *true* when the window is advanced past the last component of the file (by the action of *read(f, x)*). This will also leave *f^* undefined. Since the number of components of a file is not explicitly held, *eof* is the usual means of controlling a loop which processes the components of a file. The following sequence writes out the components of the file *f* created above:

```
reset(f);
while not eof(f) do
  begin
    read(f, next);
    writeln(next : 8 : 2)
  end
```

(iv) *f^*. This always has as its value the component in the window of file *f* (that is, the next component). Thus it is possible to look ahead one component. On *reset(f)*, *f^* is set to the first component of *f*.

(v) *get(f)*. This advances the file window so that *f* moves on to the next component. If the original value of *f^* was not used, then *get(f)* effectively skips over that component. Thus *read (f, x)* is simply a shorthand for *x := f^; get(f)*. This procedure may also set *eof*.

We illustrate the file reading sequence pictorially, too. After *reset(f)* the values of the file and the buffer-variable are:

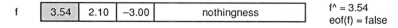

f | 3.54 | 2.10 | –3.00 | | nothingness | f^ = 3.54
                                                eof(f) = false

After *read(f, next)* is obeyed the first time:

next = 3.54

f | 3.54 | 2.10 | –3.00 | | nothingness | f^ = 2.10
                                                eof(f) = false

After it is obeyed the second time:

next = 2.10
f   3.54   2.10   –3.00   nothingness   f^ = –3.00
                                                       eof(f) = false

And after the third time:

next = –3.00
f   3.54   2.10   –3.00   nothingness   f^ = undefined
                                                       eof(f) = true

In Prog 15.1 we give a demonstration program which uses the two sequences above to read some numbers and subsequently write them out. Note that although the number of numbers is available, the sequence which reads the numbers from the file still terminates on *eof*, because in practice, the number of components in a file is not known until the whole file has been read.

Prog 15.1   An demonstration of the file facilities

```
program IllustrateInternalFiles;
{This program demonstrates the internal file facility by reading some
numbers from the keyboard, filing them and then reading them back,
and writing them out to the screen.}
  type
    natural = 0..maxint;
    realfile = file of real;
  var
    i, size : natural;
    f : realfile;
    next : real;
begin
  writeln('How many numbers are there? ');
  readln(size);
  writeln('Give them to me, one to a line. ');
  rewrite(f);
  for i := 1 to size do
    begin
      readln(next);
      write(f, next)
    end;{of loop on "i"}
  writeln('Here they are again. ');
  reset(f);
  while not eof(f) do
    begin
      read(f, next);
      writeln(next : 8 : 2)
    end {of loop on "eof(f)"}
end.
```

When run with the numbers used above it produces this output:

```
How many numbers are there?
3
Give them to me, one to a line.
3.54
2.1
-3
Here they are again.
     3.54
     2.10
    -3.00
```

To illustrate the relationship between *get* and *read* we give below two procedures for summing the elements of a file *f* of type *realfile*. Note that this is a more typical case in that it must use *eof* for loop control, since the size of the file is not explicitly known.

```
procedure SumFile(f : realfile);      procedure SumFile(f : realfile);
  var                                   var
    sum, next : real;                     sum : real;
  begin                                 begin
    sum := 0;                             sum := 0;
    reset(f);                             reset(f);
    while not eof(f) do                   while not eof(f) do
      begin                                 begin
        read(f, next);                        sum := sum + f^;
        sum := sum + next                     get(f)
      end {of loop on "eof(f)"}             end {of loop on "eof(f)"}
  end {of procedure "SumFile"}          end {of procedure "SumFile"}
```

15.4   External files

Files may be purely internal to a program (like the other structures) but more often they will be external files. We therefore have the question: how do we establish which files in the file system are to be used by the program? The answer in Standard Pascal is to use *program-parameters* which appear in the program heading, for example:

program MergeFiles(f, g, h, output);

Except for *input* and *output*, the files must still be declared within the program. Prog 15.2 gives a program which merges two external files *f* and *g,* whose components are sorted on a key, to produce another sorted external file, *h*. To use the program, the user must associate the appropriate files in the file store with the parameters, *f, g, h*. Operating systems have facilities for this.

With interactive programs, especially those running on micros, no such system facilities exist, so that program-parameters are not useful. The program itself

Prog 15.2 A standard program for merging two external files

---

program MergeFiles(f, g, h, output);
{This merges two sorted files and prints out the total number of records.
Note, the program is not complete in that keytype and informationtype
have not been defined.}
  type
    natural = 0 .. maxint;
    recordtype = **record**
      key : keytype;
      information : informationtype
    end;
  var
    f, g, h : **file of** recordtype;
    nextf, nextg : recordtype;
    norecords : natural;
    endfg : Boolean;
begin
  reset(f);
  reset(g);
  rewrite(h);
  endfg := eof(f) **or** eof(g);
  norecords := 0;
  while not endfg **do**
    begin
      if f^.key < g^.key **then**
        begin
          read(f, nextf);
          write(h, nextf);
          endfg := eof(f)
        end {of copying from "f" to "h"}
      else
        begin
          read(g, nextg);
          write(h, nextg);
          endfg := eof(g)
        end;{of copying from "g" to "h"}
      norecords := norecords + 1
    end;{of loop on "endfg"}
  while not eof(f) **do**
    begin
      read(f, nextf);
      write(h, nextf);
      norecords := norecords + 1
    end; {copying tail of "f"}
  while not eof(g) **do**
    begin

```
        read(g, nextg);
        write(h, nextg );
        norecords := norecords + 1
      end; {copying tail of "g"}
    writeln;
    writeln('Merging complete. ',  norecords:1, 'records copied.')
  end.
```

must nominate the files explicitly. The facilities vary unfortunately; one common method is to open a file, explicitly associating its name with the identifier of the parameter. For example:

```
    open(f, 'WEEK 1 DATA');
    open(g, 'WEEK 2 DATA');
    open(h, 'WEEKS 1 AND 2 DATA')
```

More often the program asks the user to type the name, which it stores in a string variable, using that variable as the second parameter in an open statement. Check your User Manual before you try this.   We will hide the details in subsequent programs inside a procedure, so that changes can be made easily.

Note that the *MergeFiles* program uses output to give a positive indication that it worked.   All file handling programs should do this: indeed, in some implementations of Pascal it is obligatory to specify *output* in the program heading.

15.5   Textfiles

The components of a file may be of any type, simple or structured, provided that they do not contain (sub)components of a file-type. At one extreme we have files of quite complex records, and at the other files of characters. There is a special class of files of characters, the *textfile*, with two important properties:

(i) Not only can we can read single characters of the text one at a time as one would expect, we can also read whole groups of characters and have them converted to an integer or a real appropriately. (A similar statement applies to writing a textfile.) This is an important advantage since the process of decimal-to-binary conversion is non-trivial as we saw in Chapter 12, where we considered only integers! Note the difference between a textfile whose characters make up a sequence of numbers separated by spaces and a file of real numbers in which the numbers are stored in binary in individual words.

(ii) Textfiles are composed of lines and there are facilities to handle this structure. At the end of each line of text a special space character is included to represent the break between one line and the next. If read, this acts like a normal space character, but there is a procedure which detects it, and others which deal with it specially. The procedures are:

- *eoln(f)*. This function returns true if the special space is in the file-buffer *f^*.

- *readln(f)*. This procedure skips over all characters of *f* up to and including the special space.

- *writeln(f)*. This procedure appends the special space to *f*.

- *page(f)*. On printers this causes future output to start at the head of the next page of paper. On terminals its action is not specified.

Note in particular the difference between reading a file of reals and a textfile containing real numbers. With a file of reals, reading the last number will set *eof true*. With a textfile reading the last character will also set *eof true*; but reading the last number will not because there will remain unread possibly some spaces and certainly the special space into which the last end of line is converted.

15.6 Input and output

In Standard Pascal, the program-heading (almost) always includes the names of two standard files, *input* and *output*.

> **program** Payroll(input, output)

The user may associate *input* and *output* with any textfile in the system. For interactive work it is natural to associate the keyboard with *input* and the screen with *output*. Their existence is assumed by all interactive systems. Further we have as abbreviations:

read(x)	read(input, x)	readln(x)	readln(input, x)
eoln	eoln(input)	eof	eof(input)
write(x)	write(output, x)	writeln(x)	writeln(output, x)

Note that there are no abbreviations for *input^* or *page*. The procedures *get* and *put* are available too, so that the procedure for skipping blanks:

```
procedure SkipBlanks;
{This procedure reads the blanks up to the next non-blank character.}
  var
    ch : char;
begin
  while input^ = ' ' do
    read(ch)
end {of procedure "SkipBlanks"}
```

can also be written as below, avoiding the need for the local variable *ch*:

```
procedure SkipBlanks;
{This procedure reads the blanks up to the next non-blank character.}
begin
  while input^ = ' ' do
    get(input)
end {of procedure "SkipBlanks"}
```

Note that the operation *reset* should not be applied to the file *input* and that the operation *rewrite* should not be applied to the file *output*.

15.7   A more typical example – the *Payroll* program

We have emphasized the importance of dividing our program into procedures, based on the essentially distinct activities that are required: input of an individual's data; calculation of tax, and so on. Often we go further, particularly in data processing, and use two separate programs which communicate by a file. The first program will read the data, possibly with extensive checking to ensure its correctness, and produce a file; the second will process this file, assuming it to be correct, and write out the appropriate results. We consider again the payroll program. As we left it, its main program was:

```
program Payroll;
begin
  Announce;
  FindStaffSize(paysheet.staffsize);
  GiveInstructions;
  for employee := 1 to paysheet.staffsize do
    with paysheet do
      begin
        ReadWorkDetails(payslip[employee]);
        CalculateGross(payslip[employee]);
        CalculateTax(payslip[employee]);
        CalculateNett(payslip[employee])
      end; {of loop on "employee"}
  SortPaySheet(paysheet);
  WriteWagesDetails(paysheet)
end.
```

Suppose now we break it in two along the lines discussed above.

The first program *PayrollInput*, will, after the appropriate preliminaries, simply read in each employee's details in turn and write them out to a file *paydata*, which is of a type *payfile* defined:

```
type
  payfile = file of payslip;
```

Its main program might be:

```
program PayrollInput;
begin
  Announce;
  Initialize(paydata);
  FindStaffSize(paysheet.staffsize);
  GiveInstructions;
  for employee := 1 to paysheet.staffsize do
    with paysheet do
      begin
        ReadWorkDetails(payslip[employee]);
        WriteWorkDetails(paydata, payslip[employee])
      end; {of loop on "employee"}
  SignOff
end.
```

The changes are simple:

- *Announce* must be modified to reflect the modified operation of the program.

- *Initialize* must be written to associate *paydata* with the appropriate file and to rewind it ready for writing.

- *WriteWorkDetails* must be written to write the payslip record to the file. Its body is simply:

  ```
  write(paydata, payslip)
  ```

- *SignOff* must be written to give a positive indication that the program actually completed. It may be quite different if the program is modified to run in batch mode.

We could, too, eliminate the paysheet, since it is redundant, and return to the single payslip, and, of course, *paydata* must be declared.

The second program *PayrollProcess* will read the file and process it. Its main program might be:

```
program PayrollProcess;
begin
  Announce;
  Initialize(paydata, employee);
  while not eof(paydata) do
    with paysheet do
      begin
        ReadWorkDetails(paydata, payslip[employee]);
        CalculateGross(payslip[employee]);
        CalculateTax(payslip[employee]);
```

```
                    CalculateNett(payslip[employee]);
                    employee := employee + 1
                  end; {of loop "eof(paydata)"}
                SortPaySheet(paysheet);
                WriteWagesDetails(paysheet)
              end.
```

The changes are simple:

  • *Announce* must be modified to reflect the modified operation of the program.

  • *Initialize* must be written to reset *paydata* and to initialize *employee*, because we had to change the for-statement into a while-statement.

  • *ReadWorkDetails* must be modified to read the payslip record to the file. Its body is simply:

            read(paydata, payslip)

15.8   Arrays or files?

When do we use a file? In some situations, of course, we have no option: where the data to be used by the program was produced by another program and so exists in a file, or where the output is to be used by another program and must be produced in a file. Within a program the choice between a file or an array is based on the different characteristics of these two structures. A file may be arbitrarily long (though only a small part is resident in the store at any one time), it may be accessed only serially and it is slower to access than a one-dimensional array (perhaps by a factor of two). An array, on the other hand, has to be relatively small (since all of it must be resident in the store) but it may be accessed randomly.

Exercises

15.1 Recast the program *IllustrateInternalFiles* (Prog 15.1) to use buffer-variables instead of the read- and write-statements.

15.2 Recast the program *MergeFiles* (Prog 15.2) as a procedure which uses buffer-variables instead of the read- and write-statements.

15.3 Consider again the *MergeFiles* program of Prog 15.2. It is sometimes possible to add to the end of a set of files a record with a special key which is larger than all the possible real keys. This record is called a *sentinel*. This enables a simpler merging procedure to be written. Do so.

15.4 As we have already noted, sets in Pascal are usually restricted in size.

We can use files for large sets. Suppose we define:

type
largeset = **file of** natural;

and suppose that we hold a set as a file of naturals in ascending order of magnitude. Write procedures with the headings:

(i) **procedure** Union(**var** f, g, h : largeset)
(ii) **procedure** Intersection(**var** f, g, h : largeset)

which set *h* to the union and intersection of *f* and *g* respectively.

Problems

15.1 A postal auction is a method of selling in which potential customers are sent a catalogue of, say, antique maps. Each customer then posts in a list containing, for each item he is interested in, its lot number together with his bid. At the closing time of the auction the letters are opened, and for each item the successful customer is the one with the highest bid provided it is not less than the previously determined reserve price. If two customers make the same bid, the one which arrived first is the winner. Suppose we have two files, one containing for each item its lot number, a descriptive piece of text and its reserve price, and one containing the bids in order of arrival. Write a program to run the auction and produce:

(i) A list of the items and the price fetched (if sold).

(ii) For each customer, at least one of whose bids was successful, an invoice which gives the number, description and price of all items bought and a total price. If some of his bids were unsuccessful, the successful bid for these should be indicated at the bottom of the invoice.

(iii) For each customer who was completely unsuccessful, a statement of the prices fetched for the items he bid for.

15.2 A treasurer of an organization maintains accounts for that organization. An active member of the community may well be treasurer of several organizations and so a method of automating the maintenance of the different accounts would be a great asset. The following method, using a card index, may be suitable. The card index is divided into sections, one for each organization. Initially each section contains a single card on which is written the name of the organization, its account number and its opening balance. As any income is received or expenses paid the treasurer records the appropriate information on a card and inserts it into its section. The information consists of five parts:

- The account number (3 digits) which must agree with the account number of the section it is filed in. This is to ensure the detection of any mistake involving storing a card in the wrong section.

- The date in the format dd/mm/yy, for example, 14/7/89.

- The letters CR or DB representing credit (for income) and debit (for expenses) respectively.

- A 6-digit reference number, corresponding to the number of the cheque involved.

- The amount involved.

The treasurer wishes periodically (say weekly) to know the state of all the accounts without bothering the bank. Write a program which will read in data corresponding to the card index and produce statements, one for each account, laid out like this:

```
ACCOUNT 137 NEDLANDS GYMNASTIC CLUB
STATEMENT TO 21 NOV 89

DATE          REFERENCE   CREDIT   DEBIT   BALANCE

OPENING BALANCE                             18.76

 2 NOV 89     173846                19.96    1.20DB
 2 NOV 89     363172      20.00             18.80
10 NOV 89     481641      20.00             38.80
15 NOV 89     173847               14.50    24.30
```

Any card not in its correct section should be rejected with an appropriate message even if it detracts from the appearance of a statement.

15.3   Most computer facilities provide a filing system for the storage of programs, data and so on, and an editor, which allows an edited file to be constructed from an original file and some editing commands. The problem is to write an editor. The system may be visualized as shown in Fig 15.4. Files may be large (say 10 000 lines) and so it would be unreasonable to list the file after each editing run. However, it is important for the user to know that what he wanted to happen did happen. Thus there will be an output called *monitoring information* which will show actually what the editor did. The design of this is important since it is the only confirmation the user has of what editing actually took place. There are a number of different ways of designing editors. We will restrict the scope though by specifying that the file to be edited will contain a Pascal program and that the editing will be on a line-by-line basis. That is, the user will be allowed to delete, insert or replace lines. He will specify the editing to take place in his input (called in the diagram *editing commands*). When designing the editor commands some points to be considered are:

(i) What commands to provide.

(ii) Whether to provide both a long form (perhaps for occasional users) and a shorter form (for regular users).

(iii) How deletion and insertion of groups of lines should be indicated.

(iv) Whether the commands should be originally in line number sequence (and what happens if the data should be out of sequence) or whether the editor should sort them.

(v) Whether the line numbering should be *absolute* or *relative*.

These notions are illustrated below in two sequences which describe the same editing sequence.

Relative	**Absolute**
| ```
Copy 26 lines
Delete
Copy 18 lines
Insert
procedure PrintBills
        .
        .
        .
end
``` | ```
Delete line 27
Replace line 46 by
procedure PrintBills;
        .
        .
        .
end
``` |

Fig 15.4 An editor

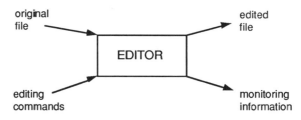

original file → EDITOR → edited file

editing commands → EDITOR → monitoring information

15.4   In any long sequence of characters, there will generally be sub-sequences in which a character is repeated a number of times. Write a procedure which, given a textfile, will determine the longest repetitive sub-sequence, and will produce the character repeated and the length of the sequence. For example, in the sequence:

   a b b a b c d d d a a b

the longest repetitive sub-sequence consists of 3 *d*s. (If there are two or more sub-sequences which tie for being longest, the procedure should produce the first.)

16

Program design with data structures

The essence of many programs lies in the creation and manipulation of the data structures. These are generally few in number, often one or two. Once the data structures are recognized and defined, the statement-part almost writes itself. In this chapter we consider a typical example.

16.1   *Bibit Magus* winery

The *Bibit Magus* vineyard and winery grows red grapes and makes red wine. This is sold from the winery and for every customer a sales record is kept of the transaction, consisting of the date, the customer's name and the quantity of the various wines bought. These records are entered into a computer as they are created and are subsequently processed by a collection of programs.

16.2   The type definitions for records on the file

Before we consider these programs we define the data structure of the records and of the file containing them. Let us start with the sales record and the sales file. From what we said above *salesrecord* is a simple three-field record, and *salesfile* a file of those records:

```
type
  salesrecord = record
     date : datetype;
     name : nametype;
     sales : quantity
  end;
  salesfile = file of salesrecord;
```

We now proceed to define the components. (It is a great pity that Pascal insists that we put the refinements first, but it is a simple editing operation to rearrange them that way.) *Date* and *name* are easy. We have used them before:

```
type
  daytype = 1..31;
  monthtype = (Jan, Feb, Mar, Apr, May, Jun, Jul, Aug, Sep, Oct,
                                                    Nov, Dec);
```

```
yeartype = 1583..maxint;
datetype = record
    day : daytype;
    month : monthtype;
    year : yeartype
  end;
nametype = record
    size : 1..20;
    characters : array[1..20] of char
  end;
```

Now for *sales*! *Bibit Magus* grows 5 varieties of grape from which it makes 5 varietal wines. They are *Cabernet Sauvignon, Merlot, Pinot Noir, Shiraz, Zinfandel*. The vintages currently available are 1982, 1983, 1984 and 1985. (Earlier wines have all been sold; younger wines are not yet — at the time of writing — drinkable.) Hence the definitions:

```
type
    variety = (cabernet, merlot, pinot, shiraz, zinfandel);
    vintage = 1982..1985;
```

Note the use of single word identifiers for those varieties whose name has two words. In this context they are precise and we can always write out the full spelling in our output if that is required. A customer may buy cases of any or all of the wines and *quantity*, which is the type describing the sales to a customer, must accommodate this. Clearly an array is called for. Our first thought might be to define its elements as being records of three fields, *variety, vintage* and *quantity* bought, which is, of course, how the sale would be written down initially. The array would have to contain 20 elements because a customer can buy all the wines on offer. By its very nature we would have to search through such an array to find what was actually sold to a customer. We can do better by using:

```
type
    quantity = array[variety, vintage] of natural;
```

Thus the complete definition is:

```
type
    natural = 0..maxint;
    daytype = 1..31;
    monthtype = (Jan, Feb, Mar, Apr, May, Jun, Jul, Aug, Sep, Oct,
                                                    Nov, Dec);
    yeartype = 1583..maxint;
    datetype = record
        day : daytype;
        month : monthtype;
        year : yeartype
      end;
```

```
nametype = record
   size : 1..20;
   characters : array[1..20] of char
   end;
variety = (cabernet, merlot, pinot, shiraz, zinfandel);
vintage = 1982..1985;
quantity = array[variety, vintage] of natural;
salesrecord = record
   date : datetype;
   name : nametype;
   sales : quantity
   end;
salesfile = file of salesrecord;
```

16.3   Producing a summary

The processing program we are going to write will take a sales file and from it produce a summary of the wines sold over the period of the file. The information will be classified by variety and vintage. An example is given below:

```
Bibit Magus Winery
Summary of sales from 2 Jun 1988 to 20 Jun 1988
```

VARIETY	1982	1983	1984	1985	TOTAL
Cabernet Sauvignon	22	15	11	27	75
Merlot	22	11	14	11	58
Pinot Noir	22	11	14	13	60
Shiraz	16	17	11	7	51
Zinfandel	8	11	8	10	37
TOTALS	90	65	58	68	281

16.4   The type definitions for the summary record

Looking at this example we see that there are 5 distinct components: the *start date*, the *end date*, a rectangular array of the *total sales* of the varieties, a column of *variety totals* and a row of *vintage totals*. We are led to the definition:

```
type
summaryrecord = record
   startdate, enddate : datetype;
   totalsales : quantity;
   varietytotals : quantitybyvariety;
   vintagetotals : quantitybyvintage
   end;
```

The types *datetype* and *quantity* we have already, being important components of the records in the file. The types *quantitybyvariety* and *quantitybyvintage* are obviously related to *quantity*:

type
    quantitybyvariety = **array**[variety] **of** natural;
    quantitybyvintage = **array**[vintage] **of** natural;

16.5   The summary program

The broad action of the summary program is clear. There will be a loop in which records, which we will call *transactions*, are read one at a time from the file, and used to update *totalsales*. We could also update *varietytotals* and *vintagetotals*, but it is more efficient to update those fields after the loop. *Totalsales* must be initialized before the loop. But what about *startdate*, and *enddate*? The start date is the date of the first transaction, and can be established before the loop by using the file-buffer variable; the end date is the date of the last transaction and can be set after the loop. Given the declarations:

var
    summary : summaryrecord;
    transaction : salesrecord;
    currentfile : salesfile;

the main program is:

```
begin
  EstablishLinkTo(currentfile);
  ClearTotalSales(summary);
  SetStartDate(currentfile, summary);
  while not eof(currentfile) do
    begin
      ReadNextTransaction(currentfile, transaction);
      UpdateTotalSales(summary, transaction)
    end; {of loop on "eof(currentfile)"}
  SetEndDate(summary);
  CalculateVintageTotals(summary);
  CalculateVarietyTotals(summary);
  WriteSummary(summary)
end.
```

Note that we have used the procedure *EstablishLinkTo* to camouflage the differences between operating in a batch mode and running interactively. In Prog 16.1 we give the interactive procedure.

With the exception of *WriteSummary* the procedures are generally quite straight-forward. We give *UpdateTotalSales* as an exemplar of the procedures which process *summary*.

```
procedure UpdateTotalSales (var summary : summaryrecord;
        var transaction : salesrecord);
  var
    year : vintage;
    grape : variety;
  begin
    with summary, transaction do
      for grape := cabernet to zinfandel do
        for year := 1982 to 1985 do
          totalsales[grape, year] := totalsales[grape, year] +
                                              sales[grape, year]
  end {of procedure "UpdateTotalSales"}
```

The procedure has two loops to access all the elements of a two-dimensional array, the inner one ranging over the vintages, using a local variable, *year*, and the outer one ranging over the varieties, using *grape*. Note the with-statement with its pair of record variables specified. Within the loop, *totalsales* refers to a field of *summary*, and *sales* refers to a field of *transaction*.

The *WriteSummary* procedure is a little more complex because it has a number of things to do. It must write out the heading, which requires the two dates. Then for each grape it must write out the grape's name, the quantity sold for each vintage, together with the total quantity for that variety. Finally it must write out the total quantity sold for each vintage, together with the grand total. Its body then is:

```
begin
  with summary do
    begin
      WriteHeader(startdate, enddate);
      for grape := cabernet to zinfandel do
        begin
          WriteVarietyName(grape);
          for year := 1982 to 1985 do
            write(totalsales[grape, year] : 6);
          write(varietytotals[grape] : 6);
          writeln
        end; {of loop on "grape"}
      writeln;
      WriteVintageAndGrandTotals(vintagetotals)
    end {of with "summary" do}
end {of procedure "WriteSummary"}
```

The procedures it uses are very simple and so we go straight to the complete program, given in Prog 16.1.

Prog 16.1 The program for producing a summary

---

program ProduceSummary;
{This program reads a file of Bibit Magus sale transactions and writes
out a summary.}
  type
    natural = 0..maxint;
    daytype = 1..31;
    monthtype = (Jan, Feb, Mar, Apr, May, Jun, Jul, Aug, Sep, Oct,
                                           Nov, Dec);
    yeartype = 1573..maxint;
    datetype = **record**
      day : daytype;
      month : monthtype;
      year : yeartype
    end;
    nametype = **record**
      size : 1..20;
      characters : **array**[1..20] **of** char
    end;
    variety = (cabernet, merlot, pinot, shiraz, zinfandel);
    vintage = 1982..1985;
    quantity = **array**[variety, vintage] **of** natural;
    salesrecord = **record**
      date : datetype;
      name : nametype;
      sales : quantity
    end;
    salesfile = **file of** salesrecord;
    quantitybyvariety = **array**[variety] **of** natural;
    quantitybyvintage = **array**[vintage] **of** natural;
    summaryrecord = **record**
      startdate, enddate : datetype;
      totalsales : quantity;
      varietytotals : quantitybyvariety;
      vintagetotals : quantitybyvintage
    end;
  var
    summary : summaryrecord;
    transaction : salesrecord;
    currentfile : salesfile;

  procedure EstablishLinkTo (**var** currentfile : salesfile);
  {This procedure associates "PvP Wine Data" with currentfile.}
    begin
      open(currentfile, 'PvP Wine Data')
    end; {of procedure "EstablishLinkTo" }

```
procedure ClearTotalSales (var summary : summaryrecord);
{This procedure clears all the entries of the totalsales field of
summary.}
  var
    grape : variety;
    year : vintage;
begin
  with summary do
    for grape := cabernet to zinfandel do
      for year := 1982 to 1985 do
        totalsales[grape, year] := 0
end; {of procedure "ClearTotalSales"}


procedure SetStartDate (var currentfile : salesfile;
          var summary : summaryrecord);
{This procedure sets the start date field of summary from the first
element of currentfile.}
begin
  with summary do
    startdate := currentfile^.date
end; {of procedure "SetStartDate"}


procedure ReadNextTransaction(var currentfile : salesfile;
            var transaction : salesrecord);
{This procedure reads the next transaction from currentfile.}
begin
  read(currentfile, transaction)
end; {of procedure "ReadNextTransaction"}


procedure UpdateTotalSales (var summary : summaryrecord;
          var transaction : salesrecord);
{This procedure updates the totalsales field of summary from
currentfile.}
  var
    year : vintage;
    grape : variety;
begin
  with summary, transaction do
    for grape := cabernet to zinfandel do
      for year := 1982 to 1985 do
        totalsales[grape, year] := totalsales[grape, year] +
                                        sales[grape, year]
end; {of procedure "UpdateTotalSales"}
```

```
procedure SetEndDate (var summary : summaryrecord);
{This procedure sets the enddate field of summary from the last
element of currentfile.}
begin
  with summary do
    enddate := transaction.date
end; {of procedure "SetEndDate"}

procedure CalculateVintageTotals (var summary : summaryrecord);
{This procedure calculates the vintagetotals field of summary from the
totalsales field.}
  var
    grape : variety;
    year : vintage;
begin
  with summary do
    for year := 1982 to 1985 do
      begin
        vintagetotals[year] := 0;
          for grape := cabernet to zinfandel do
            vintagetotals[year] := vintagetotals[year] +
                                        totalsales[grape, year]
      end {of loop on "year"}
end; {of procedure "CalculateVintageTotals"}

procedure CalculateVarietyTotals (var summary : summaryrecord);
{This procedure calculates the varietytotals field of summary from the
totalsales field.}
  var
    grape : variety;
    year : vintage;
begin
  with summary do
    for grape := cabernet to zinfandel do
      begin
        varietytotals[grape] := 0;
          for year := 1982 to 1985 do
            varietytotals[grape] := varietytotals[grape] +
                                        totalsales[grape, year]
      end {of loop on "grape"}
end; {of procedure "CalculateVarietyTotals"}

procedure WriteSummary (summary : summaryrecord);
{This procedure writes out the required summary.}
  var
    year : vintage;
    grape : variety;
```

```
procedure WriteHeader (startdate, enddate : datetype);
{This procedure writes out the 5-line header of the summary.}
  var
    year : vintage;

procedure WriteDate (date : datetype);
{This procedure writes out the date in the form typified by "5 Nov
1989"}
  begin
    with date do
      begin
        write(day : 1);
        case month of
          Jan :
            write(' Jan ');
          Feb :
            write(' Feb ');
          Mar :
            write(' Mar ');
          Apr :
            write(' Apr ');
          May :
            write(' May ');
          Jun :
            write(' Jun ');
          Jul :
            write(' Jul ');
          Aug :
            write(' Aug ');
          Sep :
            write(' Sep ');
          Oct :
            write(' Oct ');
          Nov :
            write(' Nov ');
          Dec :
            write(' Dec ')
        end; {of cases on "month"}
        write(year : 1)
      end {of with "date" do}
  end; {of procedure "WriteDate"}

begin
  writeln('Bibit Magus Winery');
  write('Summary of sales from ');
  WriteDate(startdate);
  write(' to ');
  WriteDate(enddate);
```

```
    writeln;
    writeln;
    write('VARIETY' : 20);
    for year := 1982 to 1985 do
      write(year : 6);
    write('TOTAL' : 6);
    writeln;
    writeln
  end; {of procedure "WriteHeader"}

procedure WriteVarietyName (grape : variety);
{This procedure writes out the full form of the name of the grape
variety.}
begin
  case grape of
    cabernet :
      write('Cabernet Sauvignon' : 20);
    merlot :
      write('Merlot' : 20);
    pinot :
      write('Pinot Noir' : 20);
    shiraz :
      write('Shiraz' : 20);
    zinfandel :
      write('Zindanfel' : 20)
  end {of cases on "grape"}
end; {of procedure "WriteVarietyName"}

procedure WriteVintageAndGrandTotals (vintagetotals :
                                             quantitybyvintage);
{This procedure writes out the vintage totals and calculates and
writes out the grand total.}
  var
    year : vintage;
    grandtotal : natural;
  begin
    write('TOTALS' : 20);
    for year := 1982 to 1985 do
      write(vintagetotals[year] : 6);
    grandtotal := 0;
    for year := 1982 to 1985 do
      grandtotal := grandtotal + vintagetotals[year];
    write(grandtotal : 6);
    writeln
  end; {of procedure "WriteVintageAndGrandTotals"}

begin {of procedure "WriteSummary"}
  with summary do
```

```
    begin
      WriteHeader(startdate, enddate);
      for grape := cabernet to zinfandel do
        begin
          WriteVarietyName(grape);
          for year := 1982 to 1985 do
            write(totalsales[grape, year] : 6);
          write(varietytotals[grape] : 6);
          writeln
        end; {of loop on "grape"}
      writeln;
      WriteVintageAndGrandTotals(vintagetotals)
    end {of with "summary" do}
  end; {of procedure "WriteSummary"}

begin
  EstablishLinkTo(currentfile);
  ClearTotalSales(summary);
  SetStartDate(currentfile, summary);
  while not eof(currentfile) do
    begin
      ReadNextTransaction(currentfile, transaction);
      UpdateTotalSales(summary, transaction)
    end; {of loop on "eof(currentfile)"}
  SetEndDate(summary);
  CalculateVintageTotals(summary);
  CalculateVarietyTotals(summary);
  WriteSummary(summary)
end.
```

Problems

16.1 Write a procedure which will enable the user to add a new record to the current sales file. Your program must capture the data and validate it. If your computer provides graphics facilities put them to good use.

16.2 In a multichoice test several answers are supplied for each question and candidates have to choose the correct one. For example:

What are the roots of $x^2 - (a + 1/a) x + 1 = 0$?

A	a^2, 1/a
B	2a, 2/a
C	−a, −1/a
D	1, 1/a
E	a, 1/a

Terminology. The question part is called the *stem* and the answers (A to E) are called *responses* and there are usually 5 supplied. The correct response (E in this case) is called the *key* and the others are called *distractors*. The whole is called an *item*. The main advantage of these tests is that they are easy to mark because each answer is either right or wrong.

The scripts can be marked quite easily by a computer. Suppose a textfile has been created, with the first line containing the number of items, the second containing the keys for all the questions and the others containing the name and answers supplied by each candidate. Write a program which will produce:

  (i) A list of the candidates with the marks they obtained, either in alphabetical order or order of marks attained, or both.

 (ii) An analysis of the test consisting of:

  • The mean and standard deviation of the marks.

  • An item analysis giving, for each item, the key, the proportion of candidates giving each of the five responses and the proportion giving no response.

  • A measure of the reliability of the test given by:

$$r = \frac{n}{n-1} \left\{ 1 - \sum_{i=1}^{n} \frac{P_i \, Q_i}{S^2} \right\}$$

where n = total number of items,
       P_i = proportion of candidates giving the correct response to item i,
       Q_i = proportion of candidates giving the wrong response or no response to item i (i.e. $P_i + Q_i = 1$),
       S = standard deviation of the marks.

16.3 Consider a simple preferential voting system in which there are n candidates and the voters assign an order of preference to each candidate. Below is an example of a completed voting slip.

Biggs, R.   4
Famen, N.G   2
Godfrey, W.   5
Albert, V.G.   1
Williams, G.J.   6
Court, S.C.   3

For each candidate we count the number of votes in which he is ranked first. If the candidate with the most "first" votes has more than half of the total votes, he is the winner. If he does not then we eliminate the candidate who achieved fewest "first" votes and for each voter who voted for this candidate as his first choice we assign his vote to the candidate he ranked second. This process is call *redistribution*. Now if any candidate has over half of the total votes he is the winner. If, when redistributing votes, we find a vote is to be given to an eliminated candidate, then that vote is given to the next candidate in order of preference. The problem is to write a program to process votes in the preferential voting system described above. If there is more than one candidate with the lowest number of votes, then any of these may be eliminated and the votes redistributed. If at the end, two candidates tie, then the election is to be declared a *tie*.

16.4   In medium to large companies the production of an up-to-date internal telephone directory is something of a problem. Suppose we have a textfile, the lines of which contain:

- the person's name (fewer than 30 characters),
- the person's department (fewer than 30 characters),
- the person's room number,
- the person's telephone number,

which is continually kept up-to-date. Write a program which will create from this file a directory in four parts, the parts being ordered on:

- person's name
- departmental name
- room number
- telephone number.

17

Program structure and scope

So far, the development of the programs has been quite straight-forward. The variables used by any procedure are either parameters or local variables, and in the development of each procedure we create further procedures as necessary, embedding them inside the original one. A typical example is given in Fig 17.1. These procedures are called only by the enclosing procedure; and it calls only them. Well, almost. We call *read* and *write* procedures from anywhere. And, of course, the procedures inherit the types and constants from enclosing procedures or the main program. Clearly, it is time to look at the structure of programs again.

Fig 17.1 A typical program structure

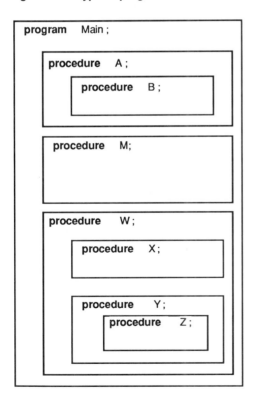

17.1 Static structure diagrams

In order to illustrate the structure of a program, we sometimes use *structure diagrams*. Fig 17.2 gives a *static structure diagram* corresponding to the schematic diagram of Fig 17.1.

Fig 17.2 Static structure diagram corresponding to Fig 17.1

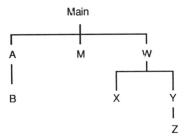

This is just a more graphic representation of the same information; three procedures, *A, M* and *W*, are *directly nested* within the main program; *B* is directly nested within *A*; and so on. All procedures are nested within the main program. Those not directly nested (*B, X, Y* and *Z*) are *indirectly nested*.

17.2 The accessibility of variables

Despite the evidence of the programs we have written, there is no rule in Pascal forcing a programmer to use local variables, but allowing him to define type-denoters and constants non-locally. We introduce the concept of a *non-local variable*. For any procedure its non-local variables are the variables of any of the enclosing procedures and those of the main program. The latter are called *global variables*. From within a procedure it is possible to access all local and non-local variables except that, if an identifier is used for more than one purpose, the most local one takes precedence. Table 17.1 shows this for Fig 17.2.

Table 17.1 The accessibility of variables

Statements within	May access variables declared in
Main	Main
A	A, Main
B	B, A, Main
M	M, Main
W	W, Main
X	X, W, Main
Y	Y, W, Main
Z	Z, Y, W, Main

With respect to the static structure diagram, we can say that a procedure *P1* may access the variables of procedure *P2* provided *P2* can be reached by moving any distance up the structure diagram. When a program has been written, as all of ours have, with the interfaces between procedures formalized completely as parameters, all of this discussion is irrelevant (since the procedures refer only to local variables and parameters) – as long as the program is correct. If, however, a variable has accidentally been left undeclared, then the rule for accessibility may associate the variable with another of the same identifier with erratic results. A common example occurs when the same identifier, *i* say, is used for the control-variables in nested procedures and is accidentally undeclared in one of them. When the procedure with the missing declaration is called, it will use as its control-variable the variable *i* of the enclosing procedure. This will cause the enclosing procedure either to miss some passes through the loop, if its control-variable is given a value by the enclosed procedure greater than its final value; or to loop forever, if its control-variable is continually reset by the enclosed procedure to a value lower than its final value. Of course, you should not be using such uninformative identifiers, but the principle remains valid.

There is another style of programming, which has now become quite unfashionable, in which procedures are not fully parameterized, especially where the interface between them is large. That is, some variables, generally data structures, are accessed non-locally, the procedures being seen as operations on those data structures. This style, in which all variables are declared in the main program, ensures their accessibility, but mitigates against robustness since any procedure can accidentally overwrite any variable.

Clearly our design strategy has been, and will continue to be, to declare as few variables as possible globally and as many as possible locally. We are led to what might be called *the principle of deepest declaration*: variables should be declared as deeply within the structure as possible. With respect to Fig 17.2, we have the situation described in Table 17.2.

During the top-down design process, these considerations are very often irrelevant – the strategy itself ensures that variables are declared at the right place. However, when we modify a program for another purpose, and where

Table 17.2   The declaration of variables

Variables accessed by	Should be declared in
B	B
A, A & B	A
M	M
X	X
Z	Z
Y, Y & Z	Y
W, W & X, W & Y, W & Z, W & Y & Z	W
Main, Main & A, etc	Main

therefore large parts of the program exist already, we need to be aware of them.

17.3 The accessibility of type-denoters and constants

Note that we cannot always use local types. Indeed most often we will have to use non-local, and even global types. All parameters, for example, have a type which, by definition, is non-local to the called procedure. And, of course, where the parameter is a structure, it is likely that local variables will be of a type describing some part of the structure. Perhaps because of this, many authors define all their types and all their constants as global quantities, the rationale being that they are easier to find and change if they are all together at the head of the program. Thus if the tax bands are altered in the Budget, the changes to the constants of the payroll program can be effected very quickly. This argument has certain merits, but we prefer the merits of the deepest declaration principle. When the Budget changes tax rates, it seems quite natural to go to the *CalculateTax* procedure to determine the changes required.

17.4 Scope

There is an inverted notion called *scope*. The scope of a variable is defined to be the set of statements in the program in which the variable can be accessed. In Pascal, the scope of any variable is the procedure in which it is declared together with all procedures nested directly or indirectly within it, except those procedures in which the identifier of the variable has been re-used.

17.5 Accessing procedures and forward references

Procedures are introduced by means of procedure declarations and the scope rules introduced earlier are relevant. There is, however, an important distinction to be made: while the variables of a procedure "belong to" that procedure, the procedure itself "belongs to" the procedure in which it is declared. Thus in Fig 17.2 *A, M* and *W* belong to the main program, and the main program can call each of them, and they can call each other. Table 17.3 summarizes the situation for the program of Fig 17.2. The asterisk indicates that the procedure must be "forward declared" as described in the next section.

Table 17.3   The accessibility of procedures

Statements within	May call procedures
Main program	A, M, W
A, B	A, B, M*,W*
M	A, M, W*
W	A, M, W, X, Y
X	A, M, W, X, Y*
Y, Z	A, M, W, X, Y, Z

From this we see that one procedure may call another in different contexts.

(i) A procedure may call any procedure nested directly within it. For example, *A* calls *B*. This is precisely why *B* was created, of course.

(ii) A procedure may call any procedure nested directly within the same procedure as it itself is directly nested. For example, *Y* calls *X*. That is *Y* was created to help *W* perform its task, which it may do directly and through *X*. There is, however, a technicality to be considered. One important characteristic of Pascal (which is concerned with the speed of its compilers) is that, with one exception to be considered in a later chapter, identifiers must be declared before they are referred to. So far the syntax of block has ensured that, and for variables there is no problem. With procedures, however, there is. Consider two procedures, which are both nested within the same procedure. If one is called by the other, then it must be declared after the first one. Normally this is no problem (as above in the case of *Y* calling *X*). This is not possible when each procedure calls the other. This is known as *indirect recursion*, the subject of the next chapter, and we must resort to the *forward reference* facility. We effectively separate the procedure-heading from the procedure-block forming its body. The heading is inserted in front of the other procedure with a dummy block, consisting of the word *forward*, and the body is given a dummy heading in which the parameters are omitted. For example if *X* called *Y*, and *Y* called *X*, we would have, in outline:

> **procedure** Y(<formal parameters>);
>   **forward**;
>
> **procedure** X(<formal parameters>);
> **begin**
>
>   .
>   .
>   Y(<actual parameters>);
>   .
>   .
>
> **end**; {of procedure "X"}
>
> **procedure** Y; {N.B. No formal parameters}
> **begin**
>
>   .
>   .
>   X(<actual parameters>);
>   .
>   .
>
> **end** {of procedure "Y"}

There are those who forward declare all their procedures, and then declare the procedures in some ordered way, often alphabetically.

(iii) A procedure may call any procedure which is directly nested within a procedure within which it is itself indirectly nested. For example, *Z* calls *X*.

(iv) A procedure may call the procedure within which it is directly nested. This is another form of indirect recursion. For example, *B* calls *A*.

(v) A procedure may call itself. This is *direct recursion*.

Pictorially with respect to the static structure diagram a procedure *P1* may call a procedure *P2* provided *P2* can be reached by moving any distance up the structure diagram, or by moving any distance up followed by a movement down of one level. From this discussion we see that the shallower the nesting of a procedure, the more accessible it is. Conversely, the more a procedure uses other procedures not nested within it, the less robust it becomes.

17.6   Dynamic structure diagrams

The discussion about the accessibility of procedures implies that a program has another structure, its dynamic structure, which indicates how its procedures actually call each other. *Dynamic structure diagrams*, such as that of Fig 17.3, represent this structure.

Fig 17.3   A dynamic structure diagram corresponding to Fig 17.1

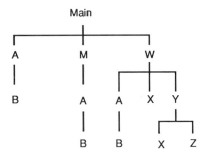

This indicates that Main calls *A*, *M* and *W*; that *A* calls *B*; that *M* calls *A* which calls *B*; that *W* calls *A*, *X* and *Y*; and so on. From the diagram we see:

- *B* is called only by *A* and so should be nested within it.

- *A* is called by both *M* and *W* and so must be placed in a mutually accessible place. Here the only such place is the main program.

- *X* is called by *W* and *Y*, and so must be placed in a mutually accessible place. The principle of deepest declaration implies that it should be *W*.

• *Y* is called only by *W* and so should be nested within it; *Z* is called only by *Y* and so should be nested within *Y*.

Thus a corresponding static structure diagram is that of Fig 17.2. Indeed, it is often by producing a dynamic structure diagram (implicitly or explicitly) that we arrive at an appropriate static diagram. Note that if all procedures are purely structural, then the static and dynamic structure diagrams are the same.

17.7   Procedure structure and top-down design

We have stressed the fact that Pascal's procedure structure is very sympathetic to the top-down design process. The components of the top-level abstract program may be coded as procedures. Further, these procedures may be developed independently, producing a hierarchy of abstract programs. Ultimately, the lower-level procedures will be coded directly.

It must be said, however, that design is an iterative process and that decisions made early may turn out later to be wrong. In this context, we may find that during the development of a procedure at the top level we nest within it a procedure to perform what seems to be a local sub-task. During the development of other procedures we may discover that the sub-task is required more generally. Then the sub-task procedure will be moved to a mutually accessible place.

17.8   Parametric procedures

Suppose we wish to write a procedure which will tabulate, over a given range of values, any given function of one natural variable which returns a natural result. Following the design strategy of Chapter 8, we first ask what are the parameters of the procedure. They are the function being tabulated and the limits of the range. Thus we must be able to have functions (and procedures) as parameters. The expanded syntax of formal-parameter-list is given in Fig 17.4.

Fig 17.4   The final syntax diagram of formal-parameter-list

formal-parameter-list

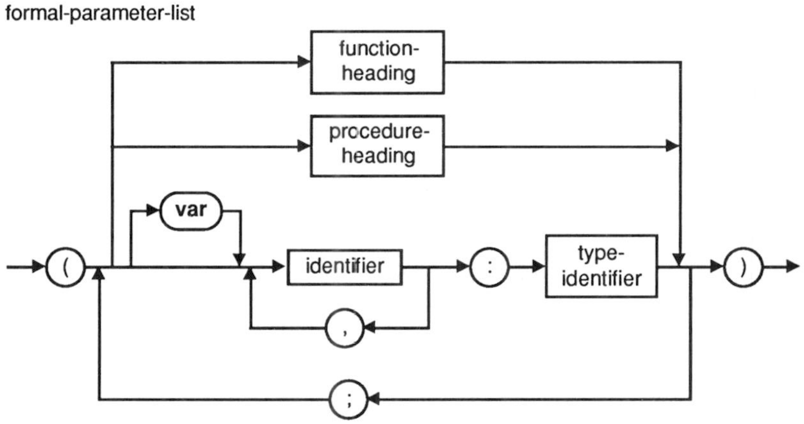

The procedure-heading is:

    procedure Tabulate (**function** F (n : natural) : natural;
           start, finish : natural)

The body is trivial, assuming that the values can be written in 4 places:

```
var
  argument : natural;
begin
  for argument := start to finish do
    writeln(argument : 3, F(argument ) : 4)
end {of procedure "Tabulate"}
```

To tabulate the integer square root function of Exercise 9.3, we use Prog 17.1.

Prog 17.1   Tabulating some integer square roots

```
program TabulateIntegerSquareRoots;
{This program tests the Tabulate procedure on IntegerSqrt.}
type
  natural = 0..maxint;

  procedure Tabulate (function F (n : natural) : natural;
                 start, finish : natural);
  {This procedure tabulates F between the start and finish limits.}
    var
      argument : natural;
  begin
    for argument := start to finish do
      writeln(argument : 3, F(argument ) : 4)
  end; {of procedure "Tabulate"}

  function IntegerSqrt (n : natural) : natural;
  {This function returns the integer square root of n.}
    var
      trial : natural;
  begin
    trial := 0;
    while sqr(trial) < n do
      trial:=trial + 1;
    IntegerSqrt := trial
  end; {of procedure "IntegerSqrt"}

begin
  Tabulate(IntegerSqrt, 1, 20)
end.
```

Note that the program includes both *Tabulate* and *IntegerSqrt*. The main program includes a single call:

Tabulate(IntegerSqrt, 1, 20)

As a more complex example, consider the problem of comparing two procedures (or functions) which are intended to calculate the same quantity. Perhaps the second is a refined version of the first, or perhaps it operates over a more restricted range. Such a procedure will invoke the two procedures with the appropriate arguments, compare the results and write out any discrepancies. We will take a particular example. In Chapter 10 we designed a program which tabulated Easter using O'Beirne's general algorithm. In Chapter 13 we introduced structures and take the opportunity now to rephrase it to use:

```
type
  datetype = record
    day : daytype;
    month : monthtype;
    year : Gregorian
  end;
```

The procedure, renamed *GeneralOBeirne* and modified to set the *day* and *month* fields of *date* to those of the Easter Day for the *year* field, is given below.

```
procedure GeneralOBeirne (var date : datetype);
{This procedure calculates the day and month of Easter.}
  var
    a, b, c, d, e, g, theta, phi, psi, i, k, lambda : natural;
begin
  with date do
    begin
      a := year mod 19;
      b := year div 100;
      c := year mod 100;
      d := b div 4;
      e := b mod 4;
      g := (8 * b + 13) div 25;
      theta := (11 * (b - d - g) - 4) div 30;
      phi := (7 * a + theta + 6) div 11;
      psi := (19 * a + (b - d - g) + 15 - phi) mod 29;
      i := c div 4;
      k := c mod 4;
      lambda := ((32 + 2 * e) + 2 * i - k - psi) mod 7;
      month := (90 + (psi + lambda)) div 25;
      day := (19 + (psi + lambda) + month) mod 32
    end
  end {of procedure "GeneralOBeirne"}
```

You may well have written a procedure for O'Beirne's restricted algorithm described in the problems section at the end of that chapter. Let us suppose you have, and that its heading is:

> **procedure** RestrictedOBeirne (**var** date : datetype)

Given that the extended algorithm is correct, we can compare the new one against it. You may have had to do it by hand earlier, now we do it by using a procedure. There are other algorithms for Easter, such as Gauss's, so we will write a general procedure for comparing Easter procedures over a given range. Its parameters are the two procedures and the range:

> **procedure** CompareEasterAlgorithms (
> **procedure** Easter1 (**var** date : datetype);
> **procedure** Easter2 (**var** date : datetype);
> start, finish : yeartype)

Within the procedure we successively set the year fields of two local *datetype* variables to all the values of the range, and invoke the Easter procedures. If the *day* and *month* fields of the two dates are different, then there is a discrepancy between the procedures and this should be written out. The procedure is given in Prog 17.2.

Prog 17.2   A procedure for comparing Easter procedures

```
procedure CompareEasterAlgorithms (
        procedure Easter1 (var date : datetype);
        procedure Easter2 (var date : datetype);
        start, finish : yeartype);
{This procedure compares the results of the procedures Easter1 and
Easter2 over a range of years, and reports any discrepancies.}
  var
    year : yeartype;
    date1, date2 : datetype;
begin
  for year := start to finish do
    begin
      date1.year := year;
      Easter1(date1);
      date2.year := year;
      Easter2(date2);
      if (date1.day <> date2.day) or
                            (date1.month <> date2.month) then
        writeln(year : 4, ' gives different answers.')
      end {of loop on "year"}
end {of procedure "CompareEasterAlgorithms"}
```

To test the new algorithm against the old, we embed the two of them in a program and call:

CompareEasterAlgorithms (GeneralOBeirne, RestrictedOBeirne,
1900, 2099)

As a final example we consider an essentially mathematical problem: the integration of a function of one real variable, *F(x)*, between the limits *a* and *b*. Clearly this function requires as parameters the function whose integral is required and the interval of integration. Given that we are going to use what is known as Simpson's Rule we will call it *Simpson*. Its heading is simply:

function Simpson (**function** F (x : real) : real;
a, b : real) : real

Simpson's Rule, whose derivation is outside the scope of this book, approximates the integral by the weighted values of the function at the limits, *a* and *b*, of the range and at the mid-point (*(a+b)/2*). More precisely the rule is:

$$\int_a^b F(x) = \frac{b-a}{3} \times \left[F(a) + 4 \times F(\frac{a+b}{2}) + F(b) \right]$$

The function follows immediately:

function Simpson (**function** F (x : real) : real;
a, b : real) : real;
begin
Simpson := (F(a) + 4 * F((a + b) / 2) + F(b)) * (b − a) / 3
end {of function "Simpson"}

To find the integral over some interval of, say, *eˣ cos x* we write a function, which, given *x*, will return the corresponding value:

function ExpCos (x : real) : real;
begin
ExpCos := exp(x) * cos(x)
end {of function "ExpCos"}

A complete program to calculate:

$$\int_0^1 e^x \cos x \, dx$$

is given in Prog 17.3.

It is important to note that the required functions such as *sin* and *cos* are usually treated specially in Pascal and cannot be used as actual parameters, so

Prog 17.3 **Evaluating an integral**

---

program TestSimpson;
{This program tests Simpson's Rule for integration.}

    function Simpson (**function** F (x : real) : real;
           a, b : real) : real;
    {This function returns the integral of F between a and b using
    Simpson's Rule.}
    begin
      Simpson := (F(a) + 4 * F((a + b) / 2) + F(b)) * (b - a) / 3
    end; {of function "Simpson"}

    function ExpCos (x : real) : real;
    {This function returns e^x cos x.}
    begin
      ExpCos := exp(x) * cos(x)
    end; {of function "ExpCos"}

begin
  write('The integral of e^x cos x from 0 to 1 is ');
  writeln(Simpson(ExpCos, 0, 1) : 1 : 2, '.')
end.

---

that to integrate, say, *cos(x)* we must first write a formal function to evaluate *cos*:

    function Cosine (x : real) : real;
    begin
      Cosine := cos(x)
    end;{of function "Cosine"}

Exercises

17.1   Draw static and dynamic structure diagrams for the payroll program as we left it.

17.2   Draw static and dynamic structure diagrams for your exam marks program.

Problems

17.1   Gauss's algorithm for determining the day, *D*, and month, *M*, on which Easter day falls given the year, *T*, is given below. (The description is from *Graded Problems in Computer Science* by McGettrick and Smith.)

If

$$k = [T/100]$$
$$a = T \text{ modulo } 19$$
$$b = T \text{ modulo } 4$$
$$c = T \text{ modulo } 7$$
$$q = [k/4]$$
$$p = [(13 + 8k)/25]$$
$$m = (15 - p + k - q) \text{ modulo } 30$$
$$d = (19a + m) \text{ modulo } 30$$
$$n = (4 + k - q) \text{ modulo } 7$$
$$e = (2b + 4c + 6d + n) \text{ modulo } 7$$

where $[x]$ is the largest integer not greater than x then D and M are determined as follows:

If $d + e \leq 9$ then $D = 22 + d + e$ and $M = 3$,
if $d = 29$ and $e = 6$ then $D = 19$ and $M = 4$,
if $d = 28$ and $e = 6$ and $a > 10$ then $D = 18$ and $M = 4$,
otherwise $D = d + e - 9$ and $M = 4$.

Write a procedure with the heading:

procedure Gauss (**var** date : datetype);

and use *CompareEasterAlgorithms* to compare this algorithm against O'Beirne's over the next 5000 years.

17.2   Write a function with the heading:

procedure Tabulate (**function** F (x : real) : real;
                numberofpoints : natural;
                start, step : real);

which will tabulate a real function, *F*, of one real argument, *x*, at *numberofpoints* points starting at *start* with increments of *step*. Use it to tabulate the function $e^x \cos x$ over the interval 0 .. 1 at 0.1 increments.

18

Recursion

In Chapter 17, we considered the accessibility of procedures and noted, without comment, that a procedure can call itself. The notion of a procedure's calling itself is called *recursion*, and is, without doubt, the most powerful facility available in Pascal.

18.1   A simple recursive function: *Factorial*

The traditional (and not terribly useful) example is the factorial function. In Chapter 8 we gave the function as:

```
function Fact (n : natural) : natural;
{This function returns the value of n!}
  var
    p, i : natural;
begin
  p := 1;
  for i := 1 to n do
    p := p * i;
  Fact := p
end {of function "Fact"}
```

This clearly reflects the definition:

$$n! = 1 \times 2 \times \ldots \times (n-1) \times n$$

That is $n!$ is the product of all the natural numbers from 1 up to n.

An alternative definition, which is often proved as a theorem when starting from the original definition, is:

$$n! = \begin{cases} 1, & n = 0 \\ n \times (n-1)!, & n > 0 \end{cases}$$

which simply defines $n!$ in terms of $(n-1)!$ except that $0!$ is defined explicitly. This form of definition maps very simply into a recursive function as shown in Prog 18.1. Note that, within the body of the function, the identifier *Fact* is used in two different ways. The means by which the programmer specifies the value of

Prog 18.1   A recursive function for factorial

---

function Fact (n : natural) : natural;
{This function returns the value of n!}
begin
  if n = 0 **then**
    Fact := 1
  else
    Fact := n * Fact(n–1)
end {of function "Fact"}

---

the function is an assignment-statement in which the left-hand side is the function-identifier. The first two appearances of *Fact* in Prog 18.1 are of this type. The other use is the recursive call. It, of course, has a parameter.

Which function is the better? Before we answer that question it is important to appreciate that we never set out to write a recursive procedure regardless of the nature of the problem. If the solution to a problem can be naturally expressed in a recursive manner then a recursive procedure is an obvious choice. In practice, the question has always been whether we can recast a recursive procedure in a non-recursive form. The reason is simply that, in the past, recursive procedures have tended on many computers to run more slowly than the non-recursive ones. Thankfully, modern compilers and machines handle recursion much more efficiently, and the drive to convert recursive procedures to iterative ones for efficiency reasons has stopped. This, at a gross level, answers the question as to which of the two versions of *Fact* is better. We can, however, be a little more precise. In both procedures there are essentially the same number of increments (or decrements), multiplications and tests. The difference is that with the recursive version there are as well the *n* procedure calls, as against *n* iterations of the loop of the non-recursive version. It is the cost of these procedure calls which has in the past counted against recursive procedures. In modern Pascal compilers, procedures are handled quite efficiently and the objections have very little weight. For *Fact* the difference is about 34% and, of course, would be smaller for more significant functions. There are even recorded instances of a recursive version being faster than the iterative equivalent.

18.2   How it works

One implication of recursion is that for each recursive activation of a function, space must be allocated on the stack beyond the previous activation. Suppose that the main program called the recursive function to set:

  f := Fact(p **div** 2 – 1)

If *p* has the value 8, then at the point at which *Fact* has just been called by the main program, the store would appear like this:

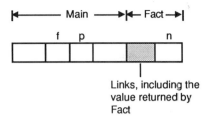

Links, including the
value returned by
Fact

just as it would do after the call of any other function. The body of *Fact* is
entered, and, because $n \neq 0$, the statement:

Fact := n * Fact(n–1)

must be obeyed. Thus *Fact* is called again to evaluate *Fact(2)*. Space is
allocated for the new activation of *Fact* beyond the existing one, and the
variables of the old one become inaccessible:

The body of *Fact* is (re)entered. The value of the new variable $n \neq 0$, so *Fact* is
called again, this time to evaluate *Fact(1)*. Space is allocated for this third
activation of *Fact* beyond the second one, and the variables of that one become
inaccessible, too:

Once again $n \neq 0$, so *Fact(0)* must be evaluated:

This time $n = 0$, so that the value of *Fact* is known explicitly as 1. This value is
stored as one of the links, and the control returned to the previous activation:

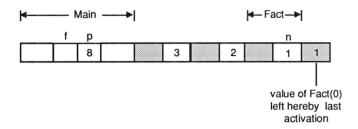

value of Fact(0)
left hereby last
activation

Now the third activation, which was trying to set :

$$Fact := n * Fact(n-1)$$

when it called itself to evaluate *Fact(0)*, can continue since it can now access *Fact(0)* from the links. It can therefore evaluate *Fact(1)* by multiplying this link value by *n*, which is 1, giving 1. It leaves this as the link and returns to the second activation:

The second activation can now complete its work, calculating *Fact(2)* as 2*1 and storing it in the links.

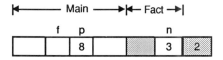

Likewise the original activation can complete its work, storing the value of *Fact(3)*, which it evaluates as 3*2 = 6 in its links:

And finally, on return to the main program, 6 is assigned to *f.*

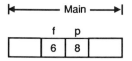

18.3   Another simple recursive function: *Greatest Common Divisor*

Consider another simple example, the *GCD* function described in Chapter 9. We gave there the following description of an algorithm for finding the GCD of natural numbers *p* and *q*:

- Divide *p* by *q* to give a remainder *r*;

- If *r* = 0 then the GCD is *q*,

- Otherwise repeat this procedure with *q* and *r* taking the place of *p* and *q*.

From this we derived the following function:

```
function GCD (p, q : natural) : natural;
{This function returns the GCD of p and q.}
  var
    r : natural;
begin
  r := p mod q;
  while r <> 0 do
    begin
      p := q;
      q := r;
      r := p mod q
    end; {of loop "while r <> 0"}
  GCD := q
end {of function "GCD"}
```

From the same description the following recursive version can equally well be written:

```
function GCD (p, q : natural) : natural;
{This function returns the GCD of p and q.}
  var
    r : natural;
begin
  r := p mod q;
  if r = 0 then
    GCD := q
  else
    GCD := GCD(q, p mod q)
end {of function "GCD"}
```

In practice we do not do it quite this way. First we rephrase the function to eliminate the variable *r*, at the cost of evaluating *p **mod** q* twice as many times:

```
function GCD (p, q : natural) : natural;
{This function returns the GCD of p and q.}
begin
  if p mod q = 0 then
    GCD := q
  else
    GCD := GCD(q, p mod q)
end {of function "GCD"}
```

Note that this function and the two earlier ones implement the definition:

$$GCD(p,q) \quad = \quad \begin{cases} q, & p \bmod q = 0 \\ GCD(q, p \bmod q), & p \bmod q > 0 \end{cases}$$

In Chapter 9 we gave the example of finding the GCD of 366 and 150. The procedure stopped when $p = 12$ and $q = 6$, when $p \bmod q$ then became 0. However, if we continue for one more iteration, $p = 6$ and $q = 0$, and we can stop when $q = 0$, in which case the GCD is p. This implements the definition:

$$GCD(p,q) \quad = \quad \begin{cases} p, & q = 0 \\ GCD(q, p \bmod q), & q > 0 \end{cases}$$

We quickly arrive at the traditional form given in Prog 18.2.

This choice of where the programmer stops the recursion, that is, of where he specifies the solution explicitly, is important. The trade-off is usually between an extra level of recursion on the one hand, and extra calculation, here of $p \bmod q$, on each recursive activation, on the other. Note, too, that the extra activation often extends the range of applicability of the function. Here Prog 18.2 gives an interpretation to *GCD(7,0)* whereas the other three do not. This difference may or may not be important.

Prog 18.2   A recursive function for GCD

```
function GCD (p, q : natural) : natural;
{This function returns the GCD of p and q.}
begin
  if q = 0 then
    GCD := p
  else
    GCD := GCD (q, p mod q)
end {of function "GCD"}
```

18.4   A third simple recursive function: *Integer Powering*

As a final example of simple recursive functions, consider a function for raising a real number to an integer power. We do not give the iterative version

(Exercise 8.4), but go straight to the recursive one. It uses the obvious definition:

$$x^n = \begin{cases} 1, & n = 0 \\ 1/x^n, & n < 0 \\ x * x^{n-1}, & n > 0 \end{cases}$$

A direct implementation is the following:

```
function Power (x : real;
          n : integer) : real;
{This function returns the value of x^n.}
begin
  if n = 0 then
    Power := 1
  else if n < 0 then
    Power := 1/Power(x, -n)
  else
    Power := x * Power(x, n-1)
end {of function "Power"}
```

This function suffers from two defects. First, at every call the actual-parameter *x* is evaluated and assigned to the formal-parameter of the same name, even though it is constant. Second, on every call *n* is tested to see if it is negative, when it can be negative only on the first call. These problems lead to inefficiency. They can, however, be overcome by using a two-level function (Prog 18.3).

Prog 18.3 A two-level function for powering

```
function Power (x : real;
          n : integer) : real;
{This function returns the value of x^n.}

  function P (k : natural) : real;
  begin
    if k = 0 then
      P := 1
    else
      P := x * P(k - 1)
  end; {of function "P"}

begin
  if n < 0 then
    Power := 1/P(-n)
  else
    Power := P(n)
end {of function "Power"}
```

The inner function, *P*, is the recursive one: it calculates x^k where *k* is a natural number, not an integer, so the continual testing of the sign of *n* is avoided. It also accesses *x* non-locally, avoiding the parameter evaluation. The function *Power* itself handles the case of negative *n*, with a consequent call of *P*.

It is important to be sensitive to the sources of inefficiency in recursion, and to avoid them. In normal iterative programming it is possible to write inefficient programs, too, but with recursion it is so much easier to make spectacular losses of efficiency with minor textual changes. The above example is not spectacular, but we will give a couple of examples later on which are. So beware!

18.5   More powerful recursive functions

The functions given earlier in this chapter could be recast easily in a non-recursive form because each broke down the problem of evaluating a function into one simpler, similar problem (recursing until the simpler problem was directly solvable). Recursion is much more powerful where a problem is expressible in terms of two or more simpler, similar problems. Sometimes only one of the smaller problems has to be solved, sometimes both. We consider the first case first. All the powering functions so far given take a time proportional to $|n|$ because they multiply 1 by *x* a total of *n* times. Such functions, which take a time proportional to the size of their arguments, are said to be *linear*. For large *n* this is slow. For example, for a 20-year mortgage with interest calculated weekly, the repayment calculation requires x^{1043} to be calculated, which needs 1043 multiplications. We can do better by a technique called "*squaring and halving*". To take an example to calculate x^{10} this technique calculates x^5 and squares it. The definition, taking into account the fact that *n* will often be odd, is:

$$x^n = \begin{cases} 1, & n = 0 \\ 1/x^{-n}, & n < 0 \\ x * x^{n/2} * x^{n/2}, & n \text{ odd} \\ x^{n/2} * x^{n/2}, & n \text{ even} \end{cases}$$

A simple change to the inner function *P* implements this as shown in Prog 18.4.

Prog 18.4   An inner function of a logarithmic function for powering

```
function P (k : natural) : real;
begin
  if k = 0 then
    P := 1
  else if odd(k) then
    P := sqr(P(k div 2)) * x
  else
    P := sqr(P(k div 2))
end {of function "P"}
```

The gain in speed is phenomenal. To calculate x^{1043} takes only 2 $\log_2 1043$, that is 22, multiplications instead of 1043! Naturally enough this function is said to be *logarithmic*. Of course, this is not attributable to recursion. You could design an iterative function with the same performance, but the formal mathematical definition mapped directly onto the recursive solution. You might like to see whether you can write an iterative version which uses this definition.

Consider again the problem of integration discussed in the last chapter, but suppose this time we have a procedure *Quadrature* with the heading:

> **procedure** Quadrature(**function** F(x : real) : real;
> a, b : real;
> **var** approximation, eps : real);

which sets *approximation* to the value of the integral and *eps* to an estimate of the relative accuracy, and that we wish to create a function which will find the integral to a relative error *e*. One algorithm is: apply *Quadrature* to the interval *a .. b*. If that does not produce the required accuracy *e*, halve the interval and apply the procedure independently to the halves, seeking an accuracy of *e/2*. (We ignore the numerical analysis problems involved.) A function is given in Prog 18.5. The power of the procedure lies in the fact that the evaluation of the integral of each of the half-intervals is quite independent, so that one of them may be halved again while the other is not. That is, the halving process adapts itself to the nature of the function being integrated.

Prog 18.5 An adaptive integration function

```
function Integral (function F (x : real) : real;
            a, b, e : real);
{This function returns the integral of F between a and b to accuracy e.}
   var
     approx, eps : real;

   procedure Quadrature (function F (x : real) : real;
               a, b : real;
               var approx, eps : real);
   begin
     {A procedure which sets approx to an approximation to the integral
     of F between a and b, and eps to its accuracy.}
   end; {of procedure "Quadrature"}

begin
   Quadrature (F, a, b, approx, eps);
   if abs(eps) <= abs(e) then
       Integral := approx
   else
       Integral := Integral(F, a, (a+b)/2, e/2) + Integral(F, (a+b)/2, b, e/2)
end {of function "Integral"}
```

18.6 A classical counter-example

We must be careful not to assume that because a problem is naturally expressed recursively, it must be coded recursively. The classical counter-example is given by the Fibonacci numbers, whose definition we gave in the exercises to Chapter 5 as:

$$Fib_n = \begin{cases} 0, & n = 0 \\ 1, & n = 1 \\ Fib_{n-1} + Fib_{n-2}, & n > 1 \end{cases}$$

The first ten Fibonacci numbers are:

0 1 1 2 3 5 8 13 21 34

The "obvious" recursive function for generating the nth Fibonacci number, given in Prog 18.6, is appallingly inefficient.

Prog 18.6   A woeful function for Fibonacci numbers

```
function Fib (n : natural) : natural;
{This is a woeful function which returns the nth Fibonacci number.}
begin
  if n in [0..1] then
    Fib := n
  else
    Fib := Fib(n−1) + Fib(n−2)
end {of function "Fib"}
```

The diagram of Fig 18.1, illustrating the calls involved in the evaluation of *F(4)*, shows why it is so bad.

Fig 18.1   The tree of function calls for *Fib(4)*

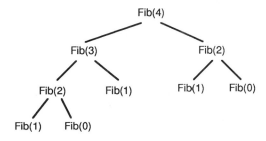

There are nine calls of *Fib* (each involving tests and many involving calculation); *Fib(1)* is evaluated three times and *Fib(0)* and *Fib(2)* twice each. In fact, to evaluate *Fib(n)* in general requires $2Fib(n+1) - 1$ calls of *Fib*. A better solution is to calculate each number once and once only, and calculate it in terms of its predecessors. This is how the standard iterative version, given in Prog 18.7, works.

Prog 18.7 The iterative version of *Fib*

```
function Fib (n : natural) : natural;
{This iterative function returns the nth Fibonacci number.}
  var
    penultimate, last, this, k : natural;
begin
  if n in [0..1] then
    Fib := n
  else
    begin
      last := 0;
      this := 1;
      for k := 2 to n do
        begin
          penultimate := last;
          last := this;
          this := penultimate + last
        end; {of loop on "k"}
      Fib := this
    end
end {of function "Fib"}
```

Many authors deduce from these two functions that recursion is inherently inefficient. Of course, it is not so. The comparison is not like with like. The recursive solution calculates one number by calculating two others directly. The iterative solution calculates a pair of numbers from the previous (overlapping) pair. We can, of course, write a recursive function which operates in the same way, and which is just as efficient. Unfortunately, Pascal's functions cannot return a pair of results, even if they were defined as a record. We have to use a procedure. This clutters up the function, requiring more statements, more **begin-end** brackettings and more local variables. See Prog 18.8. Nevertheless it is clear that it operates in the same way as the iterative version. The main function *Fib* takes care of the simple cases, calls the procedure *Get2Fibs* which calculates the nth pair, Fib_n and Fib_{n-1}, and selects Fib_n. The procedure *Get2Fibs* returns Fib_2 and Fib_1 (both 1) if $n = 2$, otherwise it calls itself to calculate the previous pair and from them trivially calculates (the new member of) the current pair.

Prog 18.8   An efficient recursive function for *Fib*

---

function Fib (n : natural) : natural;
{This linear recursive function returns the nth Fibonacci number.}
  var
    Fibn, Fibn1 : natural;

  procedure Get2Fibs (n : natural;
            var Fibn, Fibn1 : natural);
  {This procedure returns the nth and (n–1)th Fibonacci numbers.}
    var
      Fibn2 : natural;
  begin
   if n = 2 **then**
     begin
       Fibn := 1;
       Fibn1 := 1
     end
   else
     begin
       Get2Fibs (n–1, Fibn1, Fibn2);
       Fibn := Fibn1 + Fibn2
     end
  end; {of procedure "Get2Fibs"}

begin
  if n **in** [0..1] **then**
    Fib := n
  else
    begin
      Get2Fibs (n, Fibn, Fibn1);
      Fib := Fibn
    end
end {of function "Fib"}

18.7   Recursive procedures

Consider the Towers of Hanoi puzzle shown schematically below:

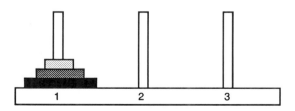

This consists of a base and three vertical pegs on one of which is placed a tower of n discs of decreasing diameter. (We have drawn only 3 discs: the real toy has 8.) The problem is to move the tower from one peg to another subject to the constraints:

- Only one disc may be moved at a time.

- No disc may ever be placed on a smaller one.

Suppose that the pegs are numbered 1 to 3, as in the picture, so that an appropriate definition would be:

type
   peg = 1..3;

Then if $n = 3$, the discs are initially on peg 1 and are to be moved to peg 2, the solution is given below:

```
Move disc 1 from 1 to 2
Move disc 2 from 1 to 3
Move disc 1 from 2 to 3
Move disc 3 from 1 to 2
Move disc 1 from 3 to 1
Move disc 2 from 3 to 2
Move disc 1 from 1 to 2
```

We want to write a procedure which will write out the moves required to move a tower of n discs from peg i to peg j. A recursive solution can be based on the observation that if we could move a tower of $n-1$ discs, we could move a tower of n discs as follows:

- move the top $n-1$ discs from peg i to the other peg

- move the bottom disc from peg i to peg j

- move the top $n-1$ discs back to peg j from the other peg

We can illustrate this for the case of a tower of 3 discs to be moved from peg 1 to peg 2 as follows:

- We move the top 2 discs from peg 1 to the other peg, peg 3. Although we are assuming this, it is easy to see how it can be done in 3 moves. (The smallest disc is moved to the peg 2, then the middle-sized disc is moved to peg 3 and finally the smallest disc is moved to peg 3.)

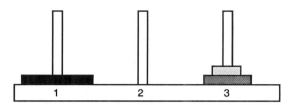

• We move the bottom disc from peg 1 to peg 2.

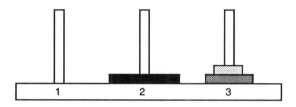

• Now we move back the tower of 2 discs from peg 3 to peg 2.

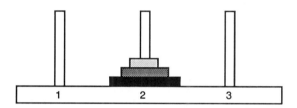

Similarly, we can move n–1 discs if we can move n–2; ... ; and we can trivially move 1 disc. This leads to the procedure of Prog 18.9.

Prog 18.9   A procedure for the Towers of Hanoi

```
procedure Hanoi (n : natural;
              p1, p2, p3 : peg);
{This procedure writes out the moves for an n-disc Hanoi problem.}
begin
  if n = 1 then
    writeln('Move disc ', n : 1, ' from ', p1 : 1, ' to ', p2 :1)
  else
    begin
      Hanoi(n–1, p1, p3, p2);
      writeln('Move disc ', n : 1, ' from ', p1 : 1, ' to ', p2 : 1);
      Hanoi(n–1, p3, p2, p1)
    end
end {of procedure "Hanoi"}
```

We give in Fig 18.2 a tree of procedure calls to which we have added branches which show the moves written out in an abbreviated form.

Fig 18.2 The tree of procedure calls for *Hanoi*

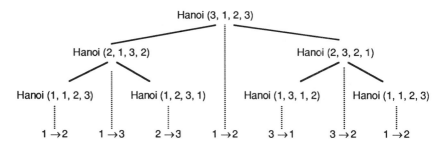

We have given as the special case, the case which is explicitly programmed, the moving of a single disc. There is an even simpler case, the moving of no discs! Prog 18.10 gives such a procedure. Note once again the choice available to the programmer. This procedure has twice as many procedure calls as the previous one, but a simpler special case. The choice between the two is difficult judging by the published versions.

Prog 18.10 An alternative procedure for the towers of Hanoi

```
procedure Hanoi (n : natural;
            p1, p2, p3 : peg);
{This procedure writes out the moves for an n-disc Hanoi problem.}
begin
  if n = 0 then
    {do nothing}
  else
    begin
      Hanoi (n–1, p1, p3, p2);
      writeln('Move disc ', n : 1, ' from ', p1 : 1, ' to ', p2 : 1);
      Hanoi (n–1, p3, p2, p1)
    end
end {of procedure "Hanoi"}
```

Notice that it is possible to define the recursive solution without ever having actually solved the problem. (It is, in fact, quite hard to use this algorithm in your head to solve the puzzle for *n* much greater than 4.) It is this characteristic which makes recursion such an effective strategy. There are many iterative solutions, of varying quality, but all rely on properties which can be established only by analysing the *solution*. We give in Prog 18.11 what appears to be the simplest one. It uses the functions *Power*, which returns the value of its first parameter raised to the value of its second, and *LS1*, which returns the position of the least significant 1 in the binary expansion of its parameter. It is based on the following observations about the solution:

- There are 2^n-1 moves for a puzzle with n discs, which we will number from 1.

- If we number the discs in order of their size starting from the smallest, then even-numbered discs always move in one direction ($1 \rightarrow 2 \rightarrow 3$ or $1 \rightarrow 3 \rightarrow 2$) and odd-numbered discs in the opposite direction.

- The position, starting from 1, of the least-significant one in the binary expansion of the move number gives the number of the disc to be moved.

- The number of the peg which is not involved in a move cycles around the pegs as if it were an even-numbered disc.

These observations are not immediately obvious even when they are given to you, and it has taken many years for this formulation to be produced.

Prog 18.11   An iterative procedure for the towers of Hanoi

```
procedure Hanoi (n : natural);
{This procedure writes out the moves for an n-disc Hanoi problem.}
   var
     moveno : natural;
     discno : disc;
   begin
    for moveno := 1 to Power(2,n) − 1 do
       begin
         discno := LS1(moveno);
         if odd(discno) then
           writeln('Move disc ', discno : 1, ' from ', (moveno − 1) mod 3 : 1,
                                              ' to ', (moveno + 1) mod 3 : 1)
         else
           writeln('Move disc ', discno : 1, ' from ', (moveno + 1) mod 3 : 1,
                                              ' to ', (moveno − 1) mod 3 : 1)
       end
   end
```

18.8   Simulating nested loops

Another situation where recursion is useful is when the program requires a variable number of nested loops. Consider the sequence of problems:

(i) Write a program which will print all 2-digit numbers which are equal to the sum of the squares of their digits. If we are happy to regard 1-digit numbers as degenerate cases of 2-digit numbers, the following program does the job.

```
program SumOfSquares;
{A program which prints all 2-digit numbers which are equal to the sum
of the squares of their digits.}
  type
    digit = 0..9;
  var
    t, u : digit;
begin
  write('This program writes out all 2-digit numbers');
  writeln('which are the sum of the squares of their digits.');
  for t := 0 to 9 do
    for u := 0 to 9 do
      if t * t + u * u = 10 * t + u then
        writeln(10 * t + u)
end.
```

(ii) Write a program which will print all 3-digit numbers which are equal to the sum of the cubes of their digits. The program below is a solution which allows 1- and 2-digit numbers as well.

```
program SumOfCubes;
{A program which prints all 3-digit numbers which are equal to the sum
of the cubes of their digits.}
  type
    digit = 0..9;
  var
    h, t, u : digit;
begin
  write('This program writes out all 3-digit numbers');
  writeln('which are the sum of the cubes of their digits.');
  for h := 0 to 9 do
    for t := 0 to 9 do
      for u := 0 to 9 do
        if h * h * h + t * t * t + u * u * u = 100 * h + 10 * t + u then
          writeln(100 * h + 10 * t + u)
end.
```

It is very similar to Prog 5.6.

(iii) Write a program which will print all the n-digit numbers which are equal to the sum of the nth powers of their digits. It is clear that if we pursue the tack used above we would require n nested loops and n variables. The n variables are no problem: we could use an array, d, to hold the digits. The n

nested loops though certainly are a problem. We can simulate these with a procedure, to be called *Choose*, which has only one loop and which calls itself recursively *n* times.

Before we do so let us look critically at *SumOfCubes*. It has a number of weaknesses, which can all be eliminated:

- The program calculates the value of say, 236, from the digits 2, 3 and 6 by multiplication and addition, when it is, of course, just one more than the previous number 235. Therefore we introduce a variable, *number*, which is initialized to 0, and incremented in the inner loop after the number is tested for the desired property.

- The program, in testing 236, calculates $2^3+3^3+6^3$ when it had done $2/3$ of the job in calculating $2^3+3^3+5^3$ during the testing of the previous number. Similarly, when testing 240 it recalculates 2^3. Therefore we introduce another variable, *sum*, which holds the sum of the cubes of the digits in the number being currently constructed. Every time another digit is chosen, the cube of that digit is added to *sum*, and after the testing is subtracted from it.

- The program calculates the cube of each digit 1000 times. Therefore we introduce an array, *cube*, which holds the cubes of all 10 digits.

This leads to the following more efficient procedure.

```
program SumOfCubes;
{A program which prints all the 3-digit numbers which are equal to the
sum of the cubes of their digits.}
  type
    natural = 0..maxint;
    digit = 0..9;
  var
    d, h, t, u : digit;
    cube : array[digit] of natural;
    sum, number : natural;
  begin
    write('This program writes out all 3-digit numbers');
    writeln('which are the sum of the cubes of their digits.');
    for d := 0 to 9 do
      cube[d] := d * d * d;
    sum := 0;
    number := 0;
    for h := 0 to 9 do
      begin
        sum := sum + cube[h];
        for t := 0 to 9 do
          begin
            sum := sum + cube[t];
```

```
for u := 0 to 9 do
   begin
      sum := sum + cube[u];
      if sum = number then
         writeln(number);
      sum := sum − cube[u];
      number := number + 1
   end;
   sum := sum − cube[t]
 end;
 sum := sum − cube[h]
end
end.
```

The loop structure is the same as in the simple version.

We said earlier that, for the n-digit case, we would simulate the n nested loops by a recursive procedure which had a single loop. The procedure has a *natural* type parameter k, which simultaneously defines the digit whose value it controls, and the depth of the loop currently being simulated. The loop control-variable is called d, for digit, since it has to count all digits, units, tens, hundreds and so on. Within the loop:

• The nth power of d is added to *sum*.

• If $k <> n$ the procedure calls itself with $k+1$ to choose the next digit; if not, then *sum* is tested against *number*, and if they are equal then the *number* is written out as a solution. *Number* is also increased in readiness for the next iteration.

• The nth power of d is subtracted from *sum*.

The main program simply calculates the nth powers of the digits, storing them in the array *power*, and, after initializing *sum* and *number* to zero, calls *Choose* with $k = 1$.

The program is given in Prog 18.12. It is quite subtle and repays careful study. It might help to note that *Choose (k+1)* really means "given the current choices of the 1st, 2nd, ..., k^{th} digits and their contribution to *sum*, make all the possible choices for the $k+1^{th}$, $k+2^{th}$, ... , n^{th} digit".

Note that this is a classical situation for the partial parameterization of procedures. The procedure *Choose* has only one parameter, k; the rest of the interface, here the *sum* and *number*, it accesses non-locally. To fully parameterize *Choose* would involve the evaluation of all the parameters for each call. The extra here would not be too burdensome but as the interface expands it would be. Note, too, that partial parameterization minimizes the space requirements.

Prog 18.12   The "sum of powers" procedure

```
program SumOfPowers;
{A program which prints all the n-digit numbers which are equal to the
sum of the nth powers of their digits.}
  const
    maxrange = 5;
  type
    natural = 0..maxint;
    digit = 0..9;
    range = 0..maxrange;
  var
    d : digit;
    i, n : range;
    power : array[digit] of natural;
    sum, number : natural;

  procedure Choose (k : range);
    var
      d : digit;
  begin
    for d := 0 to 9 do
      begin
        sum := sum + power[d];
        if k <> n then
          Choose(k + 1)
        else
          begin
            if sum = number then
              writeln(number);
            number := number + 1
          end;
        sum := sum − power[d]
      end
  end; {of procedure "Choose"}

begin
  write('This program writes out all n-digit numbers');
  writeln('which are the sum of the nth powers of their digits.');
  write('For what value of n should it run? ');
  readln(n);
  for d := 0 to 9 do
    begin
      power[d] := 1;
      for i := 1 to n do
        power[d] := power[d] * d
    end;
```

```
  sum := 0;
  number := 0;
  Choose(1)
end.
```

18.9   The power of recursion

Recursion is an extremely powerful technique, and we have been able to give only a small sample of its use here. Its area of widest applicability lies in recursive data structures, and we will give some such examples in Chapter 19. Even so, we will leave a lot unsaid. The interested reader is referred to a companion book in this series, *Recursion via Pascal*, by the first author of the current book, which covers the topic in some detail.

Exercises

18.1   Write a function with the heading:

> **function** SumOfCubes(n : natural) : natural

which returns:

$$1^3 + 2^3 + ... + n^3$$

18.2   What value is returned by each of the following functions?

(i) **function** P(**var** a : coefficient;
```
                n : natural;
                x : real) : real;
begin
  if n = 0 then
    P := a[0]
  else
    P := P(a, n–1, x) * x + a[n]
end {of function "P"}
```

(ii) **function** X(**var** a, b : arraytype;
```
                n : natural) : real;
begin
  if n = 0 then
    X := a[0]*b[0]
  else
    X := X(a, b, n–1) + a[n]*b[n]
end {of function "X"}
```

18.3   Write a third version of *Hanoi* in which the recursion stops when $n = 2$.

Problems

18.1 Write a procedure along the line of *SumOfPowers* (Prog 18.12) which
will print out all combinations of the first n integers taken r at a time.
For example, if $n = 5$ and $r = 3$, it should produce

```
1   2   3
1   2   4
1   2   5
1   3   4
1   3   5
1   4   5
2   3   4
2   3   5
2   4   5
3   4   5
```

Of course, neither the order of the combinations nor the order of the
elements in the combination is relevant, but the above sequence is one
of the easiest to produce.

18.2 A partition of an integer n is a sequence of integers whose sum is n.
Thus the partitions of 6 are:

```
6               3 1 1 1
5 1             2 2 2
4 2             2 2 1 1
4 1 1           2 1 1 1 1
3 3             1 1 1 1 1 1
3 2 1
```

Write a procedure to generate partitions. Note that, if the partitions are
generated in this order then the choices for the kth number range from
the smaller of the previous digit, on the one hand, and the difference
between n and the sum of the preceding numbers, on the other, down
to 1.

18.3 Consider an n-dimensional sphere of radius r with its centre placed at
the origin of an n-dimensional Cartesian coordinate system, and
define lattice points to be points of the Cartesian space whose co-
ordinates are all integer. Write a function with the heading:

function SpherePoints(n, r : natural) : natural

which returns the number of lattice points contained within or on the
sphere.

19

Dynamic storage

All the types we have met so far are *static*, so called since the store required for a variable is allocated at the start of the execution of the procedure. Such a variable is referred to by its identifier. *Dynamic* variables, on the other hand, are created and destroyed explicitly by statements in the program. Such a variable cannot be referred to by an identifier because of the scope rules. It is, instead, identified by means of a *pointer* variable, which is, in simple cases, a static variable. This leads to the intriguing possibility of manipulating complex data structures by manipulating pointers which point to them.

19.1   Conway's *Game of Life*

One of the more fascinating recreations to be invented in recent times is J. H. Conway's *Game of Life*. This describes the life-cycle of a colony of organisms which occupy a rectangular world composed of unit cells, each of which may either be occupied by a single organism, or be unoccupied. Two examples, of a very small world indeed, are shown below:

In practice, the world will be much larger than this with hundreds or thousands of cells, rather than 16. At regular intervals the colony moves instantaneously from one generation to the next, according to the laws:

- In an empty cell with *precisely 3* neighbours, the *birth* of an organism takes place.

- In an occupied cell with *precisely 2 or 3* neighbours, the organism *survives*.

- In an occupied cell with *fewer than 2 or more than 3* neighbours, the organism *dies*.

In the example above the colony on the right represents the next generation of the colony on the left. The organisms at the top left and bottom right corners die (of loneliness), while the other two organisms on that diagonal die from over-crowding. The two remaining organisms survive, having precisely 3 neighbours. In four other cells birth takes place. Take a minute to work out the next generation of the colony.

There are three possible fates for a given colony:

- The colony becomes *extinct.*

- The colony achieves *stability* (as the example above does).

- The colony's population *oscillates.*

Oscillation can be very difficult to detect because it may have a long period, so we ignore it, and consider a program to simulate the life of a colony over a fixed number of generations unless it previously dies or achieves stability, displaying the state of the colony at each generation. The strategy of this program is quite straightforward:

> **begin**
> Announce the purpose of the program;
>   **repeat**
>   Set up the colony to the user's specification;
>   Display the colony;
>   **repeat**
>   Move to the next generation;
>   Display the colony
>   **until** the simulation is finished;
>   Write out the reason for stopping;
>   Ask if the user wants to try another colony
>   **until** all the tries are over
> **end**.

How do we represent the colony? It is clearly a two-dimensional array whose elements are either occupied or not. If we assume that the world is square, we are lead to the definition:

> **type**
> colonytype = **array** [range, range] **of** (unoccupied, occupied);

Consider the change from one generation to the next. While it takes place "instantaneously", the program has to work serially determining the new contents of the cells one at a time. Note that, since the new occupancy of a cell depends on the original occupancy of the eight cells surrounding it, we cannot simply change the values of the elements starting from the top-left corner and moving forwards. Any such change would destroy the values required for the determination of the state of at least three cells. The simplest solution is to have two colonies, *colony* and *oldcolony*. We take the view here that they are both global:

> **var**
>   colony, oldcolony : colonytype;

We give a picture of the stack at this point which includes only the two colonies.

STACK

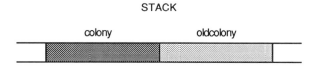

The first action of *Move to the next generation* is to copy *colony* into *oldcolony*:

> oldcolony := colony

It then creates the new generation in *colony* using *oldcolony*. (For the alternative view, that *oldcolony* should be purely local to *Move to the next generation*, see the companion book *Writing Pascal programs*, mentioned earlier.) As a result, we have the situation pictured below, where we have used a gradation of shading to indicate the age of the three generations involved.

STACK

The copying is quite expensive, especially if the world is, say, 100 cells square. (The creation of the new value of *colony* is expensive, too, but that is unavoidable.)

19.2 Pointer-variables and identified-variables

To avoid the cost of copying, we resort to *identified-variables*, which are accessed by *pointer-variables*. Consider the following definitions and declarations.

> **type**
>   colonytype = **array** [range, range] **of** (unoccupied, occupied);
>   colonyptr = ^colonytype;
> **var**
>   colony, oldcolony : colonyptr;

There is a new type, *colonyptr*, and two variables of that type. These variables have as values pointers to variables of *colonytype*. Pointer-variables reside on the stack, and occupy only a very small amount of space. The variables they point to, the identified-variables, reside on the *heap*, which is a different area of the store from the stack. If we assume that the colonies already exist on the heap, the store looks like this:

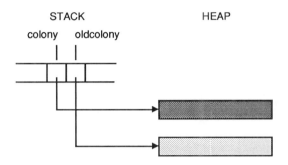

Now the first action of *Move to the next generation* is to interchange *colony* and *oldcolony* so that they point to the "other" colony:

    temp := oldcolony;
    oldcolony := colony;
    colony := temp

It then creates the new generation in *colony* using *oldcolony*. We do not give the details here, though the reader can easily fill them in. The store now looks like this:

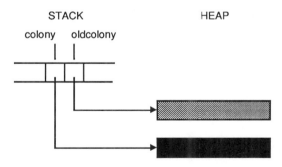

The interchange operation, since it is interchanging only pointers, is very fast, and quite independent of the size of the colonies.

The pointer-type is the last of the types of Pascal and we can now, at long last, give the complete tree of Pascal types, Fig 19.1. Note that Pascal does not treat the pointer-type as a structured-type, but gives it its own classification. As we shall see later, the pointer-variable is the means by which we may create arbitrarily complex structures. The pointer-variable is an entire-variable, of course, and there are operations appropriate to it.

Fig 19.1 The complete tree of Pascal types

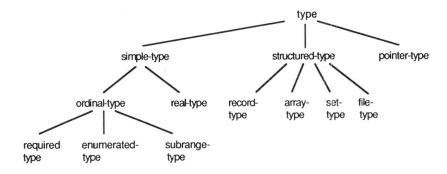

(i) We cannot read or write them. Since they refer to purely internal concepts, this is perfectly sensible.

(ii) We can assign to them. A pointer expression is very restricted. It is either a pointer-variable or **nil**. Thus we can write:

oldcolony := colony

which, by assigning the value of *colony* to *oldcolony*, makes *oldcolony* point to the same array as *colony*. **Nil** is a special pointer which identifies nothing. Once again the simplicity of the pointer expression is perfectly sensible.

(iii) We can compare them, but for equality only.

(iv) We can use them together with the indirection operator, "^", to access identified-variables. Thus *colony^* refers to the array to which *colony* is a pointer, and *colony^[r,c]* refers to the *r,c* th element of it. The identified-variable is the last of Pascal's variables, and we can give the complete tree of Pascal's variables, too. See Fig 19.2.

Note the difference between *oldcolony := colony* and *oldcolony^ := colony^*. Suppose we start with the situation used in the last section:

Fig 19.2 The complete tree of Pascal's variables

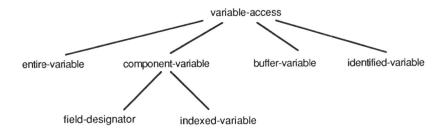

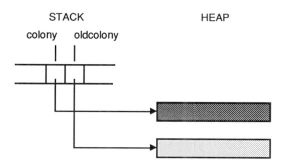

oldcolony := colony makes *oldcolony* point to the same array as *colony*. As a result the array that *oldcolony* used to point to may be quite inaccessible, a problem we will discuss shortly.

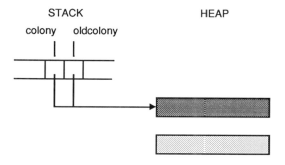

*oldcolony^ := colony^*, on the other hand, leaves the pointers unchanged, and using the full power of the array assignment, copies the value of the array itself so that *colony* and *oldcolony* point to different colonies, though these have the same value:

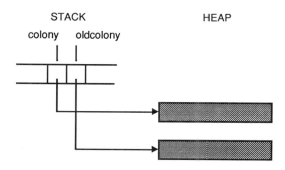

(v) We may pass them as parameters, either by value or as variables.

(vi) We may write pointer functions, i.e. functions which return pointers.

(vii) Identified-variables are created by the *required-procedure new*. This procedure has two actions. Consider the statement *new(oldcolony)*. First it creates an identified-variable of the appropriate type, here *colonytype*, on the heap, then it sets its parameter, here *oldcolony*, to point to it. It is from the parameter that the system determines the "appropriate type" of variable to create on the heap.

Note that if *oldcolony* had already been pointing to an identified-variable, as it might have in the Game of Life program if the user had wanted to try several initial colonies, that variable would have become inaccessible. To return to the example above:

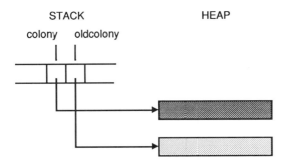

After *new(oldcolony)* we have:

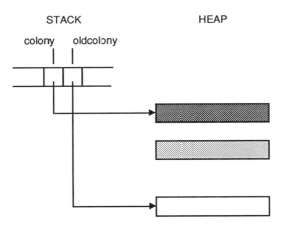

This inaccessibility can be a serious problem because in time the whole of the heap store becomes inaccessible, and so the program can run no further. How do we prevent this problem?

(viii) Identified-variables are destroyed by the required-procedure *dispose*. Thus if *dispose(oldcolony)* preceded *new(oldcolony)* in the above example, then the original value would have been destroyed before the new value was created. It is fruitful to think of the existence of a part of the Pascal system devoted to the management of the heap. When a *new* statement is obeyed, it is invoked to provide an appropriate variable from its supply of storage, and when a *dispose* statement is obeyed it recovers the variable and adds it to its supply. Clearly, if a program does a lot of *new*s, and no *dispose*s the supply will run out. For every *new* there should be an associated *dispose*.

The characteristics of static and dynamic variables are compared in Table 19.1.

Table 19.1   The characteristics of static and dynamic variables

Static variables	Dynamic variables
Live on the stack.	Live on the heap.
Are created at block entry.	Are created by a call of *new*.
Are destroyed on block exit.	Are destroyed by *dispose*.
Are accessed by "name".	Are accessed via a pointer.
Are fixed in size and shape.	Can be used to construct arbitrary structures.
	Can be left inaccessible by assigning a value to the variable pointing to them.

19.3   Interchanging rows of a matrix

The matrix is a well-known application of a two-dimensional array. If we think of it as a vector of vectors, an appropriate definition, together with two declarations, is:

```
type
  vector = array [range] of real;
  matrix = array [range] of vector;
var
  v : vector;
  m : matrix;
```

To set the elements of *m* we write, for example:

```
for i := 1 to 4 do
  for j := 1 to 4 do
    m[i][j] := i + j
```

This is, of course, nothing new! We give below a diagram of the store in which we have highlighted two rows, the *i*th and the *j*th.

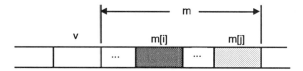

In matrix programs, it is often necessary to interchange two rows. The sequence

```
v := m[i];
m[i] := m[j];
m[j] := v
```

interchanges rows *i* and *j* of *m* leaving the store like this:

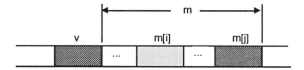

Note that this means that the *i*th row is copied twice! Alternatively, we can store the rows on the heap, and regard a matrix as a vector of pointers to vectors:

```
type
    vector = array [range] of real;
    vectorptr = ^vector;
    matrix = array [range] of vectorptr;
```

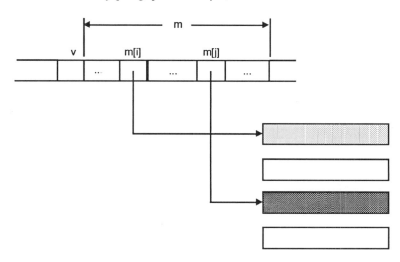

To create a matrix now, and to set its elements as before, we use a sequence:

```
for i := 1 to 4 do
  begin
    new(m[i]);
    for j := 1 to 4 do
      m[i]^[j] := i + j
  end
```

Thus within the outer loop, we create a new row, the i th, and then assign values to its elements. Note the access carefully.

m	is an array of vector pointers
m[i]	is the pointer to the i th vector
m[i]^	is the i th vector
m[i]^[j]	is the j th element of the i th vector.

To interchange rows now, we actually change the pointers:

```
v := m[i];
m[i] := m[j];
m[j] := v
```

The store now looks like this:

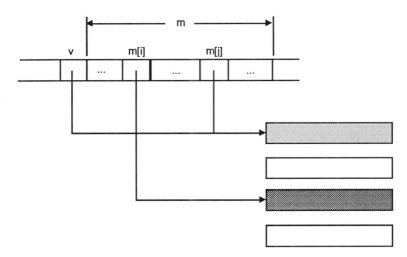

19.4   Linked lists

In many programs the relationship between items of data is as important as the data itself. It is in this situation that the use of pointers and identified-variables is most powerful. To motivate the discussion, we will consider a simple problem. Suppose we have a *sequence* of *entries*, each containing items of *information* including one field specially distinguished as a *key* field. An appropriate definition of the type of such entries is:

```
type
  entrytype = record
    key : keytype;
    information : informationtype
  end;
```

We have a sequence of these, and the problem is to insert into this sequence a new entry immediately after the entry with a given key. If the sequence is stored in an array, we have the further definitions:

```
type
  range = 1..maxsize;
  sequence = record
    size : range;
    entry : array [range] of entrytype
  end;
```

The array *entry* is assumed to be big enough to hold the new entry. If an entry with the given search key is not in the sequence, no action is to take place. For convenience, we use k in the diagrams to represent the entry with a key equal to the search key. A sequence, *seq*, might look like this in diagrammatic form:

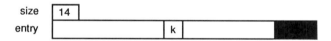

The darkly shaded area represents unused entries. The insertion process is a four-part one.

(i) Search for the entry with the key k. We assume that a variable *marker* of *range* type contains the subscript of the matching entry. We use two further shadings to distinguish the entries before (and including) and after the matching entry.

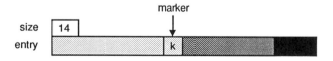

(ii) If there is a matching entry, move entries beyond it down the array, leaving space for the insertion of the new entry. This gap is unshaded below.

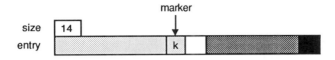

(iii) Insert the new entry into the gap. For convenience we use *n* to represent this entry.

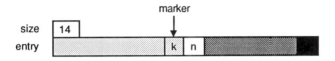

(iv) Update the size field.

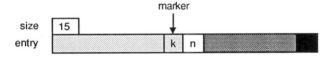

In Prog 19.1 we give a procedure which implements this, by inserting *newentry* into *seq* immediately after the entry with *searchkey* as its key.

Note that, in order to insert an entry many elements of the array have to be copied — on average half of them! If the sequence were held as a file all of the elements would have to be copied, possibly twice. The reason for this is that in both arrays and files, the successor of a component is implicit. That is, the logical successor is also the physical successor. The need to copy disappears if we make the logical successor explicit, by adding an extra field to each entry to indicate the next entry. For the last item of the sequence this field is **nil**. These structures are usually called *lists*, and the individual entries are called *nodes*, a convention we will conform to. The list itself resides on the heap, but of course there must be a variable residing on the stack to point to it. We introduce the type, *listptr*, for a pointer to a list. The variable on the stack will be of this type; so, too, will the linking field, *next*, of each node. This leads to the definition for a list structure:

```
type
  listptr = ^node;
  node = record
      entry : entrytype;
      next : listptr
    end;
```

A list, *seq*, with five entries, the third of which has a key *k*, could be drawn as shown opposite.

Prog 19.1 Inserting an entry into an array

---

procedure InsertAfter(searchkey : keytype;
       var newentry : entrytype;
       var seq : sequence);
{This procedure inserts newentry into seq immediately after the item with the given searchkey.}
  var
    marker, counter : range;
    state : (stilllooking, foundit, notthere);
begin
  with seq **do**
    begin
      {Scan over the array up to and including the key entry.}
      marker := 1;
      state := stilllooking;
      repeat
        if entry[marker].key = searchkey **then**
          state := foundit
        else if marker = size **then**
          state := notthere
        else
          marker := marker + 1
      until state **in** [notthere, foundit];
      {If the key is found, add the new entry.}
      if state = foundit **then**
        begin
          {Move the rest of the array down.}
          for counter := size **downto** marker + 1 **do**
            entry [counter + 1] := entry [counter];
          {Add the new entry in the space left.}
          entry[marker + 1] := newentry;
          {Update the size.}
          size := size + 1
        end {of "if state = foundit"}
    end {of with "seq" do}
end {of procedure "InsertAfter"}

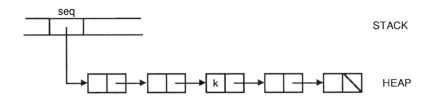

Note that there are no "unused entries": as we shall see, the list expands to include new entries as they arise. Neither is there any field holding the size of the list. Because of this, the insertion process has only three parts.

(i) Search for the entry with the key *k*. We assume that a variable *marker* of *listptr* type points to the matching entry.

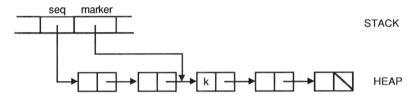

This is a straight-forward searching operation, except that the incrementing instruction for *marker* is:

      marker := marker^.next

(ii) If there is a matching entry, link in a new node to provide space for the insertion of the new entry.

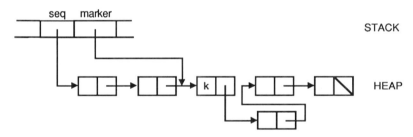

To achieve this, we require a local variable:

```
new(local);
local^ := newentry;
local^.next := marker^.next;
marker^.next := local
```

This is not shown in the diagram.

(iii) Insert the new entry. The new node is identified by *marker^.next*, which is equal to *local*. Thus:

      local^ := newentry

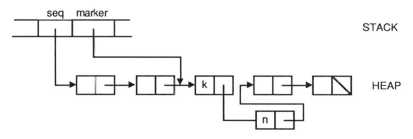

In Prog 19.2 we give a procedure which implements this.

Prog 19.2 Inserting an entry into a list

```
procedure InsertAfter (searchkey : keytype;
          var newentry : entrytype;
          seq : listptr);
{This procedure inserts newentry into seq immediately after the item
with the given searchkey.}
  var
    marker, local : listptr;
    state : (stilllooking, foundit, notthere);
begin
  {Scan along the list up to and including the key entry.}
  marker := seq;
  state := stilllooking;
  repeat
    if marker = nil then
      state := notthere
    else if marker^.entry.key = searchkey then
      state := foundit
    else
      marker := marker^.next
  until state in [notthere, foundit];
  {If the key is found, add the new entry.}
  if state = foundit then
    begin
      {Link in a new node.}
      new(local);
      local^.next := marker^.next;
      marker^.next := local;
      {Insert the new entry.}
      local^.entry := newentry
    end
end {of procedure "InsertAfter"}
```

Note that the parameter *seq* is called by value. Although the list structure can change, *seq* cannot. By definition all changes must take place after the first item, and so *seq* will always point to it.

Arrays are random-access structures, and so we can progress forwards or backwards through them. To move backwards we write:

>   marker := marker − 1

instead of:

>   marker := marker + 1

Lists, on the other hand, are asymmetric – we must always progress through them from front to rear. There is no backwards equivalent of:

>   marker := marker ^.next

Thus the procedure to insert a *newentry* into *seq* immediately before the item with the given *searchkey* is more difficult to write than the insertion procedure given earlier. It requires a *trailing pointer*, which follows along one node behind *marker*.

19.5   Recursive list-processing procedures

Notice that *listptr* is defined recursively: *listptr* is a pointer to a *node*, and a *node* contains a *listptr*-type field *next*. Consequently it is convenient to process lists recursively. We need some terminology. The *head* of a list is the first item of the list. The *tail* of a list is the list remaining when the head has been removed. With this terminology the standard strategy for processing lists is simply described:

- If the list is **nil**, then do whatever is required at the end of the list. Often, as in the *InsertAfter* procedure above, this is nothing!

- If the desired item is found in the list, then do the appropriate action on the head of the list.

- Otherwise call the procedure recursively, handing on the tail of the list.

In many situations only one of the two terminating conditions are relevant. Consider first some simple examples. To dispose a list:

- If the list is **nil**, then do nothing.

- Otherwise call the procedure recursively, handing on the tail of the list and then dispose the head.

The procedure is given in Prog 19.3.

Prog 19.3 A procedure for disposing a list

---

procedure DisposeList (l : listptr);
{This procedure disposes the list l.}
begin
  if l <> **nil then**
    begin
      DisposeList(l^.next);
      dispose(l)
    end;
end {of procedure "DisposeList"}

As a second example we give a function because the form of the reasoning is a little different. To find the size of a list, i.e. the number of elements in it:

• If the list is **nil**, then the size is 0.

• Otherwise call the procedure recursively, handing on the tail of the list and then add 1 to its size.

The function is given in Prog 19.4.

Prog 19.4 A function which returns the size of a list

---

function Size (l : listptr) : natural;
{This function returns the size of a list.}
begin
  if l = **nil then**
    Size := 0
  else
    Size := 1 + Size(l^.next)
end {of function "Size"}

Finally we return to *InsertAfter* procedure, and in Prog 19.5 give a recursive version. Note that it is a two-level procedure, with the internal (recursive) procedure doing all the work. This is another example where accessing non-local variables is both natural and efficient.

Recursion usually eliminates the need for trailing pointers. For example, suppose we wish to write a procedure *InsertBefore*, which inserts a *newitem* into *seq* before the item with the given *searchkey*. First we must notice that the parameter *seq* must be called as a variable, because it may change. If the item with the given search key is at the head of *seq* then *seq* must be changed to point to the new node into which it will be put. This is true of the inner procedure too.

Prog 19.5   Inserting an entry into a list recursively

```
procedure InsertAfter (searchkey : keytype;
                var newentry : entrytype;
                seq : listptr);
{This procedure inserts newentry into seq immediately after the item
with the given searchkey.}

    procedure Insert(marker : listptr);
    {This procedure is the recursive body of InsertAfter.}
      var
        local : listptr;
      begin
        if marker = nil then
          {Do nothing.}
        else if marker^.entry.key = searchkey then
          begin
            new(local);
            local^.next := marker^.next;
            marker^.next := local;
            local^.entry := newentry
          end {of adding the new entry}
        else
          Insert (marker^.next)
      end; {of procedure "Insert"}

begin
    Insert (seq)
end {of procedure "InsertAfter"}
```

Apart from this the changes are to the insertion sequence only. The sequence
from Prog 19.5 becomes:

```
begin
    new(local);
    local^.next := marker;
    marker := local;
    marker^ := newentry
end {of adding the new entry}
```

19.6   Binary trees

In the lists above, each node had only one (immediate) successor. In
some situations it is convenient to have two. This leads to the notion of a *binary
tree*. Such structures arise in a number of situations, including the processing of
arithmetic expressions. Fig 19.3 shows an arithmetic expression (which may

Fig 19.3   A binary tree holding an expression

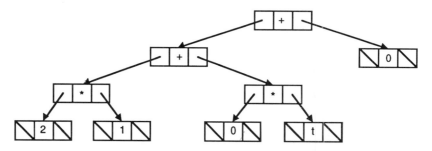

have resulted from the analytic differentiation of *2t+3* with respect to *t*).

We interpret this, starting from the top, as follows. The main (least binding) operator is the + in the item field of the top node. Its two operands are held in the left and right sub-trees. Here the first is a tree while the second is 0. We interpret the left sub-tree similarly. Its operator is + and its two operands are held in the left and right sub-trees.   Proceeding this way, we see that the expression is *2*1 + 0*t + 0*.

We wish to simplify it algebraically (rather than arithmetically) to give just *2*. For simplicity we restrict the operators to + and *. An appropriate definition is:

```
type
    treeptr = ^node;
    node = record
        left : treeptr;
        item : char;
        right : treeptr
    end;
```

To simplify a tree representing an expression, we first of all simplify the left and right sub-trees and then apply the rules of identity:

$$t + 0 \; = \; 0 + t \; = \; t$$
$$t * 1 \; = \; 1 * t \; = \; t$$
$$t * 0 \; = \; 0 * t \; = \; 0$$

Of course, if a sub-tree does not have + or * as its item, then it will have an operand and hence is as simple as it can get. The procedure is given as Prog 19.6.

It is clear that the size of the tree contracts during simplification (just as it expanded during the differentiation) and so an important part of the procedure is concerned with disposing of unwanted variables.

Prog 19.6   An expression simplification procedure

```
procedure Simplify(var t : treeptr);
{This procedure simplifies trees holding expressions, using the
identities of algebra.}
   var temp : treeptr;
begin
  if t^.item in ['+','*'] then
    begin
     Simplify(t^.left);
     Simplify(t^.right);
     if (t^.item = '+') and (t^.right^.item = '0')
        or (t^.item = '*') and (t^.right^.item = '1')
        or (t^.item = '*') and (t^.left^.item = '0') then
       begin
        {x+0=x, x*1=x, 0*x=0}
        temp := t;
        t := t^.left;
        temp^.left := nil;
        DisposeTree(temp)
       end
     else if (t^.item = '+') and (t^.left^.item = '0')
        or (t^.item = '*') and (t^.left^.item = '1')
        or (t^.item = '*') and (t^.right^.item = '0') then
       begin
        {0+x=x, 1*x=x, x*0=0}
        temp := t;
        t := t^.right;
        temp^.right := nil;
        DisposeTree(temp)
       end
    end
end {of procedure "Simplify"}
```

19.7   Managing the heap

Provided *new* and *dispose* operate universally as described above, the heap storage is used to maximum efficiency. However, in general, the heap may be required to handle variables of a number of different types and this is more difficult to handle with efficiency. Consequently the Pascal Standard allows an implementation to ignore calls for *dispose*. In this situation, if our program has structures which expand and contract frequently, the heap will soon become exhausted; and we must manage the heap ourselves.

For simplicity, let us assume that we require dynamic variables of only one type, say *node*, which are identified by variables of *listptr* type. The simplest technique consists of maintaining what is called a *free list*, a list containing all the dynamic variables that have been freed (and which would otherwise have been disposed). Thus we have the declaration:

var
    free : nodeptr;

and an initialization:

    free := **nil**

We simulate *dispose* by *SimulateDispose*, which simply adds the node to *free*, and *new* by a procedure *SimulateNew* which takes a word from *free* if *free* is contains some nodes, calling *new* only if *free* is **nil**. These are given in Prog 19.7.

Prog 19.7 Simulating *new* and *dispose*

```
procedure SimulateDispose (pointer : nodeptr);
begin
  pointer^.next := free;
  free := pointer
end {of procedure "SimulateDispose"}

procedure SimulateNew (var pointer : nodeptr);
begin
  if free = nil then
    new(pointer)
  else
    begin
      pointer := free;
      free := free^.next
    end
end {of procedure "SimulateNew"}
```

If we require dynamic variables of more than one type (say a list and a tree) then we would require separate lists for each, which might have serious effects on the efficiency of store usage.

19.8 The power of the pointer

The power of the pointer lies in flexibility; we are able to build data structures of great richness and complexity. As well as linear lists and trees, we can build arbitrary finite graphs. Study of such structures and of their relation to important abstract data structures such as the stack and the queue form an essential component of a second course in programming.

Exercises

19.1   Write a procedure for inserting an item into a list before one with a specified key.

19.2   Write a procedure for deleting from a list the item with a specified key.

19.3   Consider the simplification procedure of Prog 19.6. The if-statement after the two recursive calls has two non-null alternatives, the sequences of code for which are closely related. One can be got from the other by consistently replacing *left* with *right* and *right* with *left*. How can this similarity be capitalized on to reduce the size of the procedure?

Problems

19.1   Write a procedure for differentiating an expression stored as in Fig 19.3. Allow the operators +, * and use the formulae:

$$\frac{d}{dt}(u + v) = \frac{du}{dt} + \frac{dv}{dt}$$

$$\frac{d}{dt}(u * v) = u\frac{dv}{dt} + v\frac{du}{dt}$$

$$\frac{dt}{dt} = 1$$

$$\frac{dk}{dt} = 0$$

19.2   In number theory it is important to be able to compute with integers of very large magnitude, which means that the normal integer facilities are inadequate. Since the integers are likely to vary in magnitude, dynamic storage has obvious attractions. We can store such integers by expressing them to a large base (approximately *maxint*) and holding the individual "digits" as items in a list structure. Adding two such numbers, for example, involves adding the individual "digits" making the appropriate arrangements for "carry". Design the appropriate list structure and write functions for performing the four basic arithmetic operations and the six relational operations.

19.3   A collection of papers published in a journal will usually have an associated index. Provided the titles of the papers accurately reflect the subject of the papers, an index can be produced from key words in the titles. The problem is to write a program to produce this index which should, of course, be in alphabetical order. Clearly words such as *a*, *an, the, of, in* and so on are not keywords and should not appear in the index. Assume a text file exists containing the title, together with the name of the author (or authors) and a reference to the issue and the page numbers of the issue. The layout of the output should be carefully considered. One approach is to print the keyword on the left of the line, and then write the title next to it, replacing the keyword in the title by an asterisk. Another is to rotate the title so that the keyword appears at a standard position near the middle of the page.

Appendix 1

The syntax of Pascal

This appendix gives the complete set of syntax diagrams for Pascal. The following notes might be useful.

- All identifiers have the same (fairly trivial) syntax. They occur in two contexts: the defining context (within the definitions and declarations) and the applied context (within the statement part). The defining context classifies an identifier as, say, a constant-identifier or a type-identifier or a procedure-identifier. In the syntax of the defining context we simply use the word *identifier*. In the applied context we use a qualified form such as the three given above, as appropriate.

- A similar situation applies to variables though, because of the notion of entire-variable and component-variable, the syntax is far from trivial; and there is no notion of defining context. In the applied context we usually use a qualified form which specifies its type.

- The syntax of all function-designators is the same (and fairly simple) and in the applied context, we usually use a qualified form which specifies its type. The same is true for blocks.

- On the other hand, assignment-statements, expressions, relations and constants tend to have different syntax depending on their type. Each of these is given. We leave implicit the general notions of assignment-statement, expression, relation and constant, which are clearly defined in terms of the more specific constructs.

- Wherever an ordinal variable, function-designator or expression is referred to, it is understood that a variable, function-designator or expression of any of its sub-ranges is allowable.

We have omitted all references to labels and go-to statements, and to conformant-array-parameters, which are not covered in the text.

program

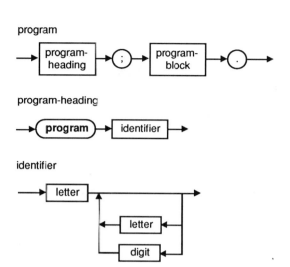

program-heading

identifier

* block

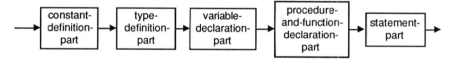

constant-definition-part

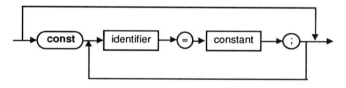

constant

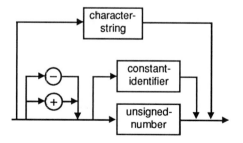

unsigned-number

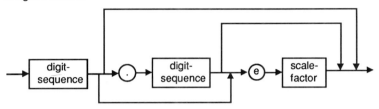

digit-sequence

scale-factor

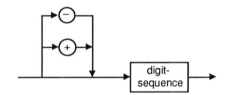

character-string

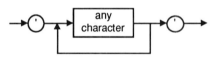

type-definition-part

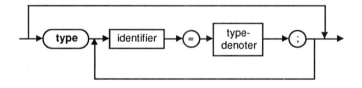

type-denoter

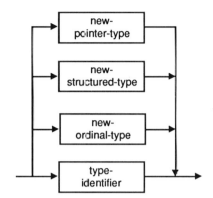

new-ordinal-type

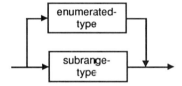

subrange-type

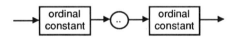

enumerated-type

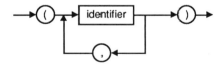

new-structured-type

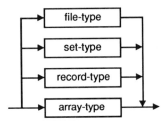

array-type

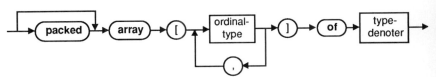

record-type

field-list

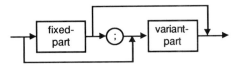

fixed-part

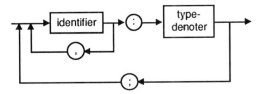

set-type

file-type

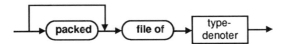

new-pointer-type

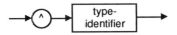

variable-declaration-part

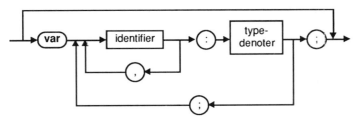

procedure-and-function-declaration-part

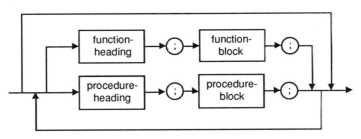

procedure-heading

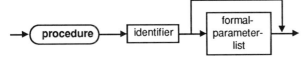

function-heading

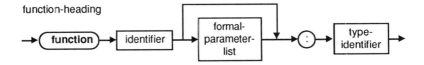

formal-parameter-list

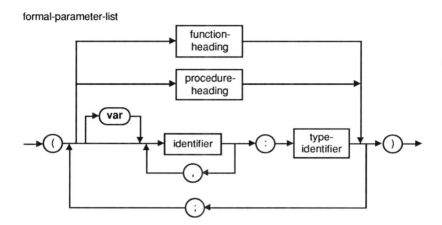

statement-part

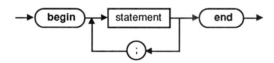

statement

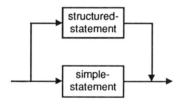

simple-statement

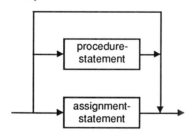

assignment-statement

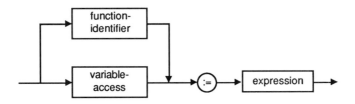

variable-access

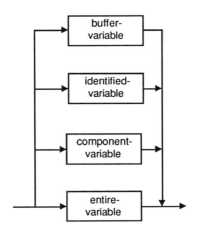

entire-variable

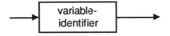

component-variable

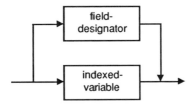

indexed-variable

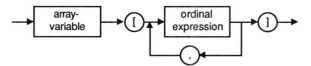

field-designator

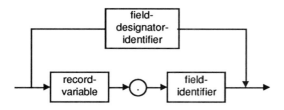

identified-variable

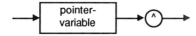

buffer-variable

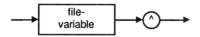

arithmetic
expression

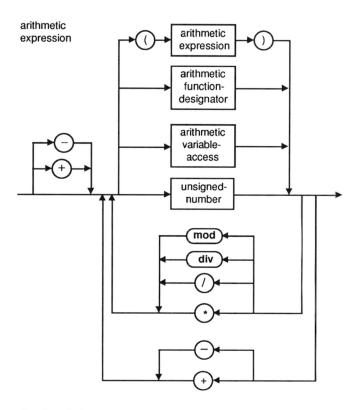

function-designator

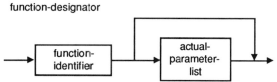

actual-parameter-list

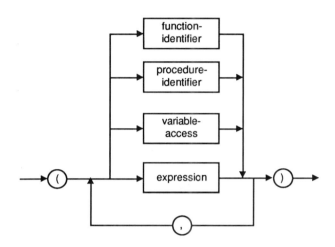

Boolean-expression

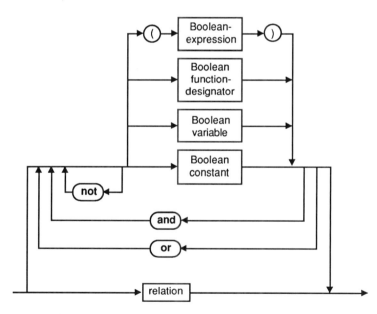

arithmetic relation

Boolean relation

set-relation

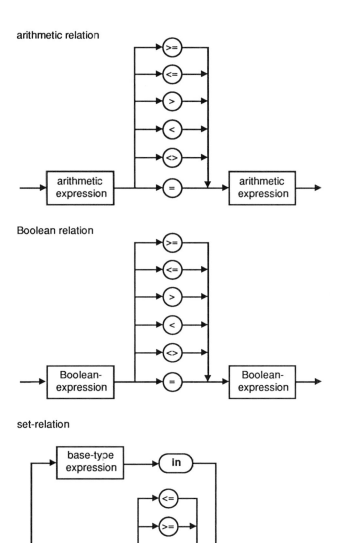

set-expression

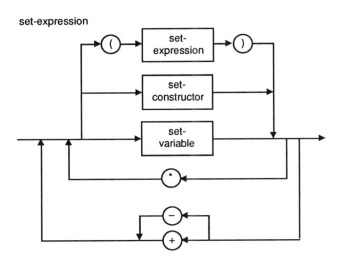

set-constructor

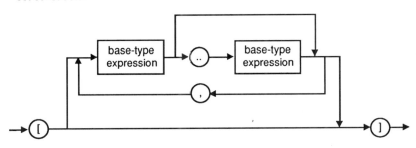

procedure-statement

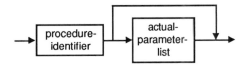

structured-statement

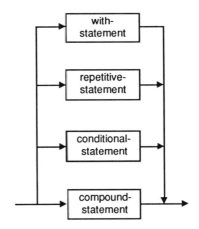

compound-statement

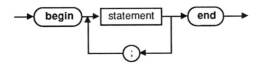

conditional-statement

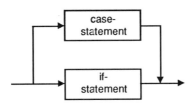

if-statement

case-statement

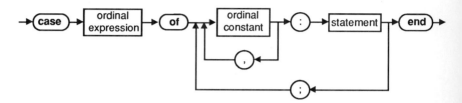

repetitive-statement

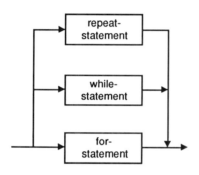

for-statement

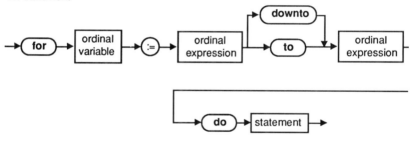

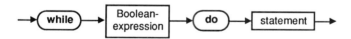

while-statement

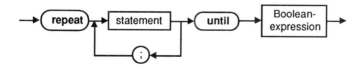

repeat-statement

Appendix 2

Reserved words, required-identifiers and operators

2.1 Reserved words

and	end	mod	repeat
array	file	nil	set
begin	for	not	then
case	forward	of	to
const	function	or	type
div	goto	packed	until
do	if	procedure	var
downto	in	program	while
else	label	record	with

2.2 Required-identifiers

(i) **Constants**:   maxint, true, false

(ii) **Types**:   integer, real, Boolean, char, text

(iii) **Files**:   input, output

(iv) **Functions**:

Name	Argument type	Function type	Comment
abs	integer	integer	The absolute value of
	real	real	the argument
arctan	real	real	Inverse tangent (in radians)
chr	integer	char	The character of the given ordinal number
cos	real	real	Cosine: the argument is in radians
eof	file	Boolean	Indicates end of file
eoln	text	Boolean	Indicates end of line
exp	real	real	Antilog (exponentiation)

ln	real	real	Natural logarithm ($\log_e$)
odd	integer	Boolean	True if the argument is odd; false otherwise
ord	ordinal	integer	Ordinal number of the argument
pred	ordinal	ordinal	Predecessor of the argument
round	real	integer	Rounded value of the argument: round(x) = trunc(x + 0.5) if $x \geq 0$ and trunc(x − 0.5) if x < 0
sin	real	real	Sine: the argument is in radians
sqr	integer real	integer real	The square of the argument
sqrt	real	real	The square root of the argument
succ	ordinal	ordinal	The successor of the argument
trunc	real	integer	Truncated value of the argument: trunc(x) = greatest integer $\leq$ x, if $x \geq 0$ and least integer > x if x < 0

(v) Procedures

Name and parameters	Description
dispose(p)	Returns to the heap the dynamic variable pointed to by *p*.
dispose(p, tag_1, tag_2... tag_n)	Returns the variable pointed to by *p*, with tag fields tag_1, tag_2 ... tag_n, to the heap.
get(f)	Advances the file *f* to the next component and assigns the value of the component to f^, the file buffer variable.
new(p)	Creates a dynamic variable (i.e. allocates storage from the heap) and assigns to *p* a pointer to the variable.
pack(u, offset, p)	Copies elements from position *offset* of array *u* to the packed array *p* starting at the first location. The number of elements copied is given by the size of *p*.
page(f)	Causes the printer to skip to the top of a new page before printing the next line of the textfile *f*.
put(f)	Appends the value of the file buffer variable, *f*^, to the file *f*.
read(f, var_1, var_2...var_n)	Reads values from the textfile *f* into the variables var_1,var_2... var_n. The variables must be of integer-type, real-type or char-type. If *f* is omitted the file *input* is assumed.
readln(f,var_1, var_2...var_n)	Reads values (of integer-type, real-type or char-type) from the textfile *f* and skips the remainder of

	the current line. If *f* is omitted the file *input* is assumed.
reset(f)	Resets the buffer variable to the start of the file for reading (i.e. *f^* is assigned the value of the first component of the file).
rewrite(f)	Resets the file so that it can be written to. Should *f* have previously been written, the old file will disappear.
unpack(p, u, offset)	Copies the elements from the first location of the packed array *p* to the array *u* starting at position *offset*.
write(f,var$_1$, var$_2$. . . var$_n$)	Writes the character strings representing the values of the variable *var$_1$*, *var$_2$*. . . *var$_n$* to the textfile *f*. The value to be written may be of integer-type, real-type, char-type, Boolean-type or string-type. If *f* is omitted the file *output* is assumed
writeln(f,var$_1$, var$_2$. . . var$_n$)	Writes the values of the variables to the textfile f and terminates the current line (so that the next write-statement begins on a new line).

NOTE: *write* and *writeln* parameters may also include field width specifications.

2.3   Operators

Operator	Operation	Type of operand(s)	Type of result
:=	Assignment	Any type except a file-type	
+	Addition	*integer* or *real*	*integer* if both operands *integer*, otherwise *real*
	Unary plus	*integer* or *real*	Same as that of the operand
	Set union	A set-type	Same set-type as that of the operands
−	Subtraction	*integer* or *real*	*integer* if both operands *integer*, otherwise *real*
	Unary minus	*integer* or *real*	Same as that of the operand
	Set difference	A set-type	Same set-type as that of the operands
*	Multiplication	*integer* or *real*	*integer* if both operands *integer*, otherwise *real*
	Set intersection	A set-type	Same set-type as that of the operands

div	Integer division	*integer*	*integer*
/	Real division	*integer* or *real*	*real*
mod	Modulus	*integer*	*integer*
not	Logical negation	*Boolean*	*Boolean*
or	Disjunction	*Boolean*	*Boolean*
and	Conjunction	*Boolean*	*Boolean*
=	Equality	A simple-,string-, set- or pointer- type	*Boolean*
<>	Inequality	A simple-,string-, set- or pointer- type	*Boolean*
<	Less than	A simple- or string-type	*Boolean*
>	Greater than	A simple- or string-type	*Boolean*
<=	Less than or equal to	A simple- or string-type	*Boolean*
	Set inclusion	A set-type	*Boolean*
>=	Greater than or equal to	A simple- or string-type	*Boolean*
	Set inclusion	A set-type	*Boolean*
in	Set membership	First operand is any ordinal variable, second operand is a set whose base type is that of the first operand	*Boolean*

Solutions to exercises

Chapter 1

1.1
```
program Menu;
begin
  writeln('          MENU');
  writeln;
  writeln;
  writeln('       Bisque de Homard');
  writeln;
  writeln('       Fried Camembert');
  writeln;
  writeln('Roast Beef and Yorkshire Pudding');
  writeln;
  writeln('          SacherTorte');
  writeln;
  writeln('          Coffee');
  writeln
end.
```

1.2
```
program Bill;
var
  callout, rate, hours, total : real;
begin
  writeln('This program calculates your total bill.');
  write('What is the call-out fee? ');
  readln(callout);
  write('What is the hourly rate? ');
  readln(rate);
  write('How many hours did it take? ');
  readln(hours);
  total := callout + hours * rate;
  writeln('The total bill is ', total : 6 : 2, '.')
end.
```

Chapter 2

2.1   (i)   s := n * (n+1) div 2

(ii) d := sqrt(sqr(E1–E2) + sqr(N1–N2))
(iii) c := sqrt(sqr(a) + sqr(b) – 2 * a * b * cos(bigC))

2.2 (i) V := 3.14159 * sqr(r)
(ii) V := 3.14159 * sqr(r) * h / 3
(iii) V := 4 / 3 * 3.14159 * r * sqr(r)

2.3   round(100 * x) / 100

2.4 (i) **M div** 2 * 2
(ii) (M–1) **div** 2 * 2 + 1

Chapter 3

3.1   Yes, it is.
3.2   Yes, no, no, yes
3.3   string = operand operand operator.
operand = string | variable.
variable = "a" | " b" | "c" | "d".
operator = "+" | "–" | "*" | "/".

Chapter 4

4.1 (i) p <= 0
(ii) (number **mod** 5 <> 0) **and** (number **mod** 7 <> 0)
(iii) (sqr(a) + sqr(b) = sqr(c)) **or** (sqr(a) + sqr(c) = sqr(b))
or (sqr(b) + sqr(c) = sqr(a))

4.2   **case** month **of**
1, 3, 5, 7, 8, 10, 12:
days := 31;
4, 6, 9, 11:
days := 30;
2:
if (year **mod** 4 = 0) **and** (year **mod** 100 <> 0)
or (year **mod** 400 = 0) **then**

days := 29
else
days := 28
end {of cases on "month"}

4.3   **case** month **of**
1:
monthstart := 0;
2:
monthstart := 31;
3:
monthstart := 59;

```
4:
   monthstart := 90;
5:
   monthstart := 120;
6:
   monthstart := 151;
7:
   monthstart := 181;
8:
   monthstart := 212;
9:
   monthstart := 243;
10:
   monthstart := 273;
11:
   monthstart := 304;
12:
   monthstart := 334
end{of cases on "month"};
daynumber := monthstart + day;
if (month in [3..12]) and ((year mod 4 = 0) and (year mod 100 <> 0) or
                                              (year mod 400 = 0)) then
   daynumber := daynumber + 1
```

4.4   (i)   n **in** [1, 3, 5, 7, 9]
     (ii)   n **in** [2, 3, 5, 7]
    (iii)   n **in** [1, 4, 9]

4.5

```
program ConcessionalExam;
var
   x, y, z : 0..100;
begin
   write('This program will determine the result of a ');
   writeln('concessional exam.');
   write('What are the student''s marks? ');
   readln(x, y, z);
   if (x >= 50) and (y >= 50) and (z >= 50) then
      writeln('The student passes with a mark of ', (x + y + z) / 3 : 1 : 1, '.')
   else if (x >= 40) and (y >= 50) and (z >= 50) and (x+y+z>=165) then
      writeln('The student passes with a mark of ', (x + y + z) / 3 : 1 : 1, '.')
   else if (x >= 50) and (y >= 40) and (z >= 50) and (x+y+z>=165) then
      writeln('The student passes with a mark of ', (x + y + z) / 3 : 1 : 1, '.')
   else if (x >= 50) and (y >= 50) and (z >= 40) and (x+y+z>=165) then
      writeln('The student passes with a mark of ', (x + y + z) / 3 : 1 : 1, '.')
   else
      writeln('The student fails.')
end.
```

Chapter 5

5.1
```
last := 0;
Fib := 1;
for k := 2 to n do
  begin
    penultimate := last;
    last := Fib;
    Fib := penultimate + last
  end {of loop on "k"}
```

5.2 (i)
```
sigma := 0;
for count := 1 to n do
  sigma := sigma + count * sqr(count)
```

(ii)
```
fact := 1;
sigma := 0;
for count := 1 to n do
  begin
    fact := fact * count;
    sigma := sigma + fact
  end {of loop on "count"}
```

5.3
```
program SumOfCubes;
{This program solves the "sum-cube-digits" problem.}
var
  number : 0..999;
  h, t, u : 0 .. 9;
begin
  writeln('The following 3-digit numbers are all equal to');
  writeln('the sum of the cubes of their digits.');
  for number := 100 to 999 do
    begin
      h := number div 100;
      t := number div 10 mod 10;
      u := number mod 10;
      if number = h * h * h + t * t * t + u * u * u then
        write(number : 5)
    end; {of loop on "number"}
end.
```

5.4
```
program xxyyPerfectsquares;
{This program writes out all 4-digit numbers of the form
xxyy which are perfect squares.}
  var
    x, y : 0..9;
    number : 0..9999;
begin
```

```
writeln('The following 4-digit numbers of the form xxyy');
writeln('are perfect squares.');
for x := 0 to 9 do
  for y := 0 to 9 do
    begin
      number := 1100*x + 11*y;
      if sqr(round(sqrt(number))) = number then
        write(number : 6)
    end {of loops on "x" and "y"}
end.
```

5.5   (i) sigma := sqr(n)
     (ii) sigma := n * (n + 1) * (2 * n + 1) / 6

Chapter 6

6.1   **program** SummerTime;

```
{This program produces a table of Summer-time dates - assuming it
to be from the last Sunday in March to the last Sunday in October.}
var
  tablesize : 1..maxint;
  firstyear, year : 1583..maxint;
  startday, endday : 25..31;
begin
  writeln('This program writes out a table of Summer-time dates.');
  write('For how many years do you want it to run? ');
  readln(tablesize);
  write('At what year should it start? ');
  readln(firstyear);
  writeln;
  writeln('YEAR' : 4, ' ' : 3, 'START' : 6, ' ' : 3, 'END' : 6);
  writeln;
  for year := firstyear to firstyear + tablesize − 1 do
    begin
      write(year : 4);
      startday := 31 − (year + year div 4 − year div 100 + year div 400
                                                                + 5) mod 7;
      write(' ' : 3, startday : 2, ' MAR');
      endday := 31 − (year + year div 4 − year div 100 + year div 400
                                                                + 2) mod 7;
      write(' ' : 3, endday : 2, ' OCT');
      writeln
    end; {of loop on "year"}
  writeln;
  writeln('SOME SUMMER-TIME DATES');
  writeln('=====================')
end.
```

Chapter 7

7.1   **type**
(i)   dayofweek = (Sun, Mon, Tue, Wed, Thu, Fri, Sat)
(ii)   subject = (SoftwareEngineering, Networks, Graphics, Database,
                Robotics, ComputerVision, ExpertSystems)
(iii)   suit = (Clubs, Diamonds, Hearts, Spades)
(iv)   punctuation = (fullstop, comma, semicolon, colon, questionmark,
                exclamationmark, invertedcommas, leftbracket, rightbracket, dash)

7.2   **program** SummerTime;
{A program which produces a table of Summer-time dates.}
```
   const
      yearwidth = 4;
      datewidth = 6;
      gap = ' ';
   type
      posint = 1 .. maxint;
      Gregorian = 1583..maxint;
   var
      tablesize : posint;
      firstyear, year : Gregorian;
      startday : 25..31;
      endday : 1..7;
begin
   writeln('This program writes out a table of Summer-time dates.');
   write('For how many years do you want it to run? ');
   readln(tablesize);
   write('At what year should it start? ');
   readln(firstyear);
   writeln;
   writeln('YEAR' : yearwidth, gap, 'END' : datewidth, gap, 'START' :
                                                      datewidth);
   writeln;
   for year := firstyear to firstyear + tablesize − 1 do
      begin
         write(year : yearwidth);
         endday := 7 − (year + year div 4 − year div 100 + year div 400
                                             + 2) mod 7;
         write(gap, endday : 2, ' MAR': datewidth − 2);
         startday := 31 − (year + year div 4 − year div 100 + year div 400
                                             + 2) mod 7;
         write(gap, startday : 2, ' OCT': datewidth − 2);
         writeln
      end; {of loop on "year"}
   writeln;
   writeln('SOME SUMMER-TIME DATES');
```

```
      writeln('=====================')
   end.
```

Chapter 8

8.1
```
      procedure CalculateGross (var gross : real;
               rate, hours : real);
        const
          normal = 37.5;
        begin
         gross := hours * rate;
         if hours > normal then
           gross := gross + (hours - normal) * 0.5 * rate;
        end {of procedure "CalculateGross"}
```

8.2
```
      procedure PolarToCart(r, theta : real;
                  var x, y : real);
      {This procedure returns the Cartesian coordinates of a
      point (x, y) given the polar coordinates (r, theta).}
      begin
        x := r * cos(theta);
        y := r * sin(theta)
      end {of procedure "PolarToCart"}
```

8.3
```
      procedure BlankLines(n : natural);
      {This procedure leaves n blank lines on output.}
        var
          i : natural;
        begin
         for i := 1 to n+1 do
           writeln
        end {of procedure "BlankLines"}
```

8.4
```
      function Power (x : real;
               n : integer) : real;
      {This function returns the value of x^n.}
        var
          p : real;
          i : integer;
        begin
         p := 1;
         for i := 1 to abs(n) do
           p := p * x;
         if n >= 0 then
           Power := p
         else
           Power := 1/p
        end {of function "Power"}
```

8.5

```
function Median(a, b, c : natural) : natural;
{This function returns the median (middle value) of a, b, c.}
begin
  if (a >= b) and (a >=c) then
    if b >= c then
      Median := b
    else
      Median := c
  else if (b >= a) and (b >=c) then
    if a > c then
      Median := a
    else
      Median := c
  else {if (c >= a) and (c >=b) then}
    if a > b then
      Median := a
    else
      Median := b
end {of function "Median"}
```

Chapter 9

9.1

```
function Digits (number : natural) : natural;
{This function returns the number of digits in the decimal expansion of
number.}
  var
    count : natural;
begin
  count := 1;
  while number >= 10 do
    begin
      count := count + 1;
      number := number div 10
    end; {of loop "while number >=10"}
  Digits := count
end {of function "Digits"}
```

9.2

```
function Digits (number, base : natural) : natural;
{This function returns the number of digits in the "base" expansion of
number.}
  var
    count : natural;
begin
  count := 1;
  while number >= base do
    begin
      count := count + 1;
```

```
        number := number div base
      end; {of loop "while number >= base"}
    Digits := count
  end {of function "Digits"}
```

9.3   **function** IntegerSqrt (number : natural) : natural;
        {This function returns the largest natural number ≤ the square root of
        number.}
```
    var
      trial : natural;
    begin
      trial := 0;
      while sqr(trial + 1) <= number do
        trial := trial + 1;
      IntegerSqrt := trial
    end {of function "IntegerSqrt"}
```

9.4   **function** IntegerLog (number : natural) : natural;
        {This function returns the largest natural number ≤ the log to the base 2
        of number.}
```
    var
      trial, twotothetrial : natural;
    begin
      trial := 0;
      twotothetrial := 1;
      while 2 * twotothetrial <= number do
        begin
          trial := trial + 1;
          twotothetrial := twotothetrial * 2
        end;
      IntegerLog := trial
    end {of function "IntegerLog"}
```

9.5   **function** LS1 (number : natural) : natural;
        {This function returns the position of the least significant 1 in the binary
        expansion of number.}
```
    var
      count : natural;
    begin
      count := 0;
      while not odd(number) do
        begin
          count := count + 1;
          number := number div 2
        end;
      LS1 := count
    end {of function "LS1"}
```

9.6   characters := digits + ord(sign = minus)

9.7   **if** odd(n) **then**
       p := **not** p

Chapter 12

12.1 (i) **function** IsADigit (ch : char) : Bcolean;
       begin
         IsADigit := ch **in** ['0'..'9']
       end {of function "IsADigit"}

   (ii) **function** IsAnOctalDigit (ch : char) : Boolean;
       begin
         IsAnOctalDigit := ch **in** ['0'..'7']
       end {of function "IsAnOctalDigit"}

12.2   **procedure** ReadHexInteger (var n : integer);
       {This procedure reads a hexadecimal integer, which may be signed,
       into n, skipping over all leading spaces, and stopping just before the
       first non-digit.}
       var
         ch, sign : char;
       begin
       {First skip over leading spaces.}
       ReadFirstNonBlank(ch);
       {If there is a sign, remember it and read the next character.}
       if ch **in** ['+', '−'] **then**
         begin
           sign := ch;
           read(ch)
         end
       else
         sign := '+';
       {Digits should follow.}
       if not (ch **in** ['0'..'9', 'A'..'F']) **then**
         writeln('There are no digits.')
       else
         begin
           if ch **in** ['0'..'9'] **then**
             n := ord(ch) − ord('0')
           else
             n := ord(ch) − ord('A') + 10;
           {Now read all the digits and accumulate the integer.}
           while input^ **in** ['0'..'9', 'A'..'F'] **do**
             begin
               read(ch);

```
        if ch in ['0'..'9'] then
          n := 16 * n + ord(ch) − ord('0')
        else
          n := 16 * n + ord(ch) − ord('A') + 10;
      end;
    {Take account of the sign.}
    if sign = '−' then
      n := −n
  end
end {of procedure "ReadHexInteger" }
```

procedure WriteHexInteger (n : integer;
         m : posint);
{This procedure writes n in hexadecimal using a minimum of m
characters. If necessary, leading spaces are written. The sign is
suppressed if n is positive, and immediately precedes the first
significant character if n is negative.}
  var
    sign : char;
    characters, i : posint;
    power, digits : natural;
begin
{First determine the sign, and replace n by |n|.}
  if n < 0 **then**
    begin
    sign := '−';
      n := −n
    end
  else
    sign := '+';
{Determine the number of digits in n, and hence the number of
characters to be written.}
  digits := 1;
  power := 1;
  while power <= n **div** 16 **do**
    begin
      digits := digits + 1;
      power := power * 16
    end;
  characters := digits + ord(sign = '−');
{Write out any leading spaces.}
  if m > characters **then**
    write(' ' : m − characters);
{Write the sign if negative.}
  if sign = '−' **then**
    write(sign);
{Now write all the digits.}
  for i := digits **downto** 1 **do**

```
        begin
          if n div power < 10 then
            write(chr(n div power + ord('0')))
          else
            write(chr(n div power − 10 + ord('A')));
          n := n mod power;
          power := power div 16
        end
      end {of procedure "WriteHexInteger" }
```

12.3
```
      procedure WriteRomanDigit (d : digit;
              one, five, ten : char);
      begin
        case d of
          0 :
            ;{write nothing}
          1 :
            write(one);
          2 :
            write(one, one);
          3 :
            write(one, one, one);
          4 :
            write(one, five);
          5 :
            write(five);
          6 :
            write(five, one);
          7 :
            write(five, one, one);
          8 :
            write(five, one, one, one);
          9 :
            write(one, ten)
        end {of cases on "d"}
      end {of procedure "WriteRomanDigit"}
```

Chapter 13

13.1 In the following some of the types and some of the constants will be left
undefined. This is not to say that they are unimportant: just that for the
moment, we are concerned with the upper level definitions.
Furthermore the definitions will be rather short, containing only the
main fields, since the details of such records varies dramatically across
different users.

(i) **type**
    student = **record**

```
            name : nametype;
            homeaddress, semesteraddress : addresstype;
            faculty : facultytype;
            credits : array [1..subjectmax] of record
                year : yeartype;
                subject : subjecttype;
                points : pointsrange
              end;
            current : array [1..subjectmax] of record
                subject : subjecttype;
                points : pointsrange
              end
          end;
```

(ii) **type**

```
        league = array [teammax] of record
            team : nametype;
            gamesplayed, gameswon, gameslost, gamesdrawn : gamesrange;
            goalsfor, goalsagainst : natural;
            points : natural;
            place : teamrange
          end;
```

(iii) **type**

```
        consumer = record
            name : nametype;
            address : addresstype;
            phone : phonetype;
            lastreading, currentreading : readingtype;
            tariff : tarifftype
          end;
```

(iv) **type**

```
        catalogue = array [1..carmax] of record
            makeandmodel : makeandmodeltype;
            colour : colourtype;
            dateofmanufacture : yeartype;
            speedoreading : natural;
            price : natural
          end;
```

13.2
```
        function Length (name : nametype) : natural;
        var
          len : natural;
          state : (searching, charfound, emptyname);
        begin
        state := searching;
        len := namemax;
```

```
          repeat
            if name[len] <> ' ' then
              state := charfound
            else if len = 1 then
              state := emptyname
            else
              len := len − 1
          until state in [charfound, emptyname];
          if len = 1 then
            Length := 0
          else
            Length := len
        end {of function "Length"}
```

13.3
```
        function HighestScorer (var team : teamrecord) : playerrange;
          var
            p : playerrange;
            bestscore : natural;
        begin
          bestscore := 0;
          with team do
            for p := 1 to noofplayers do
              with player[p] do
                if highest.runs > bestscore then
                  begin
                    HighestScorer := p;
                    bestscore := highest.runs
                  end
        end {of function "HighestScorer"}
```

13.4
```
        type
          playerrecord = record
              name : nametype;
              noinnings : natural;
              scores : array[inningsrange] of innings;
              nonotouts : natural;
              highest : innings;
              aggregate : natural;
              average : real
            end
```

(i)
```
        function Nonotouts (var player : playerrecord) : inningsrange;
          var
            count : 0..inningsmax;
            i : inningsrange;
        begin
          count := 0;
          with player do
```

```
      for i := 1 to noinnings do
        with scores[i] do
          if not out then
            count := count + 1;
    Nonotouts := count
  end {of function "Nonotouts"}
```

(ii) **function** Highest (**var** player : playerrecord) : natural;
    var
      bestscore : natural;
      i : inningsrange;
    begin
    bestscore := 0;
    with player **do**
      for i := 1 **to** noinnings **do**
        with scores[i] **do**
          if runs > bestscore **then**
            bestscore := runs;
    Highest := bestscore
    end {of function "Highest"}

(iii) **function** Aggregate (**var** player : playerrecord) : natural;
    var
      total : natural;
      i : inningsrange;
    begin
    total := 0;
    with player **do**
      for i := 1 **to** noinnings **do**
        with scores[i] **do**
          total := total + runs;
    Aggregate := total
    end {of function "Aggregate"}

(iv) **function** Average (**var** player : playerrecord) : real;
    begin
    Average := Aggregate(player) / (player.noinnings − nonotouts(player))
    end {of function "Average"}

Chapter 14

14.1 (i) ['a' .. 'z']
    (ii) ['a' .. 'z', 'A' .. 'Z']
    (iii) ['a' .. 'z', 'A' .. 'Z', '0' .. '9']
    (iv) ['g', 'j', 'p', 'q', 'y']
    (v) ['b', 'd', f', 'h', 'k', 'l', 't']

14.2   card := 0;
        for themonth := Jan **to** Dec **do**
          if themonth **in** themonthset **then**
            card := card + 1;

14.3   **function** NotIn (b : base;
                      s : setofbase) : Boolean;
        {This function returns true iff b is not in the set s.}
        begin
          NotIn := **not** (b **in** s)
        end {of function "NotIn"}

14.4   **function** Valid (d : display;
                     ndigits : length) : Boolean;
        {This function returns true iff all the digits in display are different.}
          var
            state : (digitrepeated, digitunique, alldifferent, unknown);
            i, j : length;
        begin
          i := 1;
          state := unknown;
          repeat
            j := 1;
            repeat
              if i = j **then**
                state := digitunique
              else if d[i] = d[j] **then**
                state := digitrepeated
              else
                j := j + 1
            until state **in** [digitrepeated, digitunique];
            if state <> digitrepeated **then**
              if i = ndigits **then**
                state := alldifferent
              else
                begin
                  state := unknown;
                  i := i + 1
                end
          until state **in** [digitrepeated, alldifferent];
          Valid := state = alldifferent
        end

Chapter 15

15.1   **program** IllustrateInternalFiles;
        {This is an alternative program for demonstrating the internal file
        facility.}

```
type
  natural = 0..maxint;
  realfile = file of real;
var
  i, size : natural;
  f : realfile;
  next : real;
begin
  writeln('How many numbers are there? ');
  readln(size);
  writeln('Give them to me, one to a line. ');
  rewrite(f);
  for i := 1 to size do
  begin
    readln(next);
    f^ := next;
    put(f)
  end; {of loop on "i"}
  writeln('Here they are again. ');
  reset(f);
  while not eof(f) do
    begin
      writeln(f^ : 8 : 2);
      get(f)
    end {of loop on "eof(f)"}
end.
```

15.2
```
procedure MergeFiles (var f, g, h : filetype);
{This merges two sorted files f and g to produce the sorted file h.}
  var
    endfg : Boolean;
begin
  reset(f);
  reset(g);
  rewrite(h);
  endfg := eof(f) or eof(g);
  while not endfg do
    begin
      if f^.key < g^.key then
        begin
          h^ := f^;
          get(f);
          put(h);
          endfg := eof(f)
        end {of copying from "f" to "h"}
      else
        begin
          h^ := g^;
```

```
            get(g);
            put(h);
            endfg := eof(g)
          end {of copying from "g" to "h"}
        end; {of loop on "endfg"}
      while not eof(f) do
        begin
          h^ := f^;
          get(f);
          put(h)
        end; {copying tail of "f"}
      while not eof(g) do
        begin
          h^ := g^;
          get(g);
          put(h)
        end {copying tail of "g"}
    end {of procedure "MergeFiles"}
```

15.3   **procedure** MergeFiles (**var** f, g, h : filetype);
{This merges two sorted files f and g to produce the sorted file h. All
files use a sentinel.}

```
      var
        endfg : Boolean;
      begin
        reset(f);
        reset(g);
        rewrite(h);
        endfg := false;
        while not endfg do
          begin
            if f^.key < g^.key then
              begin
                h^ := f^;
                get(f);
                put(h)
              end {of copying from "f" to "h"}
            else if f^.key > g^.key then
              begin
                h^ := g^;
                get(g);
                put(h);
              end {of copying from "g" to "h"}
            else
              begin
                if f^.key = sentinel then
                  endfg := true;
                h^ := f^;
```

```
            get(f);
            put(h);
            if not endfg then
              begin
                h^ := g^;
                get(g);
                put(h)
              end
          end {of copying from both "f" and "g" to "h"}
        end {of loop on "endfg"}
      end {of procedure "MergeFiles"}
```

15.4 (i) **procedure** Union (**var** f, g, h : largeset);
{This procedure sets h to the union of f and g.}

```
    var
      endfg : Boolean;
      nextf, nextg : natural;
    begin
     reset(f);
     reset(g);
     rewrite(h);
     endfg := eof(f) or eof(g);
     while not endfg do
       begin
         if f^ < g^ then
           begin
             read(f, nextf);
             write(h, nextf);
             endfg := eof(f)
           end {of copying from "f" to "h"}
         else if f^ = g^ then
           begin
             read(f, nextf);
             write(h, nextf);
             read(g, nextg);
             endfg := eof(f) or eof(g)
           end {of putting the common element to "h"}
         else
           begin
             read(g, nextg);
             write(h, nextg);
             endfg := eof(g)
           end {of copying from "g" to "h"}
       end; {of loop on "endfg"}
     while not eof(f) do
       begin
         read(f, nextf);
         write(h, nextf);
```

```
        end; {copying tail of "f"}
      while not eof(g) do
        begin
          read(g, nextg);
          write(h, nextg);
        end {copying tail of "g"}
      end {of propcedure "Union"}
```

(ii) **procedure** Intersection (var f, g, h : largeset);
      {This procedure sets h to the intersection of f and g.}
```
      var
        endfg : Boolean;
        nextf, nextg : natural;
    begin
      reset(f);
      reset(g);
      rewrite(h);
      endfg := eof(f) or eof(g);
      while not endfg do
        begin
          if f^ < g^ then
            begin
              read(f, nextf);
              endfg := eof(f)
            end {of skipping element on"f".}
          else if f^ = g^ then
            begin
              read(f, nextf);
              write(h, nextf);
              read(g, nextg);
              endfg := eof(f) or eof(g)
            end {of putting the common element to "h"}
          else
            begin
              read(g, nextg);
              endfg := eof(g)
            end {of of skipping element on "g".}
        end {of loop on "endfg"}
    end {of procedure "Intersection"}
```

Chapter 17

17.1

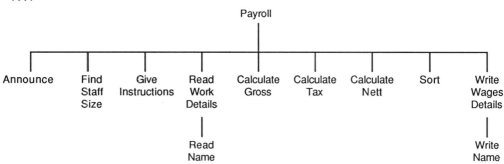

Chapter 18

18.1   **function** SumOfCubes (n : natural) : natural;
    {This procedure returns the sum of the first n cubes.}
    begin
      if n = 0 **then**
        SumOfCubes := 0
      else
        SumOfCubes := SumOfCubes(n − 1) + n * n * n
    end {of function "SumOfCubes"}

18.2 (i) *P* returns the value of the polynomial, $a_0 x^n + a_1 x^{n-1} + \ldots + a_{n-1} x + a_0$

    (ii) *x* returns the value of the scalar product of *a* and *b*.

18.3   **procedure** Hanoi (n : natural;
                      p1, p2, p3 : peg);
    {This procedure writes out the moves for an n-disc Hanoi problem.}
    begin
      if n = 2 **then**
        begin
          writeln('Move disc ', n − 1 : 1, ' from ', p1 : 1, ' to ', p3 : 1);
          writeln('Move disc ', n : 1, ' from ', p1 : 1, ' to ', p2 : 1);
          writeln('Move disc ', n − 1 : 1, ' from ', p3 : 1, ' to ', p2 : 1)
        end
      else
        begin
          Hanoi(n − 1, p1, p3, p2);
          writeln('Move disc ', n : 1, ' from ', p1 : 1, ' to ', p2 : 1);
          Hanoi(n − 1, p3, p2, p1)
        end
    end {of procedure "Hanoi"}

Chapter 19

19.1

```
procedure InsertBefore (searchkey : keytype;
        var newentry : entrytype;
        var seq : listptr);
{This procedure inserts newentry into seq immediately in front of the
item with the given searchkey.}
  var
    marker, trailer, local : listptr;
    state : (stilllooking, foundit, notthere);
begin
  if seq = nil then
    {The list is empty.}
  else if seq^.entry.key = searchkey then
    {Deal with the case where the number is to go at the front.}
    begin
      new(local);
      local^.next := seq;
      seq := local;
      local^.entry := newentry
    end {of dealing with initial case}
  else {The general case}
    begin
      {Scan along the list up to and including the key entry.}
      trailer := seq;
      marker := seq^.next;
      state := stilllooking;
      repeat
        if marker = nil then
          state := notthere
        else if marker^.entry.key = searchkey then
          state := foundit
        else
          begin
            trailer := marker;
            marker := marker^.next
          end
      until state in [notthere, foundit];
      {If the key is found, add the new entry.}
      if state = foundit then
        begin
          new(local);
          local^.next := marker;
          trailer^.next := local;
          local^.entry := newentry
        end
    end {of the general case}
end {of procedure "InsertBefore"}
```

19.2
```
        procedure Delete (searchkey : keytype;
                var seq : listptr);
        {This procedure deletes from seq the item with the given searchkey.}
          var
              marker, trailer : listptr;
              state : (stilllooking, foundit, notthere);
        begin
          if seq = nil then
              {The list is empty.}
          else if seq^.entry.key = searchkey then
              {Deal with the case where the number is at the front.}
              begin
                marker := seq;
                seq := seq^.next;
                dispose(marker);
              end {of dealing with initial case}
          else {The general case}
              begin
              {Scan along the list up to and including the key entry.}
                trailer := seq;
                marker := seq^.next;
                state := stilllooking;
                repeat
                  if marker = nil then
                      state := notthere
                  else if marker^.entry.key = searchkey then
                      state := foundit
                  else
                      begin
                        trailer := marker;
                        marker := marker^.next
                      end
                until state in [notthere, foundit];
                {If the key is found, delete the entry.}
                if state = foundit then
                    begin
                      trailer^.next := marker^.next;
                      Dispose(marker)
                    end
              end {of the general case}
        end {of procedure "Delete"}
```

Index

abs, 20
abstract data structures, 197
actual-parameter, 94, 95
adding-operator, 18
addition, 16
Advance1Day procedure, 162
alternatives, 34
and, 40, 109, 112
apostrophe-image, 20
arctan, 20
arithmetic expression, 29
arithmetic relation, 37
array-type, 164–83, 208
array-variable, 165
assignment-statement, 5, 10, 21, 135

base-type, 187
batch-mode, 7
becomes-symbol, 10
begin, 4
binary tree, 278–80
block, 30, 31, 91
Boolean-expression, 35, 36, 43, 106, 109
Boolean-type, 105, 107
Boolean relation, 110
Buley's Law, 48

call as a variable, 87
call by value, 87
CartToPolar procedure, 98
case-constant, 111
case-statement, 44, 111, 153
characters, 149–56
char-type, 149
chr, 152

comment, 13
CompareEasterAlgorithms
    procedure, 235
compiler, 6
component type, 165
component-variable, 170
compound-statement, 42, 43, 137
ConcessionalExam program, 41
conditional statement, 34, 44, 46, 137
constant, 15, 71, 73
constant-definition, 72
constant-definition-part, 71, 73
control lines, 7
control unit, 1
control-variable, 52, 114
ConvertTime program, 19
cos, 20
cursor, 4

debug printing, 145
DeleteEdge procedure, 193
deterministic loop, 105
digit, 27, 29, 31
direct recursion, 231
dispose, 267
DisposeList procedure, 277
div, 17, 112
division, 17
dot notation, 159
dynamic storage, 261–81
dynamic structure diagrams, 231
dynamic variable, 261, 268

Easter day, 127, 135
Easter program, 130–2, 234–6
end, 4

entire-variable,170
enumerated-type, 76–82
eof function, 200
eoln function, 151, 205
Euclid's algorithm, 105
exp, 20
exponentiation, 17
expression, 10, 15
Extended Backus Naur Form, 29
extended if-statement, 37

Fact function, 103, 239, 240
Factorial program, 55
FactorialFloor function, 115
false, 36, 108
Fib function, 248–50
field, 159
field-designator, 159
field-list, 161, 180
field-width, 6
file-buffer variable, 150
file-type, 198, 208
final-value, 52
FindDayOfWeek program, 45
FindLargest program, 54
FindSum program, 53, 118
fixed part, 180
for-statement, 51, 58, 111, 112, 153
formal-parameter, 87, 91
formal-parameter list, 91, 233
forward references, 229
FractionalPart, 6
full-stop, 3
function, 20, 85, 99
function design, 101–3
function-designator, 20, 99
function-heading, 100

GCD function, 105–7, 243, 244
GeneralOBeirne procedure, 234
get procedure, 200
global variable, 227

Hanoi procedure, 252–4
heap, 94
HighestScorer function, 168

identified-variable, 263, 267
identifier, 7, 11, 27, 31
if-statement, 34, 36
IllustrateInternalFiles procedure, 201
ImperialToMetric program, 22
in, 112, 190
indentation, 14, 36, 52
index, 164
indexed-variable, 164, 165
indirect recursion, 230
initial-value, 52
*input^*, 150
input file, 205
input unit, 1
InsertAfter procedure, 273, 275, 278
integer function, 20
integer-type, 3, 14
Integral function, 247
interactive mode, 7
iteration, 105

layout, 13
Leap function, 110
letter, 27
linked-lists, 270–6
links, 93, 96, 101
In, 20
local variable, 90
locations, 3
logical operator, 40
loop,

main program, 90
maxint, 14, 74
MergeFiles program, 203
mod, 17, 112
multiplication, 16
multiplying-operators, 18

natural, 14, 75
nested if-statement, 39
nested loops, 57
new, 267
new-type, 75
NewYearsDay program, 144
nil, 265

non-deterministic loop, 105
non-local variable, 227
not, 110, 112
Noughts and Crosses, 65–68, 134

object language, 6
odd, 110
operating system, 7
operator, 16
operator precedence, 18, 112, 189
or, 40, 109, 112
ord, 20, 80, 110, 152
ordinal-type, 76, 83
output file, 205

pack, 182
packed-array, 165, 182
packed-record, 165, 182
page procedure, 205
parameter, 87, 181
parametric procedure, 232
Payroll program, 2, 17, 35, 38, 52,
    72, 85, 86, 88, 175, 206
PINnumbers program, 122–6, 135
pointer-variable, 263–8,
posint, 75
Power function, 102
pred, 20, 79, 110, 151
Prime function, 116, 119
procedure, 85
procedure-call, 86
procedure-declaration, 86, 90
procedure design, 97–9, 101–3
procedure-heading, 90
procedure nesting, 227
procedure-statement, 86, 95
ProduceSummary procedure, 218
program, 1, 30, 31
program correction, 143–6
program design, 62–9, 122–32,
    213–23
program development, 134–46
program-heading, 3, 30, 31
program-parameters, 202
program structure, 227
program testing, 134–43
programming language, 1
put, 199

read-statement, 200
ReadFirstNonBlank procedure,
    150
ReadInteger procedure, 156
readln-statement, 4, 205
real function, 20
real-type, 3, 14, 76
record-type, 159–64, 169–9
recursion, 230, 231, 239–59
relational-operator, 37
repeat-statement, 117
repetition, 50
repetitive-statement, 51, 106, 138
required-constant, 74
required-functions, 79
required-identifiers, 7
required-procedures, 267
reset procedure, 200
rewrite procedure, 199
Roman notation, 76
round, 20, 22
run-time errors, 8

scale-factor, 15
scope, 229
semi-colon, 4
sequence, 198
set-constructor, 188
set difference, 189
set-expression, 188
set inclusion, 190
set intersection, 189
set notation, 42
set-relation, 191
set-type, 186
set union, 189
simple statement, 51
simple-type, 76
Simplify procedure, 280
SimulateDispose procedure, 281
SimulateNew procedure, 281
simulating nested loops, 254–9
sin, 20
Size function, 277
SkipBlanks procedure, 150, 205,
    206
source language, 6

sqr, 17, 20
sqrt, 20
stack, 94
state variable, 118
statement, 4, 46
statement-part, 3, 30, 31
static structure diagram, 227
storage allocation, 93, 96, 101, 163,
   169, 241–2, 263–8
store, 1, 4, 5
strategy, 90
string, 166
structure diagram, 227, 231–2
structured-statement, 51
structured-type, 76
stub, 141
subrange-type, 82
subtraction, 15
succ, 20, 79, 110, 151
SumOfCubes program, 57, 255,
   256
SumOfPowers program, 251
SummerTime program, 62–5, 134

syntax, 26
syntax diagrams, 26
syntax errors, 8

TabulateIntegerSquareRoots
   procedure, 233
tactics, 90
tag field, 180
TestSimpson procedure, 237
text, 204
textfiles, 204
TicTacToe program, 65–9, 134
token-separator, 1
TotalWidth, 6

Towers of Hanoï, 250–4
transfer function, 22
Triangle program, 21
tree of function calls, 248
tree of procedure calls, 253
tree of statements, 46, 58
tree of types, 83, 170, 198, 265
tree of variables, 170, 198, 265
true, 36, 108
trunc, 20, 22
type, 14, 74
type-definition-part, 75
type-denoter, 12, 30, 76

unpack, 182
unsigned-constant, 15
unsigned-integer, 15
unsigned-real, 15, 28
UpperCaseOf function, 152

Valid function, 195
value-parameter, 94
variable, 3, 10
variable-access, 10
variable-declaration, 12
variable-declaration-part, 3, 12, 30,
   31
variable-parameter, 94
variant-record, 179

while-statement, 106, 112
with-statement, 171, 172
WriteInteger procedure, 155
word-symbols, 6, 13
write-statement, 4, 199
writeln-statement, 4, 6, 205

Zeller's Congruence, 43, 63